How to Enter & Win Video/Audio Contests

How to Enter & Win Video/Audio Contests

By
ALAN GADNEY

Managing Editor
CAROLYN PORTER

Facts On File Publications
New York, New York

How to Enter & Win Video/Audio Contests

© Alan Gadney 1981

Published by Facts On File, Inc.
460 Park Ave. South, New York, N.Y. 10016

In cooperation with Festival Publications

Festival
Publications

Library of Congress Cataloging in Publication Data

Gadney, Alan.
    How to enter and win video/audio contests.

    Includes index.
    1. Broadcasting—Competitions.   2. Video art
—Competitions.   I. Facts on File, Inc.   II. Title.
III. Video and broadcasting contests.
PN1990.83.G3   384.54′079   81-2221
ISBN 0-87196-520-8   AACR2
ISBN 0-87196-551-8 (pbk.)

PRINTED IN THE UNITED STATES OF AMERICA

9 8 7 6 5 4 3 2 1

Computer Programming and Typesetting by Datagraphics Inc.

TO MARY M. GADNEY
whose confidence, love, and hard work
helped to make this series possible.
Thanks Mom.

EDITORIAL STAFF

Associate Editor: Darline Leslie

Assistant Editors: Christina J. Moose
                          Lois Smith

Editorial Assistants: Monica Olofsson
                          Lisa Zemelman

Research Assistant: Holly Christos

CONTENTS

INTRODUCTION

WELCOME . . . to the all new, completely updated edition of GADNEY'S GUIDE TO INTERNATIONAL CONTESTS, FESTIVALS & GRANTS (now under a new and more descriptive title). What began in the previous edition as a single-cover sourcebook for the contest competitor and grant seeker in the fields of Film, Video-Audio, TV-Radio Broadcasting, Writing, Photography, and Journalism, has now expanded into an entirely new ongoing series of books covering those and other related arts fields.

Each book in the series focuses on an individual art and media area (Video-Audio-TV/Radio Broadcasting, Film, Fiction Writing, Nonfiction Writing & Journalism, Photography, Art, Crafts, and so on).

And each book in the series lists complete entrance information for anyone wanting to:

- Enter their work in national and international contests, festivals, competitions, salons, shows, exhibitions, markets, tradefairs, and other award events and sales outlets.

- Apply for grants, loans, scholarships, fellowships, residencies, apprenticeships, internships, training and benefit programs, and free aids and services.

The books also have: ALPHABETICAL INDEXES listing each event, sponsor, and award by its various names. SUBJECT/CATEGORY INDEXES to the entrants' specific areas of interest. Extensive CROSS-REFERENCES and DEFINITIONS throughout. And introductory HELPFUL HINTS on how to analyze and enter the events, and possibly COME UP A WINNER!!

HOW THE BOOKS BEGAN

This series of contest-grant guides actually began several years ago with the first release print of *West Texas* (a one-hour featurette I made while completing my graduate work at the USC Cinema Department). One week after our first showing, I sent our premiere print off to the first film festival, and the contest entry process started to grow from there . . . with one major problem, however: The festival contact information was almost impossible to find.

After extensive research, all I could come up with were names and addresses (and an occasional brief blurb) of intriguingly titled film events in far-off places, but with no hard facts as to their entry requirements, eligibility restrictions, awards, deadlines, fees, statistics, judging procedures, etc. That sort of vital information was practically nonexistent, unless you took the time and postage to write away to every contest you discovered an address for . . . which I did.

Through several years of continuous address researching, blindly writing off for contest entry information and periodically submitting the film, *West Texas* won 48 international film awards, and a large file of information had been collected on about 180 international festivals—quite a few of which were not even open to *West Texas* for a variety of reasons (wrong gauge, length, category, the event turned out not to be a film festival, etc.).

The need was evident for an accurate, up-to-date, and detailed entry information source to the world's Contests, Festivals and Grants . . . Thus the premiere edition, which led to this book in the series.

ABOUT THE VIDEO-AUDIO BOOK

Like the previous premiere edition, this book (devoted solely to the field of VIDEO-AUDIO/TV-RADIO BROADCASTING) is a single-source reference guide, providing you with vital entry information and statistics about a contest/-grant before you even have to send away for the entry forms and shipping regulations (which you must always eventually do, as most require their own entry forms, and some have rather intricate shipping and customs requirements).

The 411 separate events listed in this volume were compiled through 3 years of active research on the first edition, an additional year of research on this edition, and thousands of questionnaires sent to worldwide video-audio events (many requiring repeated mailings to obtain complete and up-to-date entry information). During this process, we have totally updated, revised, and expanded the scope of the original video, audio, and broadcasting listings, added new competitions, and deleted a few which were too restricted or no longer in existence. (Film and Filmstriip sections of Video and Audio events have been included in a companion volume covering film contests and grants).

The individual events have been further grouped into 32 special-interest subcategories (an increase in the number of subject categories over the previous edition, particularly in the areas of independent videomaking, scholarships, fellowships, and grants). These subcategories are further divided and cross-referenced in the SUBJECT/CATEGORY INDEX at the back of the book.

We have included two general types of events:

- Those AWARD EVENTS and SALES OUTLETS to which entrants may submit their works in order to receive SOMETHING OF VALUE in return, such as Contests, Festivals, Competitions, Salons, Shows, Exhibitions, Markets, Tradefairs, and various other award and sales programs primarily for new and unknown works.

- And BENEFIT PROGRAMS to which individuals or organizations may apply for some type of AID or SERVICE, such as Grants, Money and Equipment Loans, Scholarships, Fellowships, Residencies, Apprenticeships, Internships, Training Programs, and so on.

Due to page length restrictions we have given condensed listings to those events that (1) are restricted to members of a specific organization, or limited to residents of a small city or geographical area (usually of less than state size), or (2) are not open to general entry but whose participants are nominated or invited by the sponsors or national selecting organizations. Workshops, seminars, conferences, schools, service programs, and the like, have only been listed if they are free, have free benefits attached, or encompass a contest, festival, grant, scholarship, fellowship, residency, etc.

We have listed as much detailed information about each separate event as possible (that is, as much as could be culled from the materials provided us by the event—usually including current addresses, dates, deadlines, complete entry requirements, eligibility and fee information, awards available, judging aspects, catch clauses, purpose, theme, sponsors, average statistics, where held, and various historical aspects). All information was transcribed from the questionnaires and entry materials provided us and edited to fit the format of the book. (See HOW TO USE THE BOOK for description of format.)

The information listed is the most current we could obtain, and will normally be revised and updated every two years as a continuing reference series.

We have also included older events when there was no direct confirmation that the events had gone out of existence. Many events come and go in an on-again, off-again manner, depending on their finances, administration changes, and other factors . . . again, good reason to ALWAYS WRITE TO AN EVENT BEFORE ENTERING YOUR WORK. Most events require entry forms, which they provide. Many have special shipping regulations. And, as we have condensed and edited their rules and regulations, it is best to write for the complete versions (especially important in interpreting the meanings of occational tricky "catch clauses" about the use and ownership of winning entries). Also remember to send along a Self-Addressed, Stamped Return Envelope (SASE), particularly to smaller events operating on tight postage budgets.

As to the total amount of money offered through this book, it would be almost impossible to give an exact figure. Some events give cash, others give equipment (of varying value depending on how badly you need the equipment or how much you can sell it for), and others give trophies, cups, plaques, medals, certificates, etc. (all of great value to the winner, but of little real monetary worth). Grant sources, on the other hand, may offer millions of dollars in direct financial aid. Probably the safest thing to say about the total amount of money offered through this book is that it is well into the millions.

HOW TO USE THE BOOK

In the TABLE OF CONTENTS you will find that this volume has been divided into a series of "special-interest" SUBCATEGORIES. Each contains all those events whose primary emphasis is within that particular subcategory. The listing is usually alphabetical—first those in the United States, followed by other countries in alphabetical order.

At the start of each subcategory is an italicized INTRODUCTORY SECTION giving (1) specific contents of that subcategory, (2) definitions, and (3) "also see" CROSS-REFERENCES to similar events in other subcategories in the book.

To find additional events accepting entries in your specific interest area (but which may be listed in other subcategories because their primary emphasis is stronger in those areas), use the SUBJECT/CATEGORY INDEX at the back of the book. This lists both Video and Audio areas of special interest by an identifying code number for each event. The code number is located in the box above each event.

To find a specific event, sponsor, or award by name, use the ALPHABETICAL EVENT/SPONSOR/AWARD INDEX at the back of the book (again listing entries by identifying code number). In this index, sponsors and events are usually listed by full names, abbreviations, and unique titles.

EACH EVENT consists of (1) a current address and telephone number; (2) month/season held; (3) introductory paragraph, including entry restrictions, date of establishment, former names, purpose, theme, motto, sponsors, average statistics, historical information, facilities and other aspects; (4) technical entry regulations and categories; (5) eligibility requirements; (6) awards; (7) judging aspects and catch clauses; (8) sales terms; (9) entry fees; (10) deadlines. All have a similar format designed for easy use, with the five most important aspects of each event noted in bold type:

1. Identifying Code Number (in box)
2. Name of event
3. Month/Season of event
4. Entrant restrictions
5. Type of event and subject-category

With these five main points in mind, a potential entrant can quickly skim through a series of events to find those of particular interest.

HOW TO ANALYZE AN EVENT

We have usually provided enough information about each event to help you in making various determinations before you send away for entry forms, shipping regulations, and additional instructions. These are some of the points you should consider in your analysis.

• **When is the event held?** The month/season held is designated by bold type immediately following the address.

• **When is the entry deadline?** Months of entry are found in the DEADLINES section at the end of each event listing, and are usually well in advance of the month held. The event should be contacted about the specific entry date for the year you are applying.

• **Do I qualify?** Entrant restrictions are listed in bold type in the first sentence, and may be further clarified in the ELIGIBILITY section.

• **Does my work qualify?** The type of event and specific subject categories are listed in bold type at the beginning of the second and subsequent paragraphs. Various technical entry requirements follow each.

• **How much does it cost?** Costs and hidden costs are found in the ENTRY FEE section.

• **What are the prizes?** Found in the AWARDS section are prizes varying from trophies, cups, plaques, and medallions (of personal value), to cash, trips, equipment, and services (of a more material value—meaning you may be able to resell them at a later date if you already have better equipment, cannot take the trip, or do not want the services). Exhibition, distribution, broadcast, sale, and publication may also be offered, but should always be analyzed in terms of their financial and legal implications (what you get for what you have to give in return, and how valuable your entry may become in the future).

• **What are the catch clauses?** A few events have tricky qualifying clauses, condensed in the JUDGING section. These may involve claims to use and ownership (sometimes of all entries, and on an extensive basis), or responsibility in the event of loss, damage, nonreturn, etc.

Occasionally the actual entry forms and regulations may be rather vague as to whether the sponsors just keep a copy of your winning entry or whether they receive full ownership of the work (and for what use). Possibly, in these instances, you should write to the sponsors for further clarification.

• **How is my work judged?** The number of judges, judging procedures, and criteria are listed in the JUDGING section. It is important to understand that during preliminary judging (sometimes performed by the event's staff and aides), many entries may be immediately disqualified because of failure to adhere to the various contest regulations, or eliminated because of technical flaws or oversights (good reason always to send away for, and to read carefully, the latest rules). This is especially true of large contests that thousands enter. Sponsors have to narrow the competition as rapidly and efficiently as possible, and the first to go are the rule breakers and sloppy entries.

A program of the event or listing of past winners may give you an overall feel for the event (if it is conservative or liberal, oriented in certain directions, etc.). There is the possibility of talking to past entrants and winners in order to get an idea of specific likes and dislikes of the event and its judges. Or if you know who the judges will be, you may be able to make an educated guess as to what they will choose. However, I have found that it is almost impossible to predict how judges will act on anything other than the widest of generalities. Judges change from year to year, the philosophy of the event may alter, and single-judge contests put you at the mercy of that particular year's judge. So, you can never really outguess the judges.

• **How old is the event?** Usually included in the first sentence is the founding date, the inference being that the older the event, the more stable and reputable it is.

• **How large is the event?** Average attendance, distribution, and sales figures can often be found in the first paragraph, indicating the potential promotional and sales values of participating in the event.

• **What is the duration of an event, and how long will it tie up my entry materials?** The number of days the event is usually held is found in the first paragraph; the entry and return-of-material dates are in the DEADLINES section.

• **What is the competition?** Average statistics on number of entries, entrants, countries competing, acceptances into final competition, and winners can be found in the first paragraph, giving some idea of possible competition in future events.

• **How legitimate is the event?** This can be determined to some extent by the names of familiar sponsors, cosponsors, financial supporters, and those organizations that officially recognize the event—again, all found in the opening paragraph, and giving some idea of reputability. Also important may be the purpose, theme, and motto.

These are just a few of the aspects to examine before writing away for further information, entry forms, the most current regulations . . . and before sending away your work.

YEARLY PLANNING GUIDE

This book can also serve as a planning guide for your contest entries throughout the year. By using the SUBJECT/CATEGORY INDEX, you can get an overall picture of the various world events accepting entries in your areas of interest. We would then suggest setting up a calendar, listing those events you wish to enter by (1) the date you should write away for entry forms and current rules (several months before the actual entry month), (2) the entry dates, and (3) the dates the event is held, which will give you some indication of when the sponsor will be announcing the winners and returning your materials.

HELPFUL HINTS ON HOW TO WIN

Here are a few recommendations to enhance your chances of winning:

• FOLLOW THE RULES—The contest rules (obtained directly from the event) should be studied carefully, first to find hidden clauses, and second to ensure you will not be inadvertently excluded because you entered the wrong category, sent an incorrect entry fee or no return postage, entered with improper technical aspects, or not enough supplementary information, etc. So read the rules and follow them, and fill out the entry forms completely. Rule breakers usually are disqualified, sometimes even before the preliminary judging. Then, to further cut down the number of competitors, most judges go strictly by the regulations, automatically discarding those entries that in any way deviate from the rules.

• KEEP IT CLEAN—technically perfect, that is. Again, judges will usually reject sloppy entries (sometimes these don't even reach the judges, but are weeded out by the contest staff). So send only clean entries in good condition. No poor recordings, bad splices, scratches, nicks, or tears. All of these reflect badly on your entry's artistic content. And if the sponsors tell you they want an entry mounted on a specific type of reel or cassette, you had better follow their instructions. Also, it is best to send a duplicate rather than your original work (unless they request the original, in which case you should study their rules carefully to see if you will ever get your original back).

• SEND IT AHEAD OF TIME—well in advance of the entry deadlines. Last-minute entries may get abbreviated handling by judges who have already looked over the earlier entries and have made up their minds. They may not get listed in the contest programs, which have already gone to the printers—and if they are shown, they may be scheduled during the least desirable exhibition times. And of course, *late* entries are usually sent back unopened.

• SEND PUBLICITY AND INFORMATION MATERIALS—unless positively prohibited. (Definitely send them when they are requested.) Every little bit helps: biographical, technical, and project background information; publicity and press materials; still photos of yourself, your cast, and crew; production philosophy, synopsis, translation, transcription (and advertising materials if appropriate). The judges may occasionally use some of these in making their final decisions, and the events may use the publicity in their programs, flyers, and press rooms. Remember to send along any special technical instructions or return shipping requests you feel are needed.

• USE PROPER SHIPPING—First a word about the U.S. and International Mail System (as opposed to international Air Freight; some foreign contests even prohibit the use of air freight, as the entries may become held up in customs). Provided your entries are properly packaged, sealed, marked, stamped, and insured, and have correctly filled-out customs stickers (information about all of this is available through the U.S. Post Office), they should be able to travel almost anywhere in the world with relative safety. (This is based on personal experience. *West Texas* was mailed to a large number of film festivals all over the world, and I never lost a print or received one back damaged in transit.)

Remember always to ship by air to overseas competitions (as boat mail may take as long as three months from the U.S. to Australia, for example). On domestic U.S. shipments, you can mail at various rates lower than First Class, if you take into account the time for possible delays. (Again, contact the post office for information about mailing costs and times.)

Of course, if you have a heavy international shipment (2-inch feature videotapes for example), you may be over the postal weight limitations, and have to ship by Air Freight. In this case, it may be best to contact a Customs House Broker/International Freight Forwarder about services and charges.

Short overseas messages will travel very rapidly by international telegram. And always remember to enclose sufficient return postage and a correctly sized Self-Addressed Stamped Return Envelope (SASE) when requested. Finally, if your entry arrives with "Postage Due," it could be a negative factor in the contest staff preselection process.

A WORD ABOUT GRANTS

It would take an entire volume to discuss all the "ins" and "outs" of grant solicitation. However, we can touch on a few of the more important aspects.

• FIND OUT AS MUCH AS POSSIBLE about a potential grant source before investing the time in sending a proposal. Write to the granting organization for more information—and once you have this information, analyze it and focus your energies on the most likely prospects.

• WRITE AN INQUIRY LETTER—a brief letter of introduction, to see if they are interested in your project. Include a short description of the project and its unique aspects, background information about yourself and your sponsoring organization, the proposal budget, and ask them if they would be interested in further information. Keep your introductory letter brief, to the point, well written, easy to understand, and not exaggerated. If the foundation is interested, it will request what it needs, which may run anywhere from an expanded summary to a full-scale proposal and budget.

• GET AN ORGANIZATION TO SPONSOR YOU—Many foundations restrict their granting to only nonprofit, tax-exempt organizations, institutions, etc. However, this does not necessarily prohibit you from securing a grant from them. Simply get a nonprofit organization to sponsor you and your project, and have the organization apply for the grant in their name. Many organizations offer grant solicitations as one of their services, and this can have benefits for the sponsoring organizations: You give them credit and publicity through your finished project. They have a track-record as a successful fund raiser, which may help them in obtaining future grants. And they can even be paid through your budget for handling certain administrative and bookkeeping duties.

• GET SOME NAMES ON YOUR SIDE—well-known persons in the roles of advisors, technical consultants, etc. can help greatly toward building an impressive project package.

• TRY SPECIAL INTEREST GROUPS—If you have designed a project involving a special interest (Medical Video, for example), rather than only approaching sources that grant your medium (Video), you might consider going to those grant sources that fund the special interest instead (i.e., Medical Grants). Or you may find similar money sources through special-interest organizations, associations, institutions, and businesses. The public library is a good place to start your search.

WHY ENTER CONTESTS

Finally, a word about the positive benefits of entering your work in contests, festivals, and competitions.

To start with, it is an extremely good way to test (and prove) the artistic and commercial value of your work before professional judges, critics, and the public. There is also the challenge of the competition—the excitement and glamour of knowing that your work is being seen in contests, festivals, salons, exhibitions, and publications around the world. Your entry competes with those of your peers —and if it reaches the finals and wins, there is the great personal satisfaction and certification of acceptance.

If you do win, you can win substantial cash prizes, trips, art items, equipment, services, exhibition, distribution, broadcast, publication, sales, trophies, and other awards. There can be useful free publicity for both you and your work, through (1) press information and literature released by the event, (2) the writings and reviews of others about your work, and (3) your own promotional materials designed around your winnings.

All of this can bring valuable international exposure through the print and broadcast media, and the resulting recognition and prestige can certainly help to sell both your award-winning work and yourself as an award-winning video or audiomaker.

The end benefits can be sales, valuable contacts, jobs, contracts, increased fees, and the financing of other projects.

How does this translate into real terms . . . The 48 international film awards won by *West Texas* resulted directly in: (1) a large number of valuable art objects, trophies, and awards; (2) enough cash winnings to cover all the film festival entry fees, shipping, promotion, and other costs; (3) an enormous amount of free personal publicity; (4) the eventual sale and distribution of the film; (5) the writing and directing of a subsequent feature-length theatrical, *Moonchild;* (6) several paid speaking engagements; (7) a TV script assignment; (8) a stint as a film magazine contributing editor; and (9) eventually to writing this series of books on Contests, Festivals and Grants . . . So, the entering of contests and the winning of awards in many ways can be quite profitable.

THE CHANGING NATURE OF VIDEO-AUDIO CONTESTS

In the three years since the previous edition of this book was published, several significant changes have taken place in the number and types of video-audio/TV-radio broadcasting contests and grants offered throughout the world. These changes (reflected in the updated and revised listings in this book) were no doubt precipitated by recent changes in the overall field of video and audio production (the explosive growth of independent videomaking, advances in technology, new distribution outlets through community and nonbroadcast television, noncommercial radio, and so on).

The largest increase in the number of newly formed video-audio contests can be found in the area of Independent-oriented festivals. This growth may be explained by two possible factors: (1) the expansion of independent video and audiomaking throughout the world (aided in part by new exhibition and distribution outlets), and (2) the conversion of what were once strictly amateur or student-oriented film festivals to an added emphasis on independently produced video and audio.

This growth in independent film-video-audio contests is in sad contrast to a decline in the number of student-only film-video competitions. Apparently the booming public interest in student films, beginning in the mid-1960s and incorporating video in the last decade, has begun to diminish somewhat. And the once numerous smaller student festivals that proliferated in the contest field have been superseded by a lesser number of large student festivals offering important prizes and exposure. To find the necessary outlets for their work, students have been entering their film-video-audio in the many independent festivals.

The second, and possibly more important, increase has come in the number of Video-Audio Grants, Scholarships, Fellowships, Residence and Research Grants currently available (aided in part by the leadership in government grant funding over the past few years). Let us hope that these grant outlets can continue through aid from private sources.

There has also been an interesting increase in the number of international Business-Industrial, and Health-Medical video-audio festivals. Possibly more and more special-interest groups and organizations are finding that the sponsoring of a video festival is an excellent way of keeping up with the latest film, video, and audio releases in their respective fields.

A FEW CLOSING THOUGHTS —about the conduct of some events. While I have found the vast majority of events to be highly reputable and continually striving to improve their quality, there are still a few bad exceptions (lost entries, withheld awards, judging problems, etc.).

However, the interesting thing is that just as numbers and types of events change from year to year, so do most of these questionable conditions. Just when you hear someone complain about an unfair judging process, the next year the judges change, and that same person may come out a winner. Or the rules and administration change, and what was once a suspect practice disappears.

With this in mind, there has been no attempt on our part to editorialize about the occasional bad occurrences we hear of. This is strictly a reference guide (not a critical work). We list all those events which qualify, from the largest to the smallest, the oldest to the youngest, the well-known and the not so well-known. And we have tried to print enough information about each event to give you a firm basis upon which to decide whether or not to write for further information. (See HOW TO ANALYZE AN EVENT.)

It should also be stated that we do not endorse (or accept any responsibility for the conduct of) the events listed in this book.

Finally, no book of this type can ever be all-inclusive. That would be virtually impossible. Each year hundreds of new events start up, old ones lapse or go out of business, only to be replaced by similar events in a new form. As I have mentioned, there is constant growth and progression based on general changes in the art and media fields. However, considering the many individual events we have listed, each as thoroughly as possible within the edited format, and each updated and verified to the best of our knowledge based on entry materials and questionnaires provided us, we feel that we have brought you quite a comprehensive reference guide.

A special thank you to the American Library Association (the Reference and Adult Services Division, Reference Committee) for awarding the premiere edition an "OUTSTANDING REFERENCE SOURCE OF THE YEAR" . . . and to the many readers and reviewers of the previous book for their favorable response. These honors have been extremely gratifying.

And an additional thanks and grateful appreciation to the many events, sponsors, contributors, and correspondents who have so graciously provided us with the information included in this directory.

As a final reminder, please remember that to ensure you have the latest information, complete regulations, and proper entry forms, ALWAYS WRITE TO AN EVENT BEFORE ENTERING YOUR WORK

And please advise us of any new Contests, Festivals and Grants you may know of, so that we may include them in our future editions. Thank you.

Alan Gadney
Festival Publications
P.O. Box 10180
Glendale, California 91209 U.S.A.

ABBREVIATIONS

AFI	American Film Institute
AIVF	Association of Independent Video and Filmmakers
AMPAS	Academy of Motion Picture Arts and Sciences
ASIFA	Association of Internationale de Film d'Animation (International Association of Animated Film)
BDFA	Bundes Deutscher Filmamateure (German Amateur Film Association)
BBC	British Broadcasting Corporation
BFI	British Film Institute
CPB	Corporation for Public Broadcasting
EBU	European Broadcasting Union
FIAP	Federation Internationale de l'Art Photographique (International Federation of Photographic Art)
FIAPF	Federation Internationale des Associations de Producteurs de Films (International Federation of Film Producers' Associations)
IAMPTP	International Association of Motion Picture and Television Producers
IFFPA	International Federation of Film Producers' Associations
IFPA	International Federation of Photographic Art
ITU	International Telecommunications Union
JRT	Yugoslav Radio and Television
MPAA	Motion Picture Association of America
NAB	National Association of Broadcasters
NEA	National Endowment for the Arts
NEH	National Endowment for the Humanities
NFB	National Film Board of Canada
NSF	National Science Foundation
NYSCA	New York State Council on the Arts
PBS	Public Broadcasting Service
PSA	Photographic Society of America
UNESCO	United Nations Educational, Scientific, and Cultural Organization
UNICA	Union Internationale du Cinema d'Amateurs (International Union of Film Amateurs)
UNICEF	United Nations International Children's Emergency Fund

VIDEO-AUDIO
TV-RADIO
BROADCASTING

ADVERTISING, COMMERCIALS, PROMOTION

TV-Radio Broadcasting (video, film, audio), Cinema, Photo, Print, and Specialty Advertising, including AUTOMOBILE, BROADCAST PROMOTION, RETAIL; and ANIMATED, INDUSTRIAL television. (Also see AMERICANISM, BROADCASTING, DOCUMENTARY)

1

American Advertising Federation (AAF) Best in the West Competition
50 California Street, Suite 425
San Francisco, California 94111
U.S.A. Tel: (415) 421-6867

May

Regional; **entry restricted to Western U.S.;** annual; established 1950. Considered oldest advertising awards in West. Purpose: to honor western creativity. Sponsored by AAF, Western Region. Average statistics: 1500 entries, 300 winners, 50 average sales per entrant. Tickets: $50. Held in San Francisco. Also sponsor awards for consumer magazine, newspaper, business, farm publications, outdoor, transit, direct mail, sales promotion, print material, specialty advertising; AAF NATIONAL AWARDS COMPETI-TIONS.

VIDEOTAPE CONTEST: Advertising Television Broadcast (3/4-inch cassette). First Place Winners must be converted to film for award presentation. Categories: National, Regional (Over 30 seconds, under 30 seconds), Single Market (over million, under million population), Campaign (3 examples), Public Service (single, campaign), Complete Campaign (2 or more media).

FILM CONTEST: Advertising Television Broadcast (gauge not specified). Requirements and categories same as for video.

AUDIOTAPE CONTEST: Advertising Radio Broadcast (7 1/2 ips) any length, single announcement. Categories: National, Regional; Single Market (over million, under million population), Campaign (3 examples), Public Service (single, campaign), Complete Campaign (2 or more media).

ELIGIBILITY: First appeared in previous calendar year; produced in 13 Western states or El Paso, Texas.

AWARDS: Sweepstakes Awards. First, Second Place Trophies, 2 Merit Awards, each category. Special Awards for Complete Campaign. Special trophies to 2 agencies based on total score of winning entries. Audiovisual presentation of winners distributed to individual clubs, federations. All Best of West winners eligible for entry into AAF National Awards Competition. Trophies, Certificates to production companies.

JUDGING: By 70 media, agency, client judges. No entries returned.

ENTRY FEE: Single, $45; Campaign, $50; Complete Campaign, $55.

DEADLINES: Entry, January. Materials, February. Judging, March. Awards, May.

2

ANDY Awards
Advertising Club of New York
3 West 51st Street
New York, New York 10019 U.S.A.
Tel: (212) 245-1781

Fall

International; **entry restricted to U.S.; Canadian professionals;** annual; established 1964. Purpose: to recognize, promote excellence in advertising; advance-develop advertising profession. Sponsored by Advertising Club of New York. Average statistics: 10,000 entries, 100 semifinalists, 50 finalists, 100 awards. Held in New York City. Have consumer, business-professional print, sales promotion, outdoor advertising contests. Publish *ANDY Awards Annual.*

VIDEOTAPE CONTEST: **Advertising Television Broadcast** 3/4-inch U-matic cassette) broadcast during previous calendar year. Categories: Product Message Single, Campaign (Automotive, Travel, Leisure; Business Products; Fashion; Food; Health, Beauty; Services, Utilities); Institutional-Corporate Single, Campaign; Retail Single, Campaign; Public Service; Political.

FILM CONTEST: **Advertising Television Broadcast** (16mm). Re-

quirements and categories same as for video.

AUDIOTAPE CONTEST: **Advertising Radio Broadcast** (1/4-inch, 7 1/2 ips open reel). Categories, requirements same as for Videotape.

AWARDS: First Place ANDY Head Trophy, Certificate of Excellence, each category. Second, Third Place Certificates of Distinction, each category. Merit Certificates. All accepted entries included in *ANDY Awards Annual* and Exhibit.

JUDGING: Preliminary, General Screenings, Final by professionals, based on selling concept, copy, graphics, production. All entries become property of ANDY Awards.

ENTRY FEE: Individual 16mm TV, Radio, $15; Campaign, $45. Individual video cassette, $20; Campaign, $50. Acceptance: Individual, $50; Campaign, $75.

DEADLINES: Entry, December. Public Service, January. Judging, Notification, March. Awards, Fall.

3

Art Directors Club Annual Exhibition
Jack G. Tauss, Chairman
488 Madison Avenue
New York, New York 10022 U.S.A.

Spring

International; **entry restricted to U.S., Canada;** annual; established 1922. Purpose: to search for new expressions, techniques, breakthroughs, talents, directions. Sponsored by New York Art Directors Club. Publish *Art Directors Club Annual.* Also sponsor newspaper, magazine advertising, promotion-graphic design, poster, book jackets, art illustration, photography contests.

VIDEOTAPE CONTEST: Advertising, Animation Television Broadcast (3/4-inch cassette or kinescope) produced in U.S. or Canada, first broadcast in previous calendar year. Categories: Animation, Commercial (10 seconds or IDs, 30 seconds, 60 seconds or over), Commercial Campaign (10 seconds, 30 seconds, 60 seconds each spot), Public Service, Public Service Campaign, Political, Political Campaign. Campaign is 3 spots minimum, 5 spots maximum.

FILM CONTEST: Advertising, Industrial, Educational, Promotional, Animation Television Broadcast (16mm) produced in U.S. or Canada, first broadcast in previous calendar year. Categories: Animation, Commercial (10 seconds or IDs, 30 seconds, 60 seconds or over), Commercial Campaign (10 seconds, 30 seconds, 60 seconds each spot), Public Service, Public Service Campaign, Political, Political Campaign, Film Titles-Logos-Signatures, Industrial-Educational-Promotional Film, Film Promos. Campaign is 3 spots minimum, 5 spots maximum.

AWARDS: Gold, Silver Awards, Distinctive Merit Awards, each category. Merit Certificates, each exhibited.

JUDGING: By 61 judges. No entries returned. Not responsible for loss or damage.

ENTRY FEE: Commercials and films, $15 each spot. Campaigns, $50.

DEADLINES: Entry, November. Awards, Spring.

Broadcasters Promotion Association (University of Nebraska) Awards Competition
Pat Evans
248 West Orange

Lancaster, Pennsylvania 17603
U.S.A. Tel: (717) 397-5727

June

International; entry restricted to radio, television stations; annual; established 1977. Purpose: to recognize, encourage outstanding broadcast promotion, community involvement. Sponsored by Broadcasters Promotion Association (BPA). Cosponsored by University of Nebraska (formerly cosponsored by Michigan State University). Average statistics: 1000 entries, 4 countries, 80 winners. Held during BPA seminar. Also have categories for Print Ad, Outdoor Advertising, Promotion, Sales Promotion, Syndicated Materials, Program Distributors. Second contact: Peter Mayeux, Department of Broadcasting, 203 Avery Hall, University of Nebraska, Lincoln, Nebraska 68588. Tel: (402) 472-3046.

VIDEOTAPE CONTEST: Broadcast Promotion Television (3/4-inch cassette), 525 lines, aired between April previous year, March current year. Categories: Multi-Media Campaign (Outside, In-house, Limited); Announcement (News or Public Affairs, Other, In-house); Community Involvement (includes tape, photos or print, and brief narrative). Market Divisions: 1-25, 26-75, Other Markets.

AUDIOTAPE CONTEST: Broadcast Promotion Radio (7 1/2 ips). Requirements, categories same as for videotape.

AWARDS: First Place, 2 Finalist Plaques, each category. Certificates for finalists.

JUDGING: By leading advertising, promotion experts. Community Involvement judged separately. May withhold awards. Not responsible for loss or damage.

ENTRY FEE: $30 per entry, $35 per campaign. Entrant pays postage.

DEADLINES: Entry, March. Judging, June.

5

CLIO Awards (U.S. Competitions)
Bill Evans, President
30 East 60th Street
New York, New York 10022 U.S.A.
Tel: (212) 593-1900

June

National; **entry open to U.S.**; annual; established 1959. Purpose: to honor advertising excellence. Sponsored by CLIO Organization. Average statistics: 13,000 entries, 500 finalists, 100 winners, 6000 attendance. Held during CLIO Awards Festival Week, New York City, Los Angeles. Tickets: $50. Have advertising library. Publish *CLIO Magazine.* Also sponsor awards for packaging design, special advertising, print entries; CLIO AWARDS INTERNATIONAL TV, CINEMA, RADIO COMPETITION. Second contact: CLIO Awards, 5900 Wilshire Blvd., Los Angeles, California 90036; tel: (213) 937-7337.

VIDEOTAPE CONTEST: Advertising Television Broadcast (3/4-inch VTR cassette) introduced in U.S. January previous year to January current year. Product Categories (single entry): Automotive, Apparel, Banking-Financial, Beverages, Snacks, Cosmetics-Toiletries, Entertainment, Promotion, Foods, Home, IDs, Insurance, Media Promotion, Office Equipment, Personal Items, Pet products, Pharmaceuticals, Political, Public Service, Recreation, Recruitment, Retail Dealers, Food-Specialty Stores, Toys-Games, Transportation, Utilities. TV Technique Categories (single entry): Animation, Cinematography, Copywriting, Costuming, Direction, Edit-

ing, Film Effects, Graphics, Humor, Performance, Product Demonstration, Production Design, Original Music (Scoring and Lyrics), New Arrangements of Commercial Themes. Campaign (limit 3): National, Regional, Local (large, small).

FILM CONTEST: Advertising Television Broadcast (16mm). Requirements and categories, same as video.

AUDIOTAPE CONTEST: Advertising Radio Broadcast (1/4-inch reel, 7 1/2 ips full track). Product Categories same as for Videotape. Technique Categories: Announcer Presentation, Conceived-Produced by Station, Copywriting, Humor, Sound, Original Music (Scoring and Lyrics), New Arrangements of Commercial Themes, Music with Lyrics Openings, Tags or Donuts. Campaign (limit 3): National, Regional, Local (large, small).

AWARDS: CLIO Statue, each product and technique category. Finalists and winners receive Recognition Certificates.

JUDGING: By panel of advertising professionals based on sales communication, impact, motivation, believability, tastefulness, imaginative techniques. May alter, add, delete award classifications. Independent tabulated votes and judges forms available for inspection. Require 16mm duplicate negative of TV winners for exhibition (talent residual fees assumed by entrants). CLIO owns all entries.

ENTRY FEE: TV Single, Campaign, $75. Radio Single, Campaign, $50.

DEADLINES: Entry, October. Materials, December, February. Judging, February-April. Event, June.

TV CLASSIC HALL OF FAME COMPETITION: 16mm film or film transfer of CLIO contenders and winners first telecast in U.S. or Canada during previous 5 years, may be on air currently. Purpose: to enrich CLIO Library for industry, educators, students. Judging based on longevity, sales productiveness, memorability, influence on later techniques, awards won, innovative production techniques. 135 accepted to date.

6

CLIO Awards (International Competitions)

Bill Evans, President
30 East 60th Street
New York, New York 10022 U.S.A.
Tel: (212) 593-1900

May, June

International; **entry restricted to professionals (except U.S.)**; annual; established 1959. Purpose: to honor advertising excellence worldwide. Sponsored by CLIO Organization. Average statistics: 12,873 entries, 42 countries. Held during CLIO Awards Festival Week, New York. Publish *CLIO Award Festival Annual.* Also sponsor CLIO AWARDS (U.S. COMPETITIONS). Second contact: CLIO Awards, 5900 Wilshire Blvd., Los Angeles, California 90036; tel: (213) 937-7337.

VIDEOTAPE CONTEST: Advertising Television (3/4-inch Sony U-matic cassette, NTSC, U.S. Standard) script, photo from tape. Product Categories (single entry): Automotive, Apparel, Banking-Financial, Beverages, Snacks, Cosmetics-Toiletries, Entertainment, Promotion, Foods, Home, IDs, Insurance, Media Promotion, Office Equipment, Personal Items, Pet Products, Pharmaceuticals, Political, Public Service, Recreation, Recruitment, Retail Dealers, Food-Specialty Stores, Toys-Games, Transportation, Utilities. TV Technique Categories (single entry): Animation, Cinematog-

raphy, Copywriting, Costuming, Direction, Editing, Film Effects, Graphics, Humor, Performance, Product Demonstration, Product Design, Original Music (Scoring and Lyrics), New Arrangements of Commercial Themes. Campaign (limit 3): National, Regional, Local (large, small).

FILM CONTEST: Advertising Television and Cinema (35mm, 16mm) requirements and categories same as for Videotape.

AUDIOTAPE CONTEST: Advertising Radio (7 1/2 ips tape) script. Radio Product Categories, same as for Videotape. Technique Categories: Announcer Presentation, Conceived and Produced by Station, Copywriting, Humor, Use of Sound, Original Music (Scoring and Lyrics), New Arrangements of Commercial Themes, Music with Lyrics Openings, Tags or Donuts. Campaign (limit 3).

AWARDS: CLIO Statue, each product and technique category. Finalists and winners receive Certificates of Recognition.

JUDGING: Preliminary and final by panels of 450 judges in 12 countries, based on sales communication, impact, motivation, believability, tastefulness, imaginative techniques, creative appraisal. CLIO owns all entries for film and tape library use, showing, duplication; may publish photos of winners. Require 16mm duplicate negative of TV Cinema winners for exhibition.

ENTRY FEE: TV, Cinema single, $70; Campaign, $110. Radio single, $50; Campaign, $75.

DEADLINES: Entry, February. Judging, February to May. Event, May, June.

☐7

Communication Arts Magazine CA Design and Advertising Exhibition

Jean A. Coyne
410 Sherman Avenue
P.O. Box 10300
Palo Alto, California 94303 U.S.A.
Tel: (415) 326-6040

January

International; entry open to all; annual; established 1959. Sponsored by *Communication Arts Magazine*, bimonthly design publication (41,973 circulation) including *Art Annual* (photography and illustration), and *CA Annual* (advertising and design contests). Average statistics: 18,000 entries. Have other design categories: magazine, newspaper, trade, institutional, poster, record jacket, packaging, trademark, letterhead, company literature, editorial book, self-promotion, miscellaneous.

VIDEOTAPE CONTEST: Advertising Television (3/4-inch NTSC). Categories: Commercials, Commercial Series (3 maximum in series).

FILM CONTEST: Advertising Television (16mm) requirements and categories same as for Video.

AUDIOTAPE CONTEST: Advertising Radio (7-1/2 ips) requirements and categories same as for Video.

ELIGIBILITY: Produced, published between July previous year, June current year. Request English translations.

AWARDS: Certificate of Excellence all winners; published in *CA Annual* (48,000 circulation).

JUDGING: By outstanding designers, art directors, writers. All entries owned by Communication Arts.

ENTRY FEE: $12 per commercial; $18 per series.

DEADLINES: Entry, July. Acceptance, October. Awards, January.

☐8

Creativity Awards Show

Art Direction Magazine
Ray Morrison, Director
10 East 39th Street, 6th Floor
New York, New York 10016 U.S.A.
Tel: (212) 889-6500

September

International; **entry restricted to professionals;** annual; established 1960. Purpose: to record trends in advertising design, art, illustration, photography, TV commercials; reward, nationally publicize talented art directors. Sponsored by *Art Direction Magazine.* Average statistics: 15,000 entries, 800 winners. Held at New York Coliseum for 1 week. Have print advertising, photography categories. Publish *Creativity Annual,* international yearbook of show, *Advertising Techniques Magazine, Graphic Arts Buyer.* Second contact: *Art Direction Magazine,* 19 West 44th Street, New York, New York 10036.

VIDEOTAPE CONTEST: Advertising Television Broadcast (3/4-inch cassette) aired between June previous year, June current year. Categories: Consumer, Corporate, Public Service, Political (single unit, campaign); Show Openings, IDs, Titles, Art and Illustration, Photography, Animation.

FILM CONTEST: Advertising Television Broadcast (16mm) requirements and categories same as for Video.

AWARDS: Creativity Certificate of Distinction.

JUDGING: By committee, based on concept and design.

ENTRY FEE: Single, $10; campaign, $19; over 1 minute, $25.

DEADLINES: Entry, April. Judging, May. Winners announced, June. Event, September.

International Broadcasting Awards
Hollywood Radio and Television Society
Oliver H. Crawford, Executive Director
5315 Laurel Canyon Blvd.
North Hollywood, California 91607 U.S.A. Tel: (213) 769-4313

March

International; entry open to all; annual; established 1960. Purpose: to promote, improve, honor artistic, creative, technical excellence in broadcast advertising. Sponsored by Hollywood Radio and Television Society (founded 1947), nonprofit organization of broadcast advertising executives. Average statistics: 5000 entries, 50 countries, 22 awards, 1500 attendance. Held in Los Angeles. Tickets: $40 per person. Also sponsor BROADCAST MAN, WOMAN OF THE YEAR AWARDS; COLLEGE SCHOLARSHIPS IN BROADCASTING; Luncheon Lecture Series.

VIDEOTAPE CONTEST: Advertising Commercials Television Broadcast (2-inch, 3/4-inch cassette) 3 minutes maximum. Categories: Public Service, Local Broadcast, Series TV Film.

FILM CONTEST: Advertising Commercials Television Broadcast (35mm, 16mm). Categories: Station Identifications (any technique, 10 seconds maximum); Animation, Combination, Humorous, Public Service, Series of 3, Local Broadcast in one Market (each, any technique, 3 minutes maximum); English, Non-English Divisions for Live Action (30 seconds maximum, 60 seconds maximum).

AUDIOTAPE CONTEST: Advertising Commercials Radio Broadcast (7 1/2 ips). Categories: Musical, Humorous, Open (60 seconds, 30 seconds maximum); One Market Local, Public Service (60 seconds), Series of 3 (any technique, 3 minutes total maximum).

ELIGIBILITY: Broadcast anywhere in world during previous year (December to December). Require English translation scripts.

AWARDS: Grand Sweepstakes Awards, Best of World, Television and Radio. Spike Trophies Best each category. Judges' Awards, Best Technical, Color, Music. Certificates to all finalists. Plaques to sweepstakes winners, best each medium.

JUDGING: 40 judging panels in major advertising centers around world choose finalists. International board of judges in Hollywood chooses trophy winners and sweepstakes winners from finalists. Trophy winners circulated within industry at no charge.

ENTRY FEE: $50 per TV commercial, $35 radio. No entries returned.

DEADLINES: Entry, December. Prejudging, January; final judging, March. Event, March.

[10]
McMahan's 100 Best TV Commercials Competition
Harry Wayne McMahan
P.O. Box 725
Escondido, California 92025 U.S.A.

February

National; **entry restricted to U.S.**

professionals; annual; established 1959. Purpose: to inform creative people on accomplishments and trends in advertising. Sponsored by *Advertising Age Magazine.* Average statistics: 3,-000-5,000 entries, 100-250 entrants, 225 finalists, 100 awards. Held in major U.S. cities. Publish list of winners as special feature of *Advertising Age.* Have worldwide touring exhibition of winning entries.

FILM CONTEST: Advertising Commercials Television Broadcast (16mm). Require script, stills, credits, marketing data. Broadcast in previous year.

AWARDS: 100 Award Certificates. Touring Exhibition worldwide.

JUDGING: By informal panel of advertising professionals, based on innovativeness, cost efficiency, other noteworthy qualities. Sponsor owns entries.

ENTRY FEE: None.

DEADLINES: Entry, December. Judging, January. Winners announced, February.

11

National Retail Merchants Association (NRMA) Retail Television and Radio Commercials Competition
John A. Murphy, Vice President
100 West 31st Street
New York, New York 10001 U.S.A.
Tel: (212) 244-8780

May

International; entry open to all; annual; established 1944. Purpose: to recognize retail promotional creativity. Sponsored and supported by NRMA, Television Bureau of Advertising, Radio Advertising Bureau. Average statistics: 800 entries, 50 countries, 200 winners. Held at annual NRMA Sales Promotion Conferences, New York. Publish books, newsletters, magazines on retailing. Also sponsor Newspaper and Direct Mail Competition, Gold Awards Competition for sales promotion campaigns of NRMA-member retail stores, trade shows, seminars.

VIDEOTAPE CONTEST: Retail Commercials Television Broadcast (3/4-inch cassette), aired in previous year. Require marketing objectives, results. Categories: Single Commercial, Campaign (markets ranked 1-50, 51-100, 101 plus); Multimarket, Image Producing, Foreign.

FILM CONTEST: Retail Commercials Television Broadcast (gauges not specified). Requirements and categories, same as for Videotape.

AUDIOTAPE CONTEST: Retail Commercials Radio Broadcast, aired previous year. Categories: Item, Image, Promotion-Sale, Nonstore Retailer.

AWARDS: First, Second, Honorable Mention, each category. Television Trophies, First Place each category. Plaques for Best Foreign, Image Producing, Runners-Up.

JUDGING: 5-member panel of retailers, retail agency executives, TV representatives, based on saleable use of copy, art, photography. No entries returned.

ENTRY FEE: $5 per entry.

DEADLINES: Entry, January. Event, May.

12

The One Show Awards
One Club for Art & Copy
Beverly Daniels
777 Third Avenue

New York, New York 10017 U.S.A.
Tel: (212) 935-0121

May

International; **entry restricted to advertising students and professionals;** annual; established 1974. Purpose: to recognize best advertising of year. Theme: Interdependence and interrelationship of art directors and copywriters. Sponsored by and held at One Club for Art & Copy. Average statistics: 7000 entries from English-speaking countries, 500 finalists, 200 winners. Tickets: $65. Publish *Advertising Annual.* Also have categories for newspaper, magazine, trade, collateral publication, outdoor, political, corporate print advertising. Also sponsor (pending) Scholarship Fund, Career Guidance Sponsor Network.

VIDEOTAPE CONTEST: **Advertising Television Broadcast** (3/4-inch cassette, kinescope) 10-60 seconds depending on category; English only; first broadcast in previous calendar year. Require publicity material for use in *Advertising Annual.* Classes: Single, Campaign (3 ads each). Categories: Consumer, Campaign, Public Service Over, Political Over, Corporate Over. Subcategories by length.

FILM CONTEST: **Advertising Television Broadcast** (16mm). Requirements and categories same as for Videotape.

AUDIOTAPE CONTEST: **Advertising Radio Broadcast** (1/4-inch, 7 1/2 ips) any length. Other requirements, classes same as for videotape. Categories: Consumer, Public Service, Political, Corporate. Subcategories by length.

AWARDS: Gold, Silver Awards. Merit Certificates to finalists, each category.

JUDGING: Preliminary by 10 committees (3 advertising directors, 3 writers each). Open judging by advertising directors, writers (including entrants). One Show judges may recategorize entries, withhold awards. Entries and rights become property of One Club, for use in exhibitions, telecasts. Entrant absorbs residual charges for telecasting.

ENTRY FEE: Single entries, $35. Campaign, $60. One fee covers all costs. No returns.

DEADLINES: Entry, January (may vary yearly). Event, May.

13

TVB-NADA Commercials Competition
Television Bureau of Advertising
Bob Grebe
485 Lexington Avenue
New York, New-York 10017 U.S.A.
Tel: (212) 661-8440

February

National; **entry open to U.S.;** annual; established 1976. Purpose: to recognize outstanding television commercials by auto dealers and dealer associations. Sponsored by Television Bureau of Advertising, National Automobile Dealers Association (NADA). Average statistics: 250 entries. Held in various U.S. locations. Second Contact: Dick O'Donnell, 3155 Big Beaver Road, Suite 217, Troy, Michigan 48084.

VIDEOTAPE CONTEST: **Automobile Commercials Television Broadcast** (3/4-inch tape) any length, aired in previous calendar year. Categories: Car Dealers, Dealer Associations (ADI 1-50, 51-100, 100 and over).

ELIGIBILITY: NADA members, state and local dealer associations, TV stations, Automotive accounts.

AWARDS: 6 Plaques.

JUDGING: Entries viewed in entirety. Not responsible for loss or damage.

ENTRY FEE: Varies.

DEADLINES: Entry, judging, December. Event, February.

14

U.S. Television Commercials Festival
United States Festivals Association
J. W. Anderson, Chairman
841 North Addison Avenue
Elmhurst, Illinois 60126 U.S.A.
Tel: (312) 834-7773

January

International; entry open to all; annual; established 1970. World's largest TV commercial festival; became worldwide 1980. Purpose: to showcase TV commercials; increase production excellence; promote industry growth. Sponsored by United States Festivals Association. Average statistics: 1400 entries, 8 countries. Held in Chicago for 1 day. Also sponsor U.S. INDUSTRIAL FILM FESTIVAL.

VIDEOTAPE CONTEST: Television Advertising-Commercials (3/4-inch U-matic cassette NTSC, PAL) 3 minutes maximum; produced, aired in previous year. Foreign language tapes must have English script. Divisions: Single, Series (under $6000 cost, over $6000). Categories: Automotive, Children, Clothing, Commercial, Food, Home Care, Home Furnishings, Personal Articles-Gifts, Pet, Pharmaceutical, Recreation, Services, Other. Technique categories: Art, Animation, Copywriting, Editing, Music, Direction, Production, Photography, Talent.

FILM CONTEST: Television Advertising-Commercials (16mm) 3 minutes maximum; optical, magnetic. Requirements and categories, same as for video.

AWARDS: Chairman's Special Award, Best of Show. First Place Brass Plaques, each division and category. Merit Certificates for Outstanding Creativity, International Division. Duplicates in case of tie.

JUDGING: By 100 advertising agents, film producers, TV sponsors. May withhold awards. Festival library retains all winners for educational showings. Not responsible for loss or damage.

ENTRY FEE: Varies. Sponsor pays return postage.

DEADLINES: Entry, October. Awards, November. Event, January.

15

Irish Advertising Awards Festival
Oliver P. Walsh, Director
35 Upper Fitzwilliam Street
Dublin 2, IRELAND Tel: 765991, 764876

September

International; entry open to all; annual; established 1963. Formerly part of CORK FILM FESTIVAL, independent since 1970. Purpose: to improve standard of all broadcast and cinema commercials in Ireland. Sponsored and supported by Institute of Advertising Practitioners in Ireland. Average statistics: 650 entries, 16 countries, 300 attendance. Held in Wexford, Ireland, for 5 days. Tickets: $150. Have workshops, seminars.

VIDEOTAPE CONTEST: Advertising Commercials Television, Cinema (U-matic, PAL) 240 seconds maximum; 1 print per entry. Require 35-word English synopsis for foreign language. Categories: Worldwinner (of First Prize in international TV commercial contest during previous year); Ireland (12 subcategories); International (12 subcategories); International Series of 3 Films; Low-Budget; International Cinema (under 60 seconds, under 30 seconds). Subcategories: Alcoholic, Nonalcoholic Drinks; Food; Confectionery; Household Maintenance, Appliances; Cosmetics, Toiletry, Medical; Automotive; Clothing, Footwear, Textiles; Services, Institutional; Publications, Photographic Equipment; Public Services, Social Welfare; Miscellaneous.

FILM CONTEST: Advertising Commercials Television, Cinema (35mm, 16mm) requirements and categories same as for Video.

AUDIOTAPE CONTEST: Advertising Commercials Radio (reel-to-reel, 7 1/2 ips) English language only; 1 tape each entry. Categories: under 30 seconds, over 30 seconds, 240 maximum.

ELIGIBILITY: Must have been transmitted, exhibited publicly in previous year (Worldwinners excluded). Must have permission of advertiser and (or) agency. Entries submitted to previous IAAF Festivals not eligible (Worldwinners excepted). No entries offensive to national, religious sentiments; no political party, campaign commercials.

AWARDS: Worldwinner; Grand Prix Television, Cinema. Irish Grand Prix (produced for showing on Radio Telefis Eireann-Ulster Television). National Awards, best from each country entering 20 or more films. Palme d'Or to company with highest average for minimum entry of 6 TV films. Special Awards for Best Editing, Music Track, Camera Work, Animation. Special Merit Prizes. Premier Awards each category and subcate-

gory. Diplomas at judges' discretion. Delegates Awards (Ireland only).

JUDGING: By independent international panel of 5 TV-Cinema, 4 radio judges. All entries viewed in entirety. Entries in Worldwinner section, winners, and radiotapes not returned (retained in Festival library). Not responsible for loss or damage.

ENTRY FEE: Video-Film, $90 each; Radio, $50 each. Entrant pays postage.

DEADLINES: Entry, July. Materials, August. Festival, September.

16

ACC Commercial Film Festival International Category
All Japan Radio and Television Commercial Council
Shizuo Kawaguchi, Chairman
Bunshun Building
3 Kioi-cho, Chiyoda-ku
Tokyo, JAPAN

October

International; entry open to all; annual; established 1960. Considered largest, most prestigious broadcast, cinema commercials competition in eastern hemisphere. Sponsored by All Japan Radio and Television Commercial Council. Held at Hibiya Public Hall, Tokyo.

FILM CONTEST: Advertising Commercials Television, Cinema (35mm, 16mm). Broadcast or screened June previous year to May current year. Television categories: Live Action (45 seconds or under, 46 and over), Animation (3 minutes maximum), Series of 3 (9 minutes total maximum). Cinema category: Cinema (3 minutes maximum). Also have Asian area cinema and TV categories.

AWARDS: ACC Trophies, Best

each category. Diplomas at judges' discretion.

JUDGING: By 10 advertiser, agency, film producer, broadcaster, commentator judges based on superiority of concept, uniqueness of expression. ACC may keep all entries for nonprofit study.

ENTRY FEE: $40 per entry; $80 per series; $15 Asian area.

DEADLINES: Entry, June. Materials, July. Judging, September. Festival, October.

AGRICULTURE, CONSERVATION, ENVIRONMENTAL

TV-Radio Broadcasting (video, audio) and Film, including FOOD, TREE; and WILDLIFE. (Also see BROADCASTING, EDUCATIONAL-INFORMATIONAL, JOURNALISM, SCIENTIFIC-TECHNICAL.)

17

Arbor Day Awards
National Arbor Day Foundation
John Rosenow, Executive Director
411 South 13th Street, Suite 308
Lincoln, Nebraska 68508 U.S.A.
Tel: (402) 474-5655

April

National; **entry open to U.S.;** annual; established 1972. Purpose: to recognize outstanding tree-related activities in communications, education, planting projects. Sponsored by National Arbor Day Foundation (Arbor Lodge 100, Nebraska City, Nebraska 68410), nonprofit corporation of U.S.

conservation, business leaders. Held at Steinhart Lodge (Nebraska City) for 1 weekend. Publish *Arbor Day News.* Also sponsor awards for projects, advertising, public relations, education, communities, schools, organizations, media (magazine, motion picture, newspaper, radio, television); J. STERLING MORTON AWARD to individual who has best perpetuated Morton's tree-planting heritage; NATIONAL ARBOR DAY FOUNDATION PHOTO CONTEST.

VIDEOTAPE CONTEST: Tree Television Broadcast (videotape, kinescope). Require script or synopsis. Categories: Individual Program, Spot Announcement Series, Special Feature, Tie-In Premium Promotion.

AUDIOTAPE CONTEST: Tree Radio Broadcast (audiotape). Requirements, categories same as for Videotape.

AWARDS: Arbor Day Foundation Awards. Winner may use Arbor Day logo for 1 year.

JUDGING: By panel of conservationists, communications authorities. May withhold awards, change categories.

ENTRY FEE: None. Entrant pays postage.

DEADLINES: Entry, November. Materials, December. Judging, January. Awards, April. Materials returned, May.

18

**Heath Cooper Rigdon
Conservation Writer and
Broadcaster Awards**
Soil Conservation Society of America
(SCSA)
Larry D. Davis
7515 N.E. Ankeny Road

Ankeny, Iowa 50021 U.S.A.
Tel: (515) 289-2331

Spring

International; **entry restricted to newscasters, journalists;** annual; established 1975. Purpose: to recognize outstanding efforts in communicating natural resource conservation, public understanding, appreciation of science and art of good land use. Sponsored by SCSA. Held at annual SCSA Council meeting. Also sponsor membership only COMMENDATION AWARDS for service to own chapters, council of chapters, professional achievement.

VIDEOTAPE AWARD: **Conservation Television Newscaster** (width not specified) nomination describing newscasting activities of individual. Include videotapes produced by nominee.

AUDIO TAPE AWARD: **Conservation Radio Newscaster** (width not specified) nomination describing newscasting activities of individual. Include radio tapes produced by nominee.

ELIGIBILITY: Persons actively engaged in reporting for radio or television.

AWARDS: Conservation Newscaster Award Plaques, Honorarium.

JUDGING: By special committee based on newscasting effort.

ENTRY FEE: None.

DEADLINES: Entry, December.

| 19 |

International Wildlife Film Festival
Wildlife Society, Student Chapter
Dr. Charles Jonkel
Wildlife Biology Program
University of Montana

Missoula, Montana 59812 U.S.A.
Tel: (406) 243-5272

March-April

International; entry open to all; annual; established 1977. Purpose: to promote public education on wildlife issues; encourage production of best possible wildlife films. Sponsored and supported by ASUM Programming, Montana Committee for the Humanities. Average statistics: 35-40 entries, 5 countries, 15 awards, 1500 attendance. Held at University of Montana for weekend. Tickets: $1 per night. Have workshops on filming techniques, markets, panels, wildlife art display.

VIDEOTAPE CONTEST: **Wildlife** (3/4-inch, 1/2-inch) any length. Must be about animals as they relate to habitat; produced or released in year prior to festival. Categories: Amateur, Professional.

AWARDS: Best of Festival; Runner-Up. Best Amateur; Cinematography; Scientific Research; Technical Information; Educational Entertainment; Montana Amateur; Award by audience vote. Various Certificates, Merit Awards, Honorable Mentions. Winners' list sent to organizations, individuals to encourage sale of work.

JUDGING: By biologists, zoologists, filmmakers, humanists, editors; based on artistic quality, art form, intellectual-scientific treatments, content, message, highest total quality. Festival responsible for print cost in case of loss or damage.

ENTRY FEE: Professional, $35; Amateur, $15 each entry.

DEADLINES: Entry, March. Festival, April.

20

Oscars in Agriculture
DEKALB AgResearch
Ron Scherer, Public Relations
Director
Sycamore Road
DeKalb, Illinois 60115 U.S.A.
Tel: (815) 758-3461

September

National; **entry open to U.S. professional editors-broadcasters;** annual; established 1961. Purpose: to encourage excellence in reporting of agriculture news. Sponsored by DE-KALB AgResearch. Held during DEKALB Communications Days in corporate headquarters at DeKalb, Illinois.

VIDEOTAPE CONTEST: **Agriculture Television Broadcast** (3/4-inch cassette) complete program or highlights from single program-series; 1 maximum per broadcast entrant, each limited to 1 theme-topic. Require purpose, description, broadcast dates. Categories: Television, Team Effort.

AUDIOTAPE CONTEST: **Agriculture Radio Broadcast.** Requirements same as for Videotape. Categories: Radio, Team Effort.

ELIGIBILITY: Broadcast June 1 previous year to June 1 current year, by 1 or more professional editor-broadcasters on staff of commercial U.S. radio-TV station.

AWARDS: Silver Agriculture Oscars to First Place, each category, for superior contributions furthering advancement of American agriculture. Plaques to employers.

JUDGING: By 7 judges, based on timeliness, depth of reporting, organization-clarity, production techniques-quality. May withhold awards.

ENTRY FEE: None.

DEADLINES: Entry, June. Awards, September.

21

Berlin International Agricultural Film Competition
AMK Berlin Company for Exhibitions, Fairs and Congresses
Horst-Ludwig Stein, General Manager
Messedamm 22
Postfach 191740
D-1000 Berlin 19, WEST GERMANY
(FRG) Tel: 030-3081-1

January

International; **entry restricted** (nomination by official organizations in each country); biennial (even years); established 1968. Gold, Silver, Bronze Ear Awards, Special Prizes, Certificates to **Agriculture, Food, Environment Television Films** (35mm, 16mm, Super 8mm) **and Videotapes** (1-inch, 2-inch cassettes); 90 minutes maximum; produced in previous 2-4 years; no commercials; sponsor retains one copy for library use. Alternates with BERLIN INTERNATIONAL CONSUMER FILM COMPETITION. Purpose: to improve quality of agricultural films by international comparison; provide survey of pertinent productions; promote international cooperation. Sponsored by Federal Minister for Food, Agriculture, Forestry in Bonn; Senator for Economics in Berlin. Average statistics: 158 entries, 29 countries. Also have Agricultural Film Round Table (biennial). Event, January.

AMERICANISM, PATRIOTIC

TV-Radio Broadcasting, Video, and Audio, including ADVERTISING, STUDENT. (Also see BROADCASTING, EDUCATIONAL-INFORMATIONAL, JOURNALISM.)

22

Fourth Estate Award Program
American Legion (National)
Frank C. Momsen, Adjutant
P.O. Box 1055
Indianapolis, Indiana 46206 U.S.A.
Tel: (317) 635-8411
Fall

National; **entry restricted** (nomination by members); annual; established 1958. Three awards to **American Patriotic Television, Radio Communications Media.** Purpose: to recognize outstanding services to community, state, or nation which further American Legion policies-programs; contribute to preservation of American Way of Life. Sponsored by American Legion. Held in various U.S. cities at national convention. Event, Fall.

23

Freedoms Foundation National Awards
Freedoms Foundation at Valley Forge
Valley Forge, Pennsylvania 19481 U.S.A.
February

National; **entry open to U.S.;** annual; established 1949. Purpose: to recognize deeds that support America, contribute to citizenship, suggest solutions to problems. Sponsored by Freedoms Foundation at Valley Forge. Recognized by National Association of Secondary School Principals. Held

during George Washington Birthday Celebration at Valley Forge and at local ceremonies. Have sermon, public-youth public addresses; college campus-community program; government-national activity; economic education; teacher, educator, individual contribution awards. Also sponsor other media contests; George Washington Plaque to Outstanding Individual; Principal School Award.

VIDEOTAPE CONTEST: Americanism Television Broadcast, Advertising, School (3/4-inch cassette) require script or synopsis, TV broadcast date. Complete 4-part (or less) series acceptable.

AUDIOTAPE CONTEST: Americanism Radio Broadcast, Advertising, School. Requirements same as for Videotape.

ELIGIBILITY: Developed, released, October previous year to October current awards year (school entries during academic year ending July 1); by U.S. citizens, U.S. Armed Forces personnel, on American Way of Life.

AWARDS: George Washington Honor Medals, Certificates; Valley Forge Honor Certificates. One award per person per category. Special Awards.

JUDGING: By national jury of state Supreme Court justices; patriotic, civic, service, veterans organization officers. May change classifications, amounts, withhold awards; retain or have access to winners for 3 years minimum for awards library research, display, convention, staff use.

ENTRY FEE: None.

DEADLINES: Entry, July (school), October (others). Judging, November. Awards announced, December. Event, February.

24

Voice of Democracy National Broadcast Scriptwriting Scholarship Program
Veterans of Foreign Wars of the Unites States
Lawrence LeFebvre, Director
VFW National Headquarters
Broadway at 34th Street
Kansas City, Missouri 64111 U.S.A.

March

National; **entry restricted to U.S. high school students;** annual; established 1948. Purpose: to encourage high school students to express opinions about American democracy patriotism, responsibility. Sponsored by Veterans of Foreign Wars (VFW) of the United States, VFW Ladies Auxiliary, Associations of Broadcasters. Recognized by National Association of Secondary School Principals. Average statistics: 250,000 entries, 8500 schools.

AUDIOTAPE CONTEST: Student Patriotic, (reel tape, 7 1/2 ips, single track) 3-5 minute recorded script on various yearly themes, by 10th-12th grade students in U.S. public, parochial, private schools. Classroom projects acceptable,. No foreign exchange students.

AWARDS: State winners get 5-day expense-paid trip to Washington, D.C. and compete for National College Scholarships. First Place, $14,000 Scholarship; Second Place, $7000; Third, $4500; Fourth, $3500; Fifth, $2500. Merit Certificates, Bonds, Scholarships; Awards to school, community, district, state winners.

JUDGING: Preliminary at entrant's school, followed by city-community, district, state competitions. State winners go to VFW National Headquarters; final judging based on delivery,

originality, content, theme interpretations, positive approach. State winners must attend national finals. VFW retains, owns all entries.

ENTRY FEE: None.

DEADLINES: Entry, Fall. School-community judging, November; district, December; state and national, January. National finals, March.

ANIMATED, EXPERIMENTAL, AVANT-GARDE
Includes GRAPHICS, ILLUSTRATION, INDEPENDENT, SHORT. (Also see ADVERTISING, DOCUMENTARY-SHORT, INDEPENDENT, TELEVISION FILMS.)

25

Anthology Film Archives Exhibitions of Avant-Garde Film and Video
Jonas Mekas
80 Wooster Street
New York, New York 10012 U.S.A.
Tel: (212) 226-0010

Continuous

International; entry open to all; continuous throughout year; established 1970. Purpose: to exhibit, preserve independent avant-garde film, video. Sponsored by and held at Anthology Film Archives. Supported by NEA, NYSCA, Jerome Hill Foundation, Mobil Oil Foundation. Average statistics: 250 shows (year-round). Tickets: $3 general public, $2 members. Have repertory and study collections of avant-garde independent films, video archives, reference library, film preservation program.

VIDEOTAPE EXHIBITION: Avant-Garde, Independent (width not specified). Request artists attend showings and discussions.

AWARDS: None.

ENTRY FEE: None.

DEADLINES: Open.

26

DESI Awards Competition
Graphics Design: USA Magazine
Louis J. Boasi, Director
32 Gansvoort Street
New York, New York 10014 U.S.A.
Tel: (212) 675-5867

Spring

National; **entry open to U.S. citizens;** annual; established 1977. Purpose: showcase for top, upcoming designers, illustrators, photographers from the worlds of design, advertising, promotion, public relations, publishing, television, finance. Sponsored by *Graphics Design: USA.* Held in New York City for 2 weeks. Second contact: Valerie Stewart, Graphics Design USA, 120 East 56th Street, New York, New York 10022.

VIDEOTAPE CONTEST: Design Graphics (3/4-inch cassette) created, produced in previous year. Category: TV Graphics.

AWARDS: DESI Certificates for each winner.

JUDGING: 4 judges experienced in graphics design field. Not responsible for loss or damage.

ENTRY FEE: $15 per cassette; $20, campaign series.

DEADLINES: Entry, January. Judging, February-March. Awards, April.

27

Infinite Forum Visual Recording Arts Expo
Pro Arts
1214 Webster Street
Oakland, California 94612 U.S.A.
Tel: (415) 763-7880

April

International; entry open to all; annual; established 1978. Purpose: to present creative and unique short films, videotapes, multimedia. Sponsored by Pro Arts. Held at Oakland Auditorium Theater (10th Street, Oakland, California). Also have photo exhibitions.

VIDEOTAPE CONTEST: Experimental Short (widths not specified).

MULTI-MEDIA CONTEST: Experimental.

AWARDS: Over $1200 cash awards.

ENTRY FEE: None specified.

DEADLINES: Entry, March. Event, April.

28

Society of Illustrators Annual Exhibition
Terry Brown, Curator
128 East 63rd Street
New York, New York 10021 U.S.A.
Tel: (212) 838-2560

February-April

National; **entry restricted to U.S. illustrators;** annual; established 1958. Purpose: to present best in illustration art. Sponsored by Society of Illustrators. Held in Society's Gallery and reproduced in *Illustrators Annual Book.* Have advertising, editorial, book, slide, institutional illustration categories.

VIDEOTAPE CONTEST: Illustrated (3/4-inch cassette) 5 minutes maximum per segment; made in year prior to event. Categories: Commercials, Title Slides, Promotional, Educational, Courtroom Reporting.

AWARDS: Gold, Silver Medals, Certificates for Excellence, to illustrators, art directors for Best each show. Merit Certificates.

JUDGING: By 5 judges.

ENTRY FEE: $10 per reel. $35 per acceptance.

DEADLINES: Entry, October. Event, February-March. Materials returned, April.

29

Ottawa International Animation Festival
Canadian Film Institute
Kelly O'Brien, Director
75 Albert Street, Suite 911
Ottawa, Ontario K1P 5E7 CANADA
Tel: (613) 238-6748

August

International; **entry restricted to independents, professionals;** biennial; established 1976. Alternates with ANNECY INTERNATIONAL ANIMATED FILM FESTIVAL (France), VARNA WORLD ANIMATION FILM FESTIVAL (Bulgaria), ZAGREB WORLD FESTIVAL OF ANIMATED FILMS (Yugoslavia). Purpose: to celebrate international animation art; inspire new production, forms, techniques, audiences. Sponsored by Canadian Film Institute, founded 1935 to encourage, promote study, appreciation, use of films in Canada through National Film Library, Film Theater, publications and Filmmakers Service Unit. Supported by Secretary of State Festivals Bureau, Ontario Arts Council, Canadian Film Development Corporation, Canadian Broadcasting Corporation, NFB. Recognized by ASIFA, FIAPF. Average statistics: 650 entries, 32 countries, 15 winners, 1000-7000 attendance. Held at National Arts Centre, Ottawa, for 6 days (formerly held in Mamaia, Rumania). Have press room. Tickets: $130 for series. Second contact: Canadian Film Institute, 1105-75 Albert Street, Ottawa, Ontario K1P 5E7, Canada.

VIDEOTAPE CONTEST: Animated (EIAJ standard 3/4-inch cassette). 30 minutes maximum; completed, copyrighted, or first shown after August previous year. Require description, 3 stills, biography. Categories: Animated (under 3 minutes, over 3), Promotional (commercials, public service announcements, fillers not over 5 minutes), First Film by Student, Independent Filmmaker, For Children, Instructional.

AWARDS: Grand Prize Silver Owl Trophy, Best of Festival. First, second prizes, each category. Special jury prizes for writing, music, graphics, design, coloring, other at judges' discretion.

JUDGING: Viewed in entirety by 5-10 international judges. Festival may show 1 minute of entry on television for publicity. Sponsor insures for cost of new print.

ENTRY FEE: None. Require return postage.

DEADLINES: Entry, June. Materials, July. Event, August. Materials returned, October.

30

Espaces Days of Experimental Cinema
Pro Helvetia
O Ceresa, Vice Director
Hirschengraben 22

CH-8001 Zurich, SWITZERLAND
Tel: 01-34-84-54

February

International; entry open to all; annual; established 1977. Purpose: to show experimental films without pre-screening to preserve freedoms essential for direct communication between filmmaker and audience. Sponsored by Pro Helvetia. Average statistics: 180 entries, 24 retrospectives. Held at Porte de la Suisse (11 bis, rue Scribe, Paris 9e, France). Have music programs, retrospectives, panel discussions. Second contact: Porte de la Suisse, 11 bis, rue Scribe, Paris 9e, France.

VIDEOTAPE FESTIVAL: Experimental, Independent (width not specified).

AWARDS: None.

ENTRY FEE: None.

DEADLINES: Entry, January. Event, February.

The ARTS

Video and Audio, including DANCE and POETRY. (Also see DRAMATIC-MUSICAL, BROADCASTING, CULTURE, EDUCATIONAL, INDEPENDENT.)

31

Dance and Mime Film and Videotape Festival
Dance Films Association
Susan Braun, President
250 West 57th Street, Room 2201
New York, New York 10107 U.S.A.
Tel: (212) 586-2142

April

International; entry open to all; annual; established 1971 (film), 1980 (video). Formerly called DANCE FILMS FESTIVAL. Purpose: to encourage excellence in films about dance. Sponsored and recognized by Dance Films Association, nonprofit service organization for dance audiovisual aids. Average statistics: 40-50 entries, 20 finalists. Held at Studio 58 (Wellington Hotel, 55th Street and 7th Avenue, New York City) for 2 days. Publish *Dance and Mime Film and Videotape Catalog.*

VIDEOTAPE CONTEST: Dance (3/4 to 1/2-inch) any length; must be in general distribution. Categories: Ballet; Modern (performance and technique); Folk, Ethnic, Primitive; Jazz, Theatrical; Ballroom; Experimental; Therapy; Education; Preclassic Forms; Mime.

AWARDS: Best of Festival Award. Certificates of Excellence. Honorable Mentions.

JUDGING: Preliminary by committee of dancers, filmmakers, critics. Semifinalists by 5 judges from Dance Films Association board, other experts when appropriate. Not responsible for loss or damage.

ENTRY FEE: 1-10 minutes, $5; 10-30, $10; 30-60, $15; over 60, $20.

DEADLINES: Entry, February. Event, April.

32

Dance Film Festival
Cinema Chicago
Michael J. Kutza, Jr., Director
415 North Dearborn Street
Chicago, Illinois 60610 U.S.A.
Tel: (312) 644-3400

July

International; entry open to all; annual; established 1976. Purpose: to showcase international dance trends, bring dance to the public. Motto: "Gotta dance." Sponsored by Cinema Chicago, nonprofit tax-exempt educational-cultural organization devoted to discovery, exhibition of world film and videotape. Supported by Illinois Arts Council, City of Chicago. Average statistics: 100 entries, 15 countries, 10 awards, 10,000 attendance. Held in Chicago for 7 days. Tickets: $2.50. Also sponsor CHICAGO INTERNATIONAL FILM FESTIVAL, POSTER COMPETITION, INTERCOM INDUSTRIAL FILM AND VIDEOTAPE COMPETITION. Second contact: Suzanne McCormick, Executive Director.

VIDEOTAPE CONTEST: Dance Feature, Short, Television Production, Independent (width not specified). Categories: Technique, Movement; History, Biography; Visual Essay, Experimental; Ballet Performance; Contemporary Dance Performance; Ethnic, Folk Dance Performance.

AWARDS: Gold, Silver, Bronze Hugos. Gold and Silver Plaques. Certificates of Merit.

ENTRY FEE: Not specified.

DEADLINES: Entry, June. Event, July.

33

Poetry Film Festival
Poetry Film Festival Workshop
Herman J. Berlandt, Director
2 Casa Way, #201
San Francisco, California 94123
U.S.A. Tel: (415) 921-4470

December

International; entry open to all; annual; established 1975. Purpose: to encourage experimentation, new forms of poetry presentation via film and video. Motto: "The power of poetry as handmaiden for all muses." Sponsored by Poetry Film Festival Workshop, nonprofit activity center providing location for production of poetry films, videotapes, forum for collaboration of poets, filmmakers and videomakers. Held at Fort Mason Conference Hall, San Francisco, for 3 days. Tickets: $3-$25. Have research, production facilities, editing lab, film archive, showcase theater. Also sponsor weekly POETRY FILM & VIDEO EXHIBITIONS AND DISTRIBUTION, YOUNG PEOPLE'S SUPER 8 FILM FESTIVAL. Second contact: Poetry Film Theater, Fort Mason Cultural Center, Building D, Room 295, San Francisco, California 94123.

VIDEOTAPE CONTEST: Poetry, sound or silent, incorporating verbal poetic statement (narrated or captioned).

AWARDS: $200 First, $100 Second, $75 Third, $50 Fourth Prize. 2 Honorable Mentions. Winning entries sent on American, Canadian, European touring exhibition.

ENTRY FEE: $5 per entry. Entrant pays postage.

DEADLINES: Entry and Event, December.

34

Prize Poetry Performed on Tape
Audio-Visual Poetry Foundation
W. I. Throssell, Director
400 Fish Hatchery Road
Marianna, Florida 32446 U.S.A.
Tel: (904) 482-3890

January, July

International; **entry open to English Speakers;** semiannual; established 1981. Purpose: to encourage effective presentation of quality poetry; restore appreciation for elegance, dignity, character, power, beauty, significance to spoken English language. Sponsored and supported by W. I. Throssell, Director. Average statistics: 18 entries, 4 awards. Have local school poetry contests, local service club programs, taped poetry round-robins.

AUDIOTAPE CONTEST: Poetry (C-60 cassettes) 3 minutes maximum, original only.

AWARDS: 4 cash prizes, $50 each. Written comments, 1-hour cassette of all entries to each entrant.

JUDGING: By participants and sponsor (total 20 ballots). Based on enunciation, articulation, pronunciation modulation, cadence; quality and applicability of sound effects; freedom from obscurity, pomposity, banality, triteness, sentimentality, and the like; good taste, imaginativeness, educativeness, grammar, precision. Sponsor makes copies for distribution to other participants, nonprofit institutions, blind, homebound.

ENTRY FEE: None. Entrant pays postage.

DEADLINES: Entry, January, July. Awards, February, August.

BROADCASTING (General)

TV-Radio Broadcasting (video, film, audio), including ADVERTISING, DOCUMENTARY, INDEPENDENT, STUDENT, NIGHTTIME. (Also see CHILDREN-YOUTH, DRAMATIC-MUSICAL, EDUCATIONAL, JOURNALISM, RELIGIOUS, TELEVISION FILMS.)

35

Chicago International Film Festival
Cinema Chicago
Michael J. Kutza, Jr., Director
415 North Dearborn Street
Chicago, Illinois 60610 U.S.A.
Tel: (312) 644-3400

November

International; entry open to all; annual; established 1965. Purpose: to present highest quality programs; develop audiences for fine film; promote demand for quality productions. Motto: "To encourage better understanding between people and make a positive contribution to the art form of film." Sponsored by Cinema Chicago. Supported by City of Chicago, Illinois Arts Council, Chicago Community Trust, Abbie Norman Prince Trust. Recognized by MPAA, City of Chicago. Average statistics: 2000 entries, 142 awards, 85,-000 attendance. Held in Chicago for 3 weeks. Tickets $3.50-$4. Also sponsor retrospectives, director and critic discussions, POSTER COMPETITION (feature and independent film and related fields posters), DANCE FILM FESTIVAL, INTERCOM INDUSTRIAL FILM AND VIDEOTAPE COMPETITION. Second contact: Suzanne McCormick, Executive Director.

VIDEOTAPE CONTEST: Television Production (3/4-inch cassette NTSC U.S. Standard) produced during year prior to event, not shown in Midwest U.S. Divisions: Local, Network; Open Broadcast, Cable. Categories: Features for TV, Education, Documentary, Public Affairs, Variety, Children's Program, Television Series, News Documentary, Spot Coverage, Special Events.

Television Commercials (3/4-inch cassette NTSC U.S. Standard). Divisions: Local, National, International. Categories: Apparel, Automotive, Beverages, Children's Products, Corporate and Institutional, Financial, Food, Fuel, Public Utilities, Home Furnishings and Appliances, Media and Entertainment, Personal and Home Products, Pharmaceuticals, Public Service, Political, Pet Products, Recreation, Travel and Transportation, Station Promos, Titles and Credits, Series (3 in a campaign). Technical categories: Overall Production, Direction, Cinematography, Animation, Editing, Music, Special Effects, Humor, Acting.

Student (3/4-inch cassette NTSC U.S. Standard). Require proof of student status, production details, grade level. Categories: Animation, Feature, Experimental, Educational, Documentary, Short Subject Fiction.

Independent Nonbroadcast (3/4-inch cassette NTSC U.S. Standard). Independent productions made directly on videotape but not produced specifically for broadcast television. Categories: Fiction, Documentary, Educational, Videoarts.

AWARDS: Features: Grand Prix Gold, Silver, Bronze Hugos; Gold, Silver Plaques to Best Feature Videotape, Director, Actress, Actor, Color or Black and White Cinematography, First Feature, Screenplay. Gold, Silver, Bronze Hugos, each major category; Gold, Silver Plaques each subcategory. Certificates of Merit. Norman McLaren Award, $250 and Plaque, Best Short Subject with unusual animation or innovative techniques. Niles Communications Centers Awards: $100 to 2 videotapes by students not in a film course. Illinois Award, Special Plaque to outstanding Illinois videomaker any category. Films Incorporated Award, $250 and Certificate, best creative short videotape by young videomaker. IDC Chicago Creative Award, gift, for outstanding creative talent and (or) contributions to Chicago's creative community.

JUDGING: Prescreening by 150-member national jury. International jury screens all feature tapes, 40 maximum. May change categories, withhold awards. Not responsible for loss or damage.

ENTRY FEE: Feature, $100. Invited features, no charge. Under 12 minutes, $50; 12-25 minutes, $60; 26-47 minutes, $70; 48 and over, $85. Student, $20. Television productions under 30 minutes, $60; 30-60 minutes, $100, 61 and over, $150. Television commercials, Individual $35; Series $90.

DEADLINES: Entry, September. Event, November.

36

Emmy Awards for Nighttime Programming
Academy of Television Arts and Sciences
John Leverence
4605 Lankershim Blvd., Suite 800
North Hollywood, California 91602
U.S.A. Tel: (213) 506-7880

September

National; **entry restricted to U.S. network, public broadcast, syndicated television;** annual; established 1977. Purpose: to recognize excellence in programming, creative arts and sciences of television broadcasting. Sponsored by Academy of Television Arts and Sciences. (Formerly sponsored by National Academy of Television Arts and Sciences, New York). Average statistics: 2500 entries. Held in Pasadena, California. Also sponsor LOS ANGELES AREA EMMY AWARDS, STUDENT FILM AWARDS; seminars, pre-broadcast screening of major television movies.

Publish quarterly *Emmy Magazine.*

VIDEOTAPE CONTEST: Nighttime Television Broadcast. Original airdate between July and June in Contest year, over ABC, CBS, NBC, PBS; if syndicated, available to 51% of U.S. households. Aired between 6 p.m. and 2 a.m. all time zones. Nighttime Categories: Series Program (Comedy, Drama, Comedy-Variety-Music, Limited). Special Program (Comedy or Drama, Comedy-Variety-Music, Children's). Classical Program or Series. Lead Actor, Actress (Comedy, Drama, Limited Series; Comedy-Drama Special, Single Series Appearance). Supporting Actor, Actress (Comedy, Drama Series; Variety-Music, Comedy-Drama Special, Single). Directing, Writing, Art Direction-Scenic Design (Comedy, Drama Series; Comedy-Variety-Music Series, Special; Special Program for Director, Original Teleplay, Adaptation, Dramatic Art Direction). Cinematography, Music Composition, Film Sound Editing, Videotape Editing (Series, Special). Costume Design (Drama Special, Music-Variety, Drama-Comedy Series). Film Editing (Comedy, Drama Series; Special). Choreography, Music Direction, Special Music, Graphic Design-Titles, Make-up, Film Sound Mixing, Tape Sound Mixing, Technical Direction-Electronic Camerawork, Lighting Direction; Special Event, Special Achievement (Individuals, Programs). Children Nighttime, Creative Technical Crafts.

FILM CONTEST: Nighttime Television Broadcast, requirements and categories same as for Video.

ELIGIBILITY: Network programs automatically considered. Syndicated program directors must contact awards office regarding entry requirements. TV movies in foreign theatrical release acceptable; no motion pictures released theatrically in U.S.

AWARDS: Gold Emmy Statuettes to individual winners, each category. Nomination Certificates. Production Certificates, Craft Citations available to be awarded by winners to their supporting personnel.

JUDGING: Votes cast by all Academy members determine nominees. Peer-group panels view nominees in entirety. Final winners by panels in secret ballot supervised by accounting firm. Winners become property of ATAS-UCLA Television Archives.

ENTRY FEE: None.

DEADLINES: Entry, June. Acceptance, July. Judging, August. Event, September.

37

George Foster Peabody Radio and Television Awards
University of Georgia
Dr. Worth McDougald, Director
School of Journalism and Mass Communication
Athens, Georgia 30602 U.S.A.
Tel: (404) 542-3785

Spring

International; entry open to all; annual; established 1939. Purpose: to recognize distinguished achievement, public service by networks, stations, producing organizations, individuals. Sponsored by Henry W. Grady School of Journalism and Mass Communication, University of Georgia. Considered "Pulitzer prizes" of fifth estate. Average statistics: 850 entries.

VIDEOTAPE CONTEST: Television Broadcast (2-inch, 3/4-inch U-matic) broadcast, distributed in previous calendar year. Categories: News,

Entertainment, Education, Children, Documentaries, Public Service or Organizations.

FILM CONTEST: Television Broadcast (gauges not specified). Requirements, categories same as for Videotape.

AUDIOTAPE CONTEST: Radio Broadcast (3/4-inch or 7-inch reel). Requirements, categories same as for Videotape.

AWARDS: Bronze Medallion and Engraved Certificate to all winners for Excellence in Broadcasting.

JUDGING: Prescreened by University of Georgia faculty. Final by 15-member National Advisory Board based on quality, distinguished service rather than popularity, commercial success. All entries kept by Peabody Research Collection, housed in University Libraries.

ENTRY FEE: $56 per entry.

DEADLINES: Entry, January. Judging, March. Awards, May.

38

Golden Globe Awards
Hollywood Foreign Press Association
8732 Sunset Blvd., Suite 210
Hollywood, California 90069 U.S.A.
Tel: (213) 657-1731

January

International; **entry restricted** (selection by members); annual; established 1943. Various drama, comedy, musical category awards in **Feature, Documentary Films, Television Shows.** Sponsored by Hollywood Foreign Press Association. Average statistics: 25 winners. Event, January.

39

Major Armstrong Awards in Radio Broadcasting
Armstrong Memorial Research Foundation
Patricia Hurd, Coordinator
Central Mailroom, 101 University Hall
Columbia University
New York, New York 10027 U.S.A.
Tel: (212) 666-8786

Fall

International; **entry restricted to U.S., Canada** annual, established 1964. Named after Major Edwin H. Armstrong, FM broadcasting inventor. Purpose: to reward and honor excellence, originality in AM-FM radio programs of greatest benefit to audiences. Sponsored and supported by Armstrong Memorial Research Foundation, National Radio Broadcasters Association. Average statistics: 300 entries, 6-12 awards. Second contact: Professor Kenneth K. Goldstein, Graduate School of Journalism, Columbia University, New York, New York 10027.

AUDIOTAPE CONTEST: Radio Broadcasting (1/4-inch tape, maximum 7-inch reel, head out; cassette, no 8-track cartridges), 1/2-track mono, 1/4-track stereo; produced and first broadcast previous calendar year. Scripts, explanatory material optional. Enter works in 1 category only; maximum 2 entries per category. Categories: Music, News, News Documentary, Public-Community Service, Education, Creative Use of Medium.

AWARDS: Plaques, Merit Certificates, each category.

JUDGING: By 6-member awards committee. May recategorize entries. Entries without return postage become property of Armstrong Foundation.

ENTRY FEE: $25. Entrant pays postage.

DEADLINES: Entry, June. Judging, Summer. Event, Fall.

40

Association of Canadian Television and Radio Artists (ACTRA) Awards

Jane Craig, Communications Director
105 Carlton Street
Toronto, Ontario M5B 1M2 CANADA
Tel: (416) 977-6335

April

National; **entry restricted** (nomination by ACTRA members and public); annual; established 1972. Nellie Statuette and other awards for **Canadian Television, Radio** to promote Canadian talent. Televised nationally on CBC-TV. Purpose: to promote Canadian radio-TV writers and performers. Sponsored by 6600-member ACTRA. Held in Vancouver. Event, April.

41

Banff International Festival of Films for Television

Banff Centre
J. David Gardiner, Director
P.O. Box 1020
Banff, Alberta T0L 0C0 CANADA
Tel: (403) 762-6247, 762-6100

September

International; entry open to all; annual; established 1979. Formerly called COMMONWEALTH GAMES INTERNATIONAL FILM FESTIVAL. Purpose: to recognize, celebrate world's leading television films, programs; provide competitive showcase for screening world premieres; stage professional seminars; provide marketplace; encourage Canadian film industry's development, international recognition. Sponsored by New Western Film and Television Foundation of Banff, nonprofit cultural agency devoted to promoting arts, crafts of motion picture industry. Supported by Government of Alberta. Recognized by Canadian Film Institute, Ottawa; Festivals Bureau, Department of Secretary of State, Ottawa; Department of Culture, Alberta; Alberta Motion Picture Industries Association. Average statistics: 63 entries. Held at Banff Centre for 11 days. Have conferences, seminars, retrospectives.

VIDEOTAPE CONTEST: For Television (3/4-inch NTSL cassette) in English or French or with subtitles. Require 3 stills, synopsis, credits. Categories (one only): Television Feature, Drama Special, Limited Series (or Mini-Series), Continuing Series (or Prime-Time Series), Situation Comedy, Documentary (Social-Political, Travel, Leisure, Wildlife), For Children.

ELIGIBILITY: Broadcast during previous year; not theatrically released prior to telecast; not entered in other North American film festival.

AWARDS: $5000 Grand Prize, Best of Festival. $1000, Best each category. Optional $1000, Best Dramatized Documentary (at jury's discretion). Banff Festival Trophies to winning producers; Cash, Certificates to directors. Certificates all films selected.

JUDGING: By international jury. Sponsor may use portions (3 minutes maximum) of entries for Festival promotion. Sponsor insures for print cost.

ENTRY FEE: $50 per entry. Sponsor pays return postage.

DEADLINES: Entry, August. Event, September.

42

MIP-TV International Television Programme Market
Bernard Chevry, Commissaire General
179 Avenue Victor Hugo
75116 Paris, FRANCE Tel: 505-14-03

April

International; **entry restricted to professionals;** annual; established 1965. Purpose: to facilitate selection, purchase, sale of television programs. Average statistics: 1843 features presented, 8570 television programs, 105 countries; 3500 participants. Held at the Palais des Festivals, Cannes, France, for 7 days. Publish *MIP TV Guide, MIP TV News.* Also sponsor INTERNATIONAL CO-PRODUCTION OFFICE. Second contact: Jack Kessler, International Exhibition Organisation Ltd., 9 Strafford Street, London W1X 3PE, United Kingdom; tel: (01) 499-23-17. John Nathan, 30 Rockefeller Plaza, Suite 4535, New York, New York 10112; tel: (212) 489-1360.

VIDEOTAPE SALES MARKET: Television Programs. Booths, with and without private screening rooms (video cassette and monitor can be rented). Video centers equipped with video cassette decks and monitors (SONY U-matic: NTSC, PAL, SECAM; VCR Philips: PAL, SECAM), $31 per 30 minutes.

FILM SALES MARKET: Feature (For Television); Booths, with and without private screening rooms (16mm projector and screen can be rented). Other screening rooms equipped with 16mm (standard, double track), 35mm (standard). Screening rooms, $31 per 30 minutes; 500-seat hall, $52 per 30 minutes.

AWARDS: None.

ENTRY FEE: $520 (includes salaried staff) covers unlimited entry, inclusion in *MIP TV News,* view all programs, opening reception.

DEADLINES: Not specified. Event, April.

43

German Critics Prizes
Society of German Critics
Heinz Ohff, Chairman
Jenaer Strasse 17
D-1000 Berlin 31, WEST GERMANY
(FRG) Tel: 030-8543352

Spring

National; **entry restricted to German-speaking countries** (selection by members); annual; established 1950. Critics Prizes to **German-speaking Film and Television Artists.** Purpose: to show critics' choice of year's artistic production. Event, Spring.

44

Jakob-Kaiser Television and Ernst-Reuter Radio Prizes
German Federal Ministry for Intra-German Relations
Postfach 120250
5300 Bonn 2, WEST GERMANY
(FRG)

National; **entry restricted to Germany;** biennial; established 1960. Monetary Awards to **German Television Film, Play, Documentary; Political Documentary or Feature; Radio Play, Documentary or Feature.** Purpose: to present problems of the division of Germany, relations between people in the 2 German states. Sponsored by German Federal Ministry for Intra-German Relations.

45

MIFED TV Pearl Prizes
MIFED International Film, TV Film,
and Documentary Market (MIFED)
Largo Domodossola, 1
20145 Milan, ITALY Tel: 495-495

October

International; **entry restricted to MIFED entrants;** annual; (TV Competition), semiannual (Sales Market). Purpose: to produce Cinematographic, television activities (mainly color TV programming). Sponsored by MIFED.

VIDEOTAPE CONTEST: Color Television (widths not specified) 25 minutes maximum. Require synopsis.

FILM CONTEST: Color Television Programs (gauges not specified) with soundtrack. Included in Videotape category.

ELIGIBILITY: Produced in previous year by producers enrolled in MIFED sales market.

AWARDS: 2 Great Prize MIFED TV Pearls (Artistic pearl shells containing checks for 1,500,000 lira, First Prize; 1,000,000 lira, Second Prize). Honor Certificates. 3 Great Merit Certificates at jury's discretion. Winners must accept in person or forfeit.

JUDGING: By international jury of culture, press personalitites; MIFED Customers.

ENTRY FEE: TV Competition: none. Sales Market: 18,000 lira (producers), 21,000 lira (Businessmen) per person. Entrant pays postage.

DEADLINES: Awards entry, October. Awards announced, April. Awards ceremony, October.

SALES MARKET: Feature, Short, Television, Documentary Videotape and Film. Unfinished entries accept-able for catalog listing. Held in spring (during Milan International Trade Fair) and fall. Purpose: to promote business contacts, international trade of film and TV. Have theatrical, TV monitor screening rooms, business offices, meeting center, special services (telephone, telegraph, telex, interpreters, bank, secretaries, legal advice, storage, insurance). No commission charged on sales. MIFED not responsible for ordinary damage, deterioration; may refuse entries offensive or harmful to moral, religious, national sentiments. No extreme sex or brutal violence. Average statistics: 1500 entries, 1000 attendance.

46

Yugoslav (JRT) Television Festival
RTV Ljubljana
Beno Hvala, Secretary
Tavcarjeva 17
61000 Ljubljana, YUGOSLAVIA
Tel: 061-311-922

May

National; **entry restricted** (nomination by Yugoslav TV organizations); annual; established 1966. Gold, Silver, Bronze Statuettes, Special Awards for **Yugoslavian Television Programs on Videotape** (625 CCIR PAL). Purpose: to review year's national TV productions; promote sale and international exchange of Yugoslav programs. Sponsored and supported by Yugoslav TV-radio broadcasting organizations. Held in Portoroz, Slovenia, Yugoslavia for 7 days. Have screenings, workshops, seminars. Second contact: JRT, Milan Milosavljevic, 11000 Belgrad, Borisa Kidrica 70, Yugoslavia. Event, May.

BROADCASTING (Community-Local)

TV-Radio Broadcasting (video, film, audio), including CABLE, COMMUNITY SERVICE. (Also see ADVERTISING-PROMOTION, AGRICULTURE, EDUCATIONAL, INDEPENDENT, JOURNALISM-NEWS, TELEVISION FILMS.

47

Abe Lincoln Awards to Distinguished Broadcasters
Southern Baptist Radio and Television Commission
Bonita Sparrow, Awards Coordinator
6350 West Freeway
Fort Worth, Texas 76150 U.S.A.
Tel: (817) 737-4011, ext. 240

February

National; **entry restricted to U.S. broadcasters;** annual; established 1970. Founded for North Texas broadcasters, became national 1971. Purpose: to honor broadcasters for advancing quality of American Life, contributing to community and nation. Motto: "With firmness in the right, as God gives us to see the right." Sponsored by Southern Baptist Radio and Television Commission (founded 1941), world's largest producer and distributor of internationally syndicated religious programming. Recognized by NAB. Average statistics: 50 entries, 20 semifinalists, 8 finalists, 500-1000 attendance. Held at Tarrant County Convention Center, Fort Worth, Texas. Tickets: $15. Also sponsor NATIONAL CONFERENCE ON BROADCAST MINISTRIES.

VIDEOTAPE CONTEST: Community Service Television (3/4-inch Sony U-matic compatible cassette) produced in previous year; one entry maximum per person. Classes: Commercial, Educational. Divisions: Market under 50,000-100,000; 100,000-500,000; over 500,000. Categories: Management, Programming, Promotion, Public Service, News and Public Affairs, Other.

FILM CONTEST: Community Service Television (gauge not specified). Requirements and categories same as for Videotape.

AUDIOTAPE CONTEST: Community Service Radio, cassette, produced in previous year; one entry maximum per person. Classes, Divisions, Categories same as for Videotape.

AWARDS: Abe Lincoln Award Statuette and Oval Bronze Medallion Merit Awards to broadcaster-citizen who exemplifies ideals expressed by Lincoln. Abe Lincoln Railsplitter Award, periodically to veteran broadcaster for pioneering efforts. Distinguished Communications Medal, Distinguished Communications Recognition Award, Christian Service Award, Public Service Award, Community Service Award. Vincent Wasilewski Award for improving broadcasting's image. Attendance required by winners.

JUDGING: By selection committee of broadcasters based on personal involvement; community service programming, projects, performance; industry improvement; originality; concept; content; consistency; creativity; effectiveness rather than production quality. May withhold awards. Not responsible for loss or damage.

ENTRY FEE: $25. $5 for support material.

DEADLINES: Entry, September.

Judging, November. Materials returned, January. Event, February.

48

ACE Awards for Cablecasting Excellence
National Cable Television Association (NCTA)
Gail Dosik, Assistant Director
918 Sixteenth Street N.W.
Washington, District of Columbia
20006 U.S.A. Tel: (202) 457-6700

Spring

National; **entry restricted to NCTA members;** annual. ACE Statuette, Honorable Mentions to previous year's **local cable Television Programs.** Sponsor retains all entries. Formerly called NCTA CABLECASTING AWARDS COMPETITION to 1978. Purpose: to award achievements in local and national made-for-cable programming. Sponsored and held during annual NCTA convention. Average statistics: 275 entries, 23 winners. Event, Spring.

49

Broadcast Industry Conference Broadcast Preceptor and Media Awards
San Francisco State University
Janet Lee Miller, Darryl R. Compton, Co-Chairpersons
1600 Holloway Avenue
San Francisco, California 94132
U.S.A. Tel: (415) 469-1347

April

International; entry open to all; annual; established 1950. Purpose: to honor, recognize signal accomplishments in leadership and excellence in local radio, TV programming. Sponsored by San Francisco State University (SFSU), Broadcast Industry Conference. Average statistics: 47 media,

13 Preceptor Awards. Held during Broadcast Industry Conference at SFSU. Also have VICTORIA ST. CLAIRE, ALBERT JOHNSON AWARDS for SFSU students.

VIDEOTAPE CONTEST: Local Television Broadcast (3/4-inch U-matic cassette; other formats by arrangement). Media Award Groups: Commercial, Noncommercial Television, CATV. Categories: Local News, Information or Documentary, Special Event, Instructional, Station Editorial, Entertainment, Public Affairs, Promotion.

FILM CONTEST: Local Television Broadcast (16mm) optical, magnetic. Groups and categories same as for Video.

AUDIOTAPE CONTEST: Local Radio Broadcast (1/4-inch reel or cassette). Media Award Groups: Commercial, Educational, Noncommercial Radio. Categories same as for Videotape.

PRECEPTOR AWARDS: To men and women whose accomplishments are of highest importance and have contributed to industry standards and accomplishments. Submit biography, achievement outline, 8x10-inch photo. Categories: Media Literature (published during previous year; 2 copies), Production, Performance, Industry, Academic Leadership.

ELIGIBILITY: Broadcast Media Awards open to local programming, no network. Request supporting materials.

AWARDS: Media Awards in TV, Radio groups and categories. Preceptor Awards, outstanding achievement, any category.

JUDGING: Media Awards by faculty, students of SFSU Broadcast Communication Arts Department, based on program purpose, audience, production facilities. Preceptor by SFSU faculty. Media Awards, Documentaries, Preceptor nominations placed in SFSU Broadcast Archives.

ENTRY FEE: Commercial TV Media Awards, $75; Noncommercial TV, Radio, CATV, $50. Preceptor Awards, free.

DEADLINES: Entry, February. Judges' reports, April. Awards, May.

| 50 |

Golden Mike Awards
American Legion Auxiliary (ALA)
Layton K. Hurst, Coordinator
1608 K Street N.W.
Washington, District of Columbia
20006 U.S.A. Tel: (202) 861-2795

Spring

National; **entry restricted to local U.S. radio, television stations;** annual; established 1957. Purpose: to encourage stations to attain highest standards in local broadcasting. Sponsored and supported by ALA to promote "juvenile decency over juvenile delinquency" in nation's communications media. Held at ALA National Convention for 4 days. Second contact: Miriam Junge, National Secretary, American Legion Auxiliary, 777 North Meridian Street, Indianapolis, Indiana 46204.

VIDEOTAPE CONTEST: Theme Local Television Series Broadcast (width not specified) series of 3 or more, various yearly themes. Station series aired between May 1 of previous, May 1 of current year. Require scripts or outlines, effectiveness of program, nomination reasons.

FILM CONTEST: Theme Local Television Series Broadcast Requirements same as for Videotape.

AUDIOTAPE CONTEST: Theme Local Radio Series Broadcast (3-3/4 or 7-1/2ips) series of 3 or more, various yearly themes. Requirements same as for Videotape.

AWARDS: Golden Mike National Trophies, Best Local Radio and Television Programs. Golden Mike State Certificates, winning series, each state.

JUDGING: Preliminary in each state. State winners further judged by ALA National Judging Committee.

ENTRY FEE: None. Sponsor pays return postage.

DEADLINES: Entry, May. Awards, August.

| 51 |

Video Festival: Perspectives in Community Video
Downtown Community TV Center
Karen Ranucci
87 Lafayette Street
New York, New York 10013 U.S.A.
Tel: (212) 966-4510

November

National; **entry open to U.S.;** annual; established 1980. Purpose: to give exposure to videomakers working in communities around country. Sponsored by Downtown Community TV Center, NEA, NYSCA. Average statistics: 100 entries, 120 entrants, 20 winners, 100 nightly attendance. Held at Downtown Community Television Center for 6 nights. Have minigrant and video access programs.

VIDEOTAPE CONTEST: Community Video (1/2-inch, 3/4-inch). Categories vary annually.

AWARDS: Cash Prizes. Excerpts shown on television.

JUDGING: Screened by 4 judges from the community representing minority groups and concerns.

ENTRY FEE: $10 per tape.

DEADLINES: Entry, May. Materials, July. Judging, Septmeber. Event, November. Materials returned, January.

BUSINESS, INDUSTRIAL, INFORMATIONAL

TV-Radio Broadcasting (video, film, audio), Audiovisual, Multimedia, and Video Disk, including ADVERTISING, BUILDING-CONSTRUCTION, CONSUMER, EDUCATIONAL, EXPERIMENTAL, FINANCE-ECONOMICS, FIRE FIGHTING, HOME APPLIANCE, INDUSTRIAL MANAGEMENT, INSTITUTIONAL, MEDICAL, PUBLIC RELATIONS, PUBLIC SERVICE, TRAINING. (also see ADVERTISING, BROADCASTING, EDUCATIONAL, JOURNALISM, SCIENTIFIC-TECHNICAL, TELEVISION FILMS.)

52

Association of Home Appliance Manufacturers (AHAM) Appliance Communications Award Program
Marian Johnson, Assistant General Manager
20 North Wacker Drive
Chicago, Illinois 60606 U.S.A.
Tel: (312) 984-5821

Various

International; **entry restricted to professionals;** various throughout the year; established 1958. Formerly called ALMA AWARDS PROGRAM to 1980. Purpose: to encourage communication to public about home appliances, recognize excellence in consumer appliance communications. Sponsored and supported by AHAM. Average statistics: 55-100 entries. Held at National Home Appliance Conference.

VIDEOTAPE CONTEST: Home Appliance (widths not specified). Require scripts or scenarios. Categories: Television and Radio, Utilities, USDA Extension (state, county), Classroom Education (college or university, high school, junior high).

AUDIOTAPE CONTEST: Home Appliance. Categories same as for Videotape.

AUDIO-VISUAL CONTEST: Home Appliance. Categories same as for Videotape.

ELIGIBILITY: Consumer information about small or large appliances (dehumidifiers, dishwashers, disposers, dryers, freezers, humidifiers, ranges, refrigerators, room air conditioners, trash compactors, washers). Completed August of previous year to August of current year; 3 maximum. Require announcements, handouts, publications, other publicity materials. No student projects.

AWARDS: AHAM Awards for imaginative consumer communications.

JUDGING: By panel of home economists, journalism faculty of Iowa State University (Ames), based on effectiveness, clarity, creativity, timeliness, practicality.

ENTRY FEE: None.

DEADLINES: Vary.

53

Audio Visual Department of the Year Awards Competition
Information Film Producers of America (IFPA)
Wayne Weiss
750 East Colorado Blvd., Suite 6
Pasadena, California 91101 U.S.A.
Tel: (213) 795-7866
Fall

National; **entry restricted to U.S. Audio-Visual Departments;** annual; established 1980. Purpose: to recognize total accomplishments of audiovisual departments. Sponsored by 3M, IFPA, (founded 1957, nation's largest nonprofit association of documentary, educational, industrial, business filmmakers, dedicated to professional advancement, recognition of those who create film, video, audiovisual for communications as opposed to entertainment). Average statistics: 75-100 entries, 15 winners. Location varies. Publish *The Communicator,* (bimonthly newsletter). Also sponsor CINDY COMPETITION for film and video, IFPA FILM AND VIDEO COMMUNICATORS SCHOLARSHIP, IFPA NATIONAL CONFERENCE AND TRADE SHOW, seminars.

VIDEOTAPE CONTEST: **Audio-Visual Department Production** (3/4-inch cassette); entries must represent Audiovisual Department from business, industry, education, government, (including Department of Defense agencies); single product or multimedia including 16mm film, sound slide, filmstrip, photographic stills or transparencies.

AUDIOTAPE CONTEST: **Audio-Visual Department Production** (cassette). Requirements same as for Video.

AWARDS: Gold, Silver, Bronze Awards, each category. Audio-Visual Department of the Year Grand Award (in memory of D. David Bash, past IFPA President), chosen from 6 gold winners.

JUDGING: By panel of experienced audiovisual managers selected by IFPA. Not responsible for loss or damage.

ENTRY FEE: Not specified.

DEADLINES: Entry, April.

54

Chicago
Communications Collaborative
410 South Michigan Avenue
Suite 433
Chicago, Illinois 60605 U.S.A.
Tel: (312) 633-9566
Summer

International; entry open to all; annual; established 1978. Purpose: to recognize finest examples of communications nationally and internationally through Chicago shows. Sponsored by Communications Collaborative, organization of Chicago communication associations. Recognized by Art Directors Club of Chicago, Artists Guild of Chicago, American Society of Magazine Photographers, Graphic Arts Council. Have other visual media categories. Publish *Chicago Annual* (yearbook of winners).

VIDEOTAPE CONTEST: **Business, Industrial, Educational, Experimental, Television** (3/4-inch NTSC U-matic cassette) created after March previous year. Categories: Internal, Educational, Public Relations, Sales Promotion, Experimental, Art Direction (Audiovisual), Television (Under 60-Second Spot, Campaign; Over 60-Second Spot, Campaign; Editorial or PSA).

AUDIOTAPE CONTEST: Radio, created after March previous year. Require typewritten script. Categories: Under 60-Second Single, Campaign; Over 60-Second Single, Campaign.

AWARDS: Best of Category, Best of Show at judges' discretion. TV Spot winners must submit reproducible stills. Winners exhibited for one month.

JUDGING: By media experts, based on 5-point scale.

ENTRY FEE: Single $25, Campaign $75. Not-for-Profit Public Service Single $12, Campaign $37. Acceptance: Single $70, Campaign $175. Not-for-Profit Public Service Single $45, Campaign $100.

DEADLINES: Entry, August.

55

Cindy Competition
Information Film Producers of America (IFPA)
Wayne Weiss
750 East Colorado Blvd., Suite 6
Pasadena, California 91101 U.S.A.
Tel: (213) 795-7866

Fall

International; entry open to all; annual; established 1968. Purpose: to promote, showcase finest in informational, educational, documentary, audiovisual communications. Sponsored by Eastman Kodak; IFPA (founded 1957), nation's largest nonprofit association of documentary, educational, industrial, business filmmakers dedicated to professional advancement, recognition of those who create film, video, audiovisual for communications as opposed to entertainment. Average statistics: 700-800 entries, 100 winners. Held during IFPA National Conference and Trade Show. Publish *The Communicator,* bi-

monthly newsletter; membership directory. Also sponsor IFPA FILM AND VIDEO COMMUNICATORS SCHOLARSHIP; AUDIO-VISUAL DEPARTMENT OF THE YEAR AWARDS COMPETITION; seminars.

VIDEOTAPE CONTEST: Informational (3/4-inch U-matic cassette). Categories: Television Information; Business, Industry, Government; Education; Environment, Ecology; Fund-Raising; Health, Medicine; Public Relations, Public Service Information; Documentary; Safety; Sales, Marketing; Religious; Sports, Recreation; Travel; Student Productions.

AUDIOTAPE CONTEST: Informational (1/8-inch standard cassette). Categories same as for Videotape.

MULTI-IMAGE CONTEST: Informational (AVL, Arion, Clear Light, Electrosonic, Spindler & Saupe). Require layout plan, kind of equipment, program soundtrack information. Categories same as for Videotape.

ELIGIBILITY: Completed or released between June previous, May of current year.

AWARDS: Gold, Silver, Bronze Cindy Plaques. Honor Certificates to finalists. IFPA Grand Award, Best of Best. Special Awards, Best in Show, each contest. Special Achievement Award, Exceptional Performance.

JUDGING: Preliminary in regional chapters countrywide. Finalists by Blue Ribbon Panel of 30-35 industry professionals. Request permission to make winning entries available to regional IFPA chapters for nonprofit screenings. Not responsible for loss or damage.

ENTRY FEE: Videotape: $65 IFPA members, $85 nonmembers. Audiotape: $50 IFPA members, $70 non-members. Multi-Image, special rates. Student, $25.

DEADLINES: Entry, June. Winners announced, August.

56

Council for Advancement and Support of Education (CASE) Recognition Program
Charles M. Helmken, Vice President
Eleven Dupont Circle, Suite 400
Washington, District of Columbia
20036 U.S.A. Tel: (202) 328-5917

June

International; **entry restricted to CASE members;** annual. Awards (monetary) and Certificates to **Institutional, Public Service Videotapes, Audiotapes, and Films.** Sponsored by CASE. Sponsor keeps winners. Average statistics: 3200 entries. Held in various U.S. cities. Have workshops, conferences. Event, June.

57

Industrial Management Society Audio Visual Competition
Lila Blondell, Film Library Manager
570 Northwest Highway
Des Plaines, Illinois 60016 U.S.A.
Tel: (312) 296-7189

November

International; entry open to all; annual; established 1977. Purpose: to encourage production of management-related audiovisual materials that deal with management psychology, develop greater productivity, explain free enterprise, stimulate cost reduction through methods improvement. Sponsored by Industrial Management Film Library. Held at Industrial Engineering Management Clinic, Arlington Heights, Illinois.

VIDEOTAPE CONTEST: Industrial Management (1-inch, 1/2-inch, 3/4-inch). Categories: Management Motivation, Techniques; Methods Improvement; Industrial Engineering; Hospital Management; Work Performance Rating; Safety; Work Sampling; Quality Control; Office, Clerical Operations.

AUDIOTAPE CONTEST: Industrial Management. Categories same as for Videotape.

ELIGIBILITY: Produced for training, moral incentive; to teach or demonstrate Techniques, methods. No product or service sales films.

AWARDS: Ralph Landes Award for Outstanding contributions in training, motivation, management techniques, cost reduction. Winners nominated to IMS Film Rental Library.

JUDGING: Based on story accomplishments, introduction, evidence of objectives, story organization, presentation quality (scenes, titles, narration, photography); savings realized, reduction in fatigue, tools and techniques of management. Not responsible for loss or damage.

ENTRY FEE: $25 per entry.

DEADLINES: Entry, September. Awards, November.

58

INTERCOM Industrial Film and Video Festival
Cinema Chicago
Michael J. Kutza, Jr., Director
415 North Dearborn Street
Chicago, Illinois 60610 U.S.A.
Tel: (312) 644-3400

September

International; entry open to all; annual; established 1965 as part of

CHICAGO INTERNATIONAL FILM FESTIVAL. Named after International Communication (INTERCOM). Purpose: to honor audiovisual business communications producers and distributors. Motto: "To encourage better understanding between people and nations." Sponsored by Cinema Chicago, nonprofit, tax-exempt educational-cultural organization devoted to discovery, exhibition of world film and video. Supported by Illinois Arts Council, City of Chicago. Average statistics: 700 entries, 10 countries, 52 winners. Held during Chicago International Film Festival. Second contact: Suzanne McCormick, Executive Director.

VIDEO CONTEST: Industrial, Information, Medical (3/4-inch U-matic cassette NTSC U.S. Standard) must have been originally shot on videotape. Categories: Product Sales, Point of Purchase Sales, Public Relations, Corporate Image, Employee Relations, Industrial Training, Business Training, Research and Development, Urban Development, Public Information, Recruiting, Fund Raising, Public Health, Physical Education, Medical Research, Medical Surgical Procedures, Addiction, Psychiatry or Psychology, Dentistry, Sports and Recreation, Travel, Religion, Guidance, Language Arts, Science, Ecology, Mathematics.

ELIGIBILITY: Produced in previous year. No television productions.

AWARDS: Grand Prix Gold Hugo, Silver and Bronze Hugos to outstanding entries. Gold, Silver Plaques each category. Certificates of Merit.

JUDGING: By 75 audiovisual, business professional volunteer judges, based on budget, audience, general purpose. Not responsible for loss or damage.

ENTRY FEE: Under 30 minutes, $60; 30-60 minutes $100; 61 minutes and over, $150. Sponsor pays return postage.

DEADLINES: Entry, materials, June. Event, September.

59
International Association of Fire Fighters (IAFF) International Awards Program
John A. Gannon, President
1750 New York Avenue N.W.
Washington, District of Columbia
20006 U.S.A. Tel: (202) 872-8484
April

International; **entry restricted** (nomination by local U.S. and Canadian IAFF unions); annual; established 1965. First, Second Place monetary awards and plaques, Honorable Mentions, Certificates for **Fire Fighting Television, Radio Broadcast;** news media reporting of U.S., Canadian fire fighters aired in previous year; sponsor may reproduce winners in IAFF publications. Sponsored by IAFF. Average statistics: 350 entries. Event, April.

60
International Film and TV Festival of New York
Gerald M. Goldberg, President
251 West 57th Street
New York, New York 10019 U.S.A.
Tel: (212) 246-5133
November

International; **entry restricted to professionals;** annual; established 1957. Formerly called INDUSTRIAL FILM AND A-V EXHIBITION to 1967. Purpose: to recognize excellence in production of film and video; honor producers, sponsors, advertising agencies, television stations, individuals contributing to greatness of the industry. Sponsored by International FTF Corporation. Average statistics: 1400 entrants, 37 countries, 350 winners, 1400 attendance. Held in New York for 3 days. Tickets: $60 per person.

VIDEOTAPE CONTEST: Industrial, Educational, Commercials, Television (2-inch tape or cassette) series acceptable. Require separate tape for each category. Industrial and Educational Categories: Corporate Image, Public Relations, Public Service, Services, Training, Manufacturing, Product Presentation, Sales Presentation, Consumer Goods, Agriculture, City and Urban Development, Wild Life and Ecology, Communication Media, Transportation, Health and Home Economics, Safety and Insurance, Social Welfare, Recruiting, Scientific, Medical, Medical Research, Education, Documentary, Current Events, History and Biography, Geography and Exploration, Travelog, Ocean Research, Fund Raising, Political, Art and Music, Religion, Fashion, Sports and Gymnastics, Hobbies and Recreation, Environment, Energy, Law and Order, Special Education, Animation. TV Commercials: Any Media (10 seconds maximum); Live Action, Animation and Puppets, Live and Animation (11-30 seconds, 31-60); Any Media (1 1/2-3 minutes). Cinema Commercials: Live, Animation, Mixed. TV Public Service Spots: 30 seconds maximum, 60 maximum, over 60. TV Programs, Show (require 2 and presentation book): News, Documentary, Educational, Public Service (Network, Local, Syndicated); Special, Feature Film, Syndicated Series (Drama, Comedy, Music, Adventure, Children, Games). Filmed Introductions, Lead-in Titles: Feature Movies, TV Programs, Sales Meetings, Promotional. Other: Featurettes, News Films.

MULTIMEDIA, MIXED-MEDIA CONTEST. Require 1-page resume, presentation book, releases, clippings, photos, slides.

ELIGIBILITY: Produced or released after September previous year. Require English synopsis for languages other than English, French, Spanish, German.

AWARDS: Grand Award Trophy, Most Outstanding, each section. First Place Gold, Second Silver, Third Bronze Medals, each category. Special Achievement Awards, any category. Special Mention Awards.

JUDGING: By industry panel. May change categories, withhold awards, refuse acceptance. Festival owns all commercials for presentation showing. Not responsible for loss or damage.

ENTRY FEE: Industrial, Educational (single program) $55, (series) $130. TV, Cinema Commercials, TV Public Service Spots, Filmed Introductions, Lead-in Titles, Slide Programs, $45, $110. TV Programs, $90, $180. TV Specials, Features, Syndicated, $110, $220. Featurettes, News Films, $55. Multimedia, $110. Mixed-Media, $80. Finalist Fee, $60, all categories.

DEADLINES: Entry, September. Judging, September-October. Event, November. Materials returned, December.

61

International Television Association (ITVA) Video Festival
Bobette Kandle, Operations Director
136 Sherman Avenue
Berkeley Heights, New Jersey 07922
U.S.A. Tel: (201) 464-6747

Winter

International; **entry restricted to nonbroadcast television;** annual; established 1968. Purpose: to recognize videotape creations contributing to excellence of nonbroadcast television. Sponsored by ITVA. Average statistics: 800 entries, 250 finalists, 45-60 awards. Held at International Industrial Television Association National Conference.

VIDEOTAPE CONTEST: Nonbroadcast, Industrial (3/4-inch NTSC U-matic cassette) produced prior to January previous year. Require English transcript for non-English audiotracks. No film transfers. Categories: Training, Information, Sales-Marketing, Public Service, Public Relations, Ecology, Company News, Health-Medicine, Education.

ELIGIBILITY: Produced by industrial, nonbroadcast television user, or in conjunction with production house. Total Film transfers not accepted.

AWARDS: Golden Reel of Excellence (to tapes combining creativity, innovative techniques, high production values). Golden Reel of Merit (to tapes with effective combination of message transfer, high production skills). All entries may be shown through ITVA Video Network.

JUDGING: Preliminary (minimum 10 minutes viewed) by 85 judging panels across U.S. Finals based on stated objectives, use of television medium, originality, creativity, production values, innovative techniques. Not responsible for loss or damage.

ENTRY FEE: ITVA members $35 first tape; nonmembers $85. ITVA pays return postage.

DEADLINES: Entry, January. Event, May. Materials returned, June.

| 62 |

Janus Awards for Financial Broadcasting

Mortgage Bankers Association of America
Jane DeMarines, Public Relations Director
1125 15th Street N.W.
Washington, District of Columbia
20005 U.S.A. Tel: (202) 861-6554

May

National; **entry restricted to U.S. and Canadian journalists;** annual; established 1970. Purpose: to encourage excellence in broadcast reporting of economic news. Sponsored by Mortgage Bankers Association of America (MBA). Recognized by NBA, NDA. Average statistics: 200 entries, 4 winners. Held in New York at annual MBA conference.

VIDEOTAPE CONTEST: Finance-Economics Television Broadcast (3/4-inch cassette, 2-inch high-band) 1 copy of 1-3 programs from series, dates aired. Request scripts, synopsis, analysis. Divisions: Network, Local. Categories: Regular News Programming, Documentary or Educational Programs.

AUDIOTAPE CONTEST: Finance-Economics Radio Broadcast, (1/4-inch cassette or standard, 7-inch reel, 7 1/2ips full-track). Requirements, categories same as for Videotape.

ELIGIBILITY: Business, economic, financial programs or series broadcast in U.S., Canada in previous year, by radio or TV networks, stations, CATV stations currently licensed or certified by FCC (including PBS and noncommercial stations or networks). Local or CATV must be stationed-produced.

AWARDS: Janus (Roman god) Bronze statuette for excellence in financial or economic news programming, each category, each division.

JUDGING: By panel of professional critics, former broadcasters, representatives from professional broadcasting, news director societies. Based on comprehension, information, authority, interest. MBA retains winners, other entries returned. Not responsible for loss or damage.

ENTRY FEE: None.

DEADLINES: Entry, February. Event, May.

63

JVC Business and Industry Video Festival
Burson-Marsteller Public Relations
John Bailey
866 Third Avenue
New York, New York 10022 U.S.A.
Tel: (212) 752-6500, ext. 3422

Fall

National; **entry restricted to U.S. business communicators;** annual; established 1980. Purpose: to encourage business-oriented applications of video; recognize achievements of business program producers. Sponsored by U.S. JVC Corporation (Victor Company of Japan). Average statistics: 116 entries, 55 entrants, 8 winners. Held in New York City. Also sponsor JVC TOKYO VIDEO FESTIVAL, JVC STUDENT VIDEO FESTIVAL. Second contact: Stuart Rose.

VIDEOTAPE CONTEST: **Business, Industry** (widths not specified) 20 minutes maximum. Categories: Corporate Communications, Training, Promotion-Merchandising.

AWARDS: First Prizes, over $5000; other awards, cash or equivalent in equipment.

JUDGING: By producers, directors, critics, educators.

ENTRY FEE: None. Sponsor pays return postage.

DEADLINES: Entry, August. Judging, Event, October. Materials returned, November.

64

Media Awards for Economic Understanding
Amos Tuck School of Business Administration
Jan B. Bent, Program Administrator
Dartmouth College
Hanover, New Hampshire 03755
U.S.A. Tel: (603) 643-5596

Spring

National; **entry restricted to journalists, general media employees;** annual; established 1977. Formerly called MEDIA AWARDS FOR THE ADVANCEMENT OF ECONOMIC UNDERSTANDING to 1978. Purpose: to recognize, improve quality, increase quantity of public economics reporting. Sponsored and supported by Champion International Corporation. Held at Amos Tuck School of Business Administration. Average statistics: 1400 entries.

VIDEOTAPE CONTEST: **Economics Television Broadcast** (3/4-inch) with script, telecast during previous year. TV Categories: Network, Nationally Distributed (Top 25 Markets, 26-100, 101 and smaller).

AUDIOTAPE CONTEST: **Economics Radio Broadcast** (standard cassette) with script, telecast during previous year. Radio Categories: Network (Top 50 Markets, 51 and smaller).

AWARDS: First Place, $5000; Second Place, $2500, each category.

JUDGING: By 11 judges, based on effectiveness, understanding of economic system. Sponsor has reproduction rights.

ENTRY FEE: None.

DEADLINES: Materials, March. Judging, April. Winners announced, May.

65

Public Relations Film Festival
Public Relations Society of America (PRSA)
Chairman, Film Festival
845 Third Avenue
New York, New York 10022 U.S.A.
Tel: (212) 826-1755

Fall

National; **entry restricted to PRSA members;** annual; established 1968. Certificates to **Public Relations Videotapes** (3/4-inch), **Films** (16mm) produced in previous year in English. Purpose: to identify and honor best public relations film produced by companies, organizations. Sponsored by PRSA (Nancy M. Gallagher, Coordinator). Average statistics: 160 entries, 6 winners. Held in various U.S. cities at national conference. Also sponsor Silver Anvil Program. Second contact: Jaci Locker, Director, Member Services.

66

Training Film Festival
Olympic Media Information
Walt Carroll, Publisher
71 West 23 Street
New York, New York 10010 U.S.A.
Tel: (212) 675-4500

December-April

International; entry open to all; semiannual; established 1978. Purpose: to present new, prepackaged film and video programs for human resource development. Sponsored by Olympic Media Information and *Training* magazine. Average statistics: 60 entries, 30 entrants. Held in New York City and at Disneyland, Anaheim, California, for 4 days.

VIDEOTAPE EXHIBITION: **Training** (3/4-inch cassette) 60 minutes maximum; produced in previous 12 months. Categories: Personal Productivity, Leadership Skills, Interpersonal Relations, Management-Supervision, Motivation, Communication Skills, Selling, Free Enterprise, Safety, Health, Entry-Level and Vocational Skills, Employer-Employee Orientation, Internal Communications.

AWARDS: None.

ENTRY FEE: $4-$6 per minute running time, depending on overall minutes entered.

DEADLINES: Entry, September (for December event); February (for April).

67

U.S. Industrial Film Festival
United States Festivals Association
J. W. Anderson, Chairman
841 North Addison Avenue
Elmhurst, Illinois 60126 U.S.A.
Tel: (312) 834-7773

May

International; entry open to all; annual; established 1967. World's largest exclusively industrial film media festival. Purpose: to showcase industrial films, videotapes, increase production excellence; promote audiovisual industry growth. Sponsored by United States Festivals Association, Chicago Film Council, Chicago Audiovisual Producers Association. Average statistics: 1200 entries, 18 countries, 200 attendance. Held in Chicago for 2 days. Also sponsor seminars, U.S. TELEVISION COMMERCIALS FESTIVAL.

VIDEOTAPE CONTEST: Industrial (3/4-inch NTSC American Standard U-matic cassette). Divisions: Commercially Produced, In-Plant, University, Government. Categories: Advertising, Sales Promotion; Art, Culture; Career Guidance, Recruiting Employee Communications; City, Urban Development; Conservation, Ecology, Pollution; Documentary; Education, Nonscholastic or All School Grades; Fund-Raising; History, Biography; Technical Processes; Medicine, Health; Politics; Public Relations (commercial, nonprofit, TV news or theatrical short); Recreation; Religion, Ethics; Safety, Welfare, Insurance; Sales; Science, Research; Training; Travel; Miscellaneous.

VIDEO DISK CONTEST: Industrial, compatible with MCA Model PR-7820. Divisions, categories same as for Videotape.

ELIGIBILITY: Produced during year prior to Festival for industry, associations, government, religious, charitable, educational organizations (to inform, motivate, stimulate, educate). English language, subtitle, or script. No videotapes of original 16mm film.

AWARDS: Chairman's Special Award, Best of Festival. Gold Camera and Silver Screen Brass Plaques, First Place, each category and division. Special Awards, Public Relations, International Creativity, International Audio-Visuals; Best Director, Cameraman, Chicago Area. Private industry awards. Creative Excellence Certificates. Duplicates in case of tie.

JUDGING: By 200 in various U.S. cities, based on effectiveness, audience motivation, clarity, photography, sound. May reclassify entries, retain

Best of Festival. Not responsible for loss or damage.

ENTRY FEE: $30-$90, varies with format entered. Entrant pays return postage.

DEADLINES: Entry, March. Judges' reports, April. Event, May.

International Festival of Economics and Training Films
Cercle Solvay
Didier Cloos, President
Avenue Franklin Roosevelt 48
B-1050 Brussels, BELGIUM
Tel: 02-6490030, ext. 2528

November

International; entry open to all; triennial; established 1978. Purpose: to acquaint widest possible public to film and video as aids to teaching and training. Sponsored by Cercle Solvay, Free University of Brussels, Union of Commercial Engineers. Average statistics: 400 entries, 25 countries, 12 winners. Held at University of Brussels for 8 days. Have exhibitions, conferences, seminars. Tickets: 400-4000 Belgian francs.

VIDEOTAPE CONTEST: Economics, Training (VHS 625-line PAL, VHS NTSC 443, U-matic PAL, U-matic SECAM, U-matic NTSC 443) recent productions; French language version requested (French, English, Dutch official festival languages).

AWARDS: Grand Prize, Best Production. University Teaching Prize, Best Teaching Production. Sectional Prizes.

JUDGING: By 4 5-member juries of university professors, various specialists, based on educational and technical realization. All entries viewed in entirety. Sponsor insures during Festival.

ENTRY FEE: None. Entrant pays postage.

DEADLINES: Entry, May. Materials, June. Event, November.

69

Canadian Film and Television Association Awards
Suite 512
55 York Street
Toronto, Ontario M5J 1S2 CANADA
Tel: (416) 363-8374

October

National; **entry open to Canada;** annual; established 1948. Sponsored by Canadian Film and Television Association (CFTA). Held in Toronto.

VIDEOTAPE CONTEST: **Canadian Industrial** (3/4-inch Sony U-matic cassette) 3 minutes minimum; sponsored, industrial productions produced by private production companies, completed July 1 of previous to June 30 of current year. Canadian content must qualify under CRTC regulations. Categories: Public Relations, Sales Promotion, Travel-Recreation, Nature-Wildlife, Sports, Educational-Instructional, TV Information-Public Affairs. Require separate tape each category entered.

AWARDS: Special Certificates, Best Overall Production. Certificates, each category and craft (Direction, Script, Editing, Sound, Music Score).

JUDGING: Sponsor may televise clips of all entries; hold free Canadian screenings.

ENTRY FEE: $60 members; $75 nonmembers.

DEADLINES: Entry, September.

Awards given, October. Materials returned, November.

70

British Industrial and Scientific Film Association (BISFA) International Video Festival
Keith Bennett, Director
26 D'Arblay Street
London W1V 3FH, ENGLAND
Tel: 01-439-8441

May

International; **entry restricted to OECD member countries;** annual; established 1981. Purpose: to provide international forum to view, discuss video as communications aid. Sponsored by BISFA. Supported by The Economist (international video conference), International Television Association (Video Workshops), BFI (International Video Forum). Recognized by Confederation of British Industry. Held in London during International Video Week for 3 days. Tickets: 25 pounds per day; Banquet, 25-50 pounds; International Video Week, 265 pounds (plus value-added tax). Also sponsor BRITISH INDUSTRIAL FILM AND VIDEO FESTIVAL. Second Contact: Meridian Conferences, 133 Rosendale Road, London SE21 8HE, ENGLAND. Tel: 01-670-5400.

VIDEOTAPE CONTEST: **Industrial, Educational, Social, Medical** (U-matic, separate cassette, PAL, SECAM or NTSC standard; other formats acceptable on prior notice); 45 minutes maximum; English or English translation. Categories: Education, Training, Safety, Public Welfare and Social Questions, Medical and Para-Medical, Sales Products or Services, Public Relations, Ecology (Environment and Recreation), Internal Communications, Recruitment and Induction.

ELIGIBILITY: Only entries sponsored or produced within OECD-member countries (Australia, Austria, Belgium, Canada, Denmark, Finland, France, Germany FR, Greece, Iceland, Ireland, Italy, Japan, Luxembourg, Netherlands, New Zealand, Norway, Portugal, Spain, Sweden, Switzerland, Turkey, United Kingdom, USA). No TV commercials.

AWARDS: First, Second, Third Prizes, each category (subject to number of entries). Special Prizes.

JUDGING: By panel of sponsors, producers, users in each category. Entries viewed in entirety. Judges reserve right to limit entry. Not responsible for loss or damage.

ENTRY FEES: 50 pounds plus value-added tax per entry. BISFA members 40 pounds plus value-added tax. Special Fee, 20 pounds plus value-added tax (educational institutions, community welfare groups, individual noncommercial producers). Entrant pays return postage.

DEADLINES: Entry, February. Materials, April. Event, May. Materials returned, June.

71

British Industrial Film and Video Festival
British Industrial and Scientific Film Association (BISFA)
Keith Bennett, Director
26 D'Arblay Street
London W1V 3FH, ENGLAND
Tel: 01-439-8441

Spring

International; entry open to all; annual; established 1957. Became international 1981; Videotapes added 1975. Formerly called BRITISH SPONSORED FILM FESTIVAL. Purpose: to recognize, select, discuss, promote,

improve quality of sponsored films and videotapes. Sponsored by BISFA, independent, nonprofit trade association assisting industry, government, commerce, science to achieve effective audiovisual communications. Recognized by Confederation of British Industry. Average statistics: 200 entries, 54 finalists, 33 winners. Held at various locations. Have film shows, information services, seminars, conferences. Also sponsor BISFA INTERNATIONAL VIDEO FESTIVAL. Second contact: Mrs. Judy Steele, Organizer, BISFA, 6 Devonshire Close, London W1N 1LE, ENGLAND: tel: 01-636-8520.

VIDEOTAPE CONTEST: Industrial, Educational, Medical (U-matic cassette, PAL standard) 33 minutes maximum, completed in previous 2 years. Categories: Education, Training, Safety, Public Welfare and Social Questions, Medical, Sales (Products, Services), Public Relations and Prestige (Public, Private), Ecology and Environment, Internal Communications.

AWARDS: Gold, Silver, Bronze Awards, Best each category. Times Newcomers' Award, best by first-time film sponsor. Financial Times Export Award, most suitable for promotion of British exports. Clifford Wheeler Memorial Award, most enterprise and initiative in securing distribution (previous year's award winners). Times Business News Awards (films by public or private companies expressing wider corporate concerns and responsibilities). Imperial Group Training Film Trophy (Commercial and industrial training category).

JUDGING: By selection screenings, entries viewed in entirety. 8 final specialist judges, each category. Not responsible for loss or damage.

ENTRY FEE: 100 pounds plus value-added tax per entry. BISFA members, 60 pounds plus value-added tax. 35 pounds plus value-added tax each Special Prize. Entrant pays return postage.

DEADLINES: Entry, January. Materials, judging, March. Event, March, June.

72

Biarritz Audiovisual Demonstrations
Connaissance de l'Economie par le Film (CEFILM)
Baudry Francois, Delegate General
15 bis, rue de Marignan
75008 Paris, FRANCE Tel: 359-69-40

June

National; **entry open to France;** annual; established 1958. Awards to **French Business and Industrial Videotapes and Films** (35mm, 16mm); produced in previous 2 years; no advertising, tourism films. Formerly called NATIONAL BUSINESS FILM FESTIVAL. Theme: National Meeting Concerning Business Through Audiovisual Programs. Sponsored by CEFILM. Average statistics: 111 films, 1300 attendance. Held in Casino Municipal, Casino Bellevue, Biarritz, for 4 days. Have debates, workshops. Also sponsor Days of Audiovisual Programs of Education, Industrial Diaporamas. Event, June.

73

Berlin International Consumer Film Festival
AMK Berlin Company for Exhibitions, Fairs and Congresses
Prof. Dr. Otto Blume, Chairman
Messedamm 22
Postfach 191740
D-1000 Berlin 19, WEST GERMANY
(FRG) Tel: 030-3081-1

January

International; entry open to all; biennial (odd years); established 1971. Alternates with BERLIN INTERNATIONAL AGRICULTURAL FILM COMPETITION. Purpose: improve quality, stimulate interest in consumer films; strengthen international cooperation. Sponsored by Consumers' Working Group (Arbeitsgemeinschaft der Verbraucher e.V. AGV Heilsbachstrasse 20, D-5300 Bonn 1). Held at International Congress Center (Berlin) during International Green Week.

VIDEOTAPE CONTEST: Consumer (2-inch, 625 lines, PAL system; 1-inch BCN Standard, 625 lines, PAL Norm; U-matic cassette, 625 lines, PAL Norm) 60 minutes maximum; 1 category per entry. Categories: Informational (General, Commercial Goods, Services, Food and Nutrition, Health); Education, School.

ELIGIBILITY: Premiered during previous 3 years. Require 2 dialogs or commentaries, 10-line summary (German, English or French). Request teaching material or learning aids. No advertisements for companies, products, services.

AWARDS: Gold, Silver, Bronze, Best each category. Special Awards. Participation Certificates.

JUDGING: First hour viewed by 5-member international jury, based on general treatment, specific content. Excerpts may be shown on TV.

ENTRY FEE: None. Entrant pays postage.

DEADLINES: Entry, October. Event, January.

74

South Africa Festival of Building Films
National Building Research Institute
Murray Baxter, Organizer
P.O. Box 395
Pretoria 0001, SOUTH AFRICA
Tel: (012) 74-9111

May

International; entry open to all; biennial; established 1974. Purpose: to show development of building; foster use of audiovisual media as research tool, means of communicating about building. Sponsored by National Building Research Institute of the Council for Scientific and Industrial Research. Average statistics: 50 entries. Held in Cape Town concurrent with South African Building Research Congress. Also sponsor National Competition for Building Photography.

VIDEOTAPE CONTEST: Building, Construction (Sony U-matic, Philips VCR, PAL standard) produced within last 4 years, 1 category per entry. Commentary, translation or contents summary in English. Categories: Record of Building-Construction Project, Design-Physical Planning, Building Methods-Materials-Services-Equipment, Management-Training-Safety, Career Opportunities.

AWARDS: Gold Trophy, Best of Festival. Silver Trophies, Best each category. Bronze Trophies, Certificates. GENOP Trophy for Best South African Entry.

JUDGING: Preliminary by committee. Final by independent 11-member juries. Based on effectiveness in conveying theme, production standard, contribution to knowledge in building field. May change categories.

ENTRY FEE: None. Festival pays return postage.

DEADLINES: Entry, March. Materials, April. Event, May.

For CHILDREN, YOUTH (TV)

TV Broadcasting (video and film). (Also see ANIMATED, BROADCASTING, EDUCATIONAL, TELEVISION FILMS.)

75

Achievement in Children's Television Awards
Action for Children's Television (ACT)
Natalie Rothstein
46 Austin Street
Newtonville, Massachusetts 02160
U.S.A. Tel: (617) 527-7870

Spring

International; **entry restricted to children's series TV broadcasts;** annual. Purpose: to encourage diversity, eliminate commercial abuses, award significant contributions toward improving children's broadcasting and cable. Sponsored by ACT, national nonprofit consumer organization founded 1968 to improve broadcasting practices related to children. Publish *Re:act* news magazine; books, posters, children's TV guidelines for professionals and parents. Also sponsor national conferences, symposia, workshops.

VIDEOTAPE CONTEST: Children's Series Television Broadcast (3/4-inch cassette) 15 minutes minimum, designed for and directed to children, young people; part of ongoing series (6 parts minimum); aired during previous year. Require descriptive material. No single specials, public announcements.

AWARDS: For significant contributions toward improving children's TV.

ENTRY FEE: $40 per entry.

DEADLINES: Entry, February. Event, Spring.

76

Odyssey Institute Media Awards Competition
Jean S. Elahi, Vice President
Development
656 Avenue of the Americas
New York, New York 10010 U.S.A.
Tel: (212) 691-8510

December

International; **entry restricted to U.S., Australia, New Zealand;** annual; established 1977, added books 1981. Purpose: to recognize, encourage media productions of excellence in area of children's issues, programming. Theme: Concerns of children. Sponsored by Odyssey Institute, international nonprofit organization committed to health care concerns, research, legislative action, child advocacy. Average statistics: 260 entries, 520 entrants, 70 finalists, 36 winners, 250 attendance. Held in New York City for 1 day. Tickets: by invitation. Have multimedia library with equipment to hear, view submissions. Publish *Odyssey Journal* books (publication list available). Also sponsor internships for fieldwork experience.

VIDEOTAPE CONTEST: Children's Issue Television (cassette) aired by previous September. Categories: National and Local Broadcast (Feature, Series, Documentary, Public Service Announcement, Editorial).

AUDIOTAPE CONTEST: Children's Issue Radio (cassette) aired by previous September. Categories: Same as for Videotape.

AWARDS: Awards each category. Special Mentions. Winners displayed, aired at ceremonies. Entries used as references in publications, appearances, legislative consultations prepared by sponsor.

JUDGING: Entries viewed in entirety by 15 judges from media schools, Congress, public relations firms, foundations. Institute retains copies of entries for Concerns of Children Multimedia Library, New York, New York. Not responsible for loss or damage.

ENTRY FEE: $20. No entries returned.

DEADLINES: Entry, October. Judging, November. Event, December.

77

Danube Prize-International Festival of Television Programs for Children and Youth
Czechoslovak Television
Dr. Jan Kocian, Director
Television Centre Mylnska dolina
841 01 Bratislava,
CZECHOSLOVAKIA Tel: 32-74-48

September

International; **entry restricted** (selection by official broadcasting organizations in each country); biennial (odd years); established 1971. Danube Prize, Honorable Mentions, other awards to **Children-Youth Television Films** (35mm, 16mm) and **Videotapes** (2-inch PAL, SECAM) 120 minutes maximum total (limit 4 per organization); produced in previous 2 years; no educational, sports, commercials, or former international festival entries; Czechoslovak TV telecasts all winners nationwide. Purpose: to bring to professionals, public, best television programs for children and youth. Motto: "Furtherance of a progressive relationship of children and youth to life." Sponsored by Czechoslovak Television and government. Average statistics: 75 entries, 280 entrants, 26 countries, 8 winners. Held in Bratislava for 9 days. Event, September.

CULTURE, SOCIOLOGY

Includes ALTERNATIVE-NEW AGE, ANTHROPOLOGY, ARCHITECTURE-URBAN ISSUES, FOLKLORE-FOLKMUSIC, FUTURE, HUMAN COMMUNICATION, WESTERN. (Also see AMERICANISM, EDUCATIONAL, INDEPENDENT, HUMANITARIAN, TELEVISION.)

78

Prix Jeunesse International Television Competition
Bayerischer Rundfunk
Dr. Ernst Emrich, Secretary General
Rundfunkplatz 1
D-8000 Munich 2, WEST GERMANY
(FRG) Tel: (089) 59-00-20-58

June

International; **entry restricted** (selection by official broadcasting organizations in each country); biennial; established 1964. Prix Jeunesse, Certificates, Special Awards to **Television Films** (35mm, 16mm) **and Videotapes for Children and Young People**; 60 minutes maximum per organization (90 minutes maximum for TV feature film if only entry); produced in previous 2 years; no advertising programs. Alternates with PRIX JEUNESSE SEMINAR. Purpose: to treat up-to-date subjects in children's and youth TV. Have yearly theme. Sponsored by Bavaria, City of Munich, Bavarian Broadcasting Corporation. Recognized by UNESCO, EBU. Average statistics: 86 entries, 300 entrants, 39 countries. Have seminars, workshops, training courses, research studies. Event, June.

79

Conference on Visual Anthropology (COVA) Film and Video Exhibitions
Temple University
Jay Ruby, Director
Department of Anthropology
Philadelphia, Pennsylvania 19122
U.S.A. Tel: (215) 787-1414, 787-7513

March

International; entry open to all; biennial; established 1965. Formerly called ANTHROPOLOGICAL AND DOCUMENTARY FILM CONFERENCE. Alternates with CONFERENCE ON CULTURE AND COMMUNICATION. Purpose: to explore human condition through visual means. Sponsored by Temple University Anthropology and Radio-Television-Film Departments, Lectures and Forums Committee, Center for Visual Communications; Society for Anthropology of Visual Communication (founded 1972 as organization of researchers, scholars, practitioners studying human behavior through visual means). Held at Walk Auditorium in Ritter Hall, Temple University. Have discussions, panels, workshops, exhibits. Also sponsor photo essay exhibit.

VIDEOTAPE EXHIBITION: Anthropology (1/2-inch reel, 3/4-inch cassette).

AWARDS: Small stipend to some invited participants.

JUDGING: By selection committee.

ENTRY FEE: None.

DEADLINES: Entry, November. Materials upon request. Judging, December. Exhibition, March.

80

New Earth Television (N.E.T. Works) Film and Video Broadcasts
Future Now Communications
Taylor Barcroft, Publisher
P.O. Box 1281
Santa Cruz, California 95061 U.S.A.
Tel: (408) 476-8336

Continuous

International; entry open to all; continuous; established 1981. Purpose: to provide useful information, show application of worldwide innovations for improvement in quality of life. Motto: "Solutions exist." Presented through U.S. broadcast stations, Canadian Cable TV systems, other foreign countries. Have postproduction facilities. Publish monthly newsletter.

FILM-VIDEOTAPE BROADCAST: Alternative, New Age Documentary for Television (3/4-inch minimum) shot on 3-tube camera. Require stills. Category: Documentary (Technology, Psychology, Sociology, Spirituality, Innovative Music-Visualizations, Energy, Health Care, Alternative Lifestyles, New Inventions, New Applications of Old Inventions, Learning, Shelter, Transportation, Agriculture; Consumer Electronics: Home Video, Home Computing, Home Entertainment, Programmed

Instruction, other life improvement solutions including Space Industrialization). No master tapes.

JUDGING: By staff of editors, writers based on quality journalism. Sponsor may edit. Nonexclusive agreement (exclusive if production goes into Home Videocassettes).

SALES TERMS: $100 per minute of transmitted footage.

ENTRY FEE: None.

DEADLINES: Open.

81

Speech Communication Association (SCA) Student Produced Public Service Announcement Contest
Dr. James E. Fletcher, Chairman
Henry W. Grady School of
Journalism and Mass Communication
University of Georgia
Athens, Georgia 30602 U.S.A.
Tel: (404) 542-3785

November

National; entry restricted to U.S. undergraduates; annual; established 1980. Purpose: to encourage public service announcements which advance general public understanding of human communication. Sponsored and supported by SCA. Average statistics: 20 entries, 5 winners.

VIDEOTAPE CONTEST: Human Communication Television Public Service Announcements (3/4-inch U-matic) 3 30-second public service announcements maximum.

AUDIOTAPE CONTEST: Human Communication Radio Public Service Announcement (1/4-inch reel, 7 1/2 ips). 3 30-second public service announcements maximum.

ELIGIBILITY: American junior college, college, or university under-graduates in certificate degree program in communication or related fields.

AWARDS: First Place, best TV, Radio $100. Two runners-up $50 each.

JUDGING: By 5 members, based on originality, script, production quality. Sponsor retains all entries.

ENTRY FEE: None.

DEADLINES: Entry, Winter. Materials, June. Judging, Summer.

82

Western Heritage Awards
National Cowboy Hall of Fame and Western Heritage Center
1700 Northeast 63rd Street
Oklahoma City, Oklahoma 73111
U.S.A. Tel: (405) 478-2250

April

International; entry open to all; annual; established 1961. Purpose: to honor drama and heritage of Old West. Sponsored by and held at National Cowboy Hall of Fame and Western Heritage Center (world's largest western lore exhibit), founded 1965 to perpetuate western traditions in authentic, artistic exhibits. Also sponsor music category, WESTERN PERFORMER'S HALL OF FAME AWARDS (to 1 living, 1 deceased western contributor).

VIDEOTAPE CONTESTS: Western Television (3/4-inch, 2-inch) produced in previous 2 years. Categories: Factual Television, Fictional Television.

AWARDS: Wrangler Trophies (replica of Charles Russell sculpture) for Excellence in Western Achievement, each category.

JUDGING: By panel, based on artis-

tic merit, integrity, achievement in portraying spirit of Western pioneers. May change categories, withhold awards. Sponsor retains all winners for permanent collection.

ENTRY FEE: None. Entrant pays postage.

83

Fact-Film
FACT (Forum Architecture, Communication, Territory)
Francois Confino, Director
Circa, Chartreuse
30400 Villeneauve lez Avignon, FRANCE Tel: (90) 25-05-46

October

International; entry open to all; triennial; established 1973. Purpose: to promote wider use of media to convey architectural, urban issues to general public. Theme: Architecture and urban issues. Sponsored and supported by UNESCO, French Government, Columbia University of New York. Recognized by UNESCO, French Government. Average statistics: 200 entries, 27 countries, 1500 attendance. Also sponsor FACT, INTERNATIONAL CONFERENCE ON ARCHITECTURE AND URBAN ISSUES with discussions, seminars, workshops, technical expositions. Second contact: Caroll Michells, 491 Broadway, New York, New York 10012.

VIDEOTAPE CONTEST: Architecture, Urban Issues (3/4-inch) any length, any type. Categories: Made for Television, Made for Festival (on given subject), special theme.

AWARDS: Approximately $4000 shared among winners at judges' discretion.

JUDGING: By international experts in architecture, film, communications.

Festival insures for lab costs only during Festival.

ENTRY FEE: $10 (includes return postage).

DEADLINES: Entry, March. Materials, June. Acceptance, July. Event, September-October.

84

Prix Futura International Radio and Television Competition
Sender Freies Berlin
Wilfried Zierke, Director
Masurenallee 8-14
D-1000 Berlin 19, WEST GERMANY
(FRG) Tel: (030) 308-3100

March-April

International; **entry restricted** (selection by official broadcast organizations in each country); biennial; established 1969, added radio 1979. Futura Prizes (monetary) to **Futuristic Television Films** (35mm, 16mm), **Videotapes** (2-inch, 1-inch cassette), and **Radio Audiotapes** about life, living together, survival in world of tomorrow; 90 minutes maximum; 2 limit per organization; first broadcast in previous 2 years; no advertising or former EBU festival winners. Purpose: to encourage broadcasting organizations to seek new approaches to production. Sponsored by Sender Freies Berlin and Second German Television (ZDF). Recognized by EBU. Average statistics: 100 entries, 400 entrants, 32 countries, 5 winners. Held at Sender Freies Berlin, Television Centre for 8 days. Also sponsor award to Best Third World TV Production.

85

Golden Harp Television Festival
Radio Telefis Eireann
Aindreas O'Gallchoir, Secretary General
Donnybrook

Dublin 4, IRELAND Tel: 693111

May

International; **entry restricted** (selection by official broadcasting organizations in each ITU-member country); annual; established 1966. Harp Awards, Special Mentions to **Folklore, Folkmusic Television Films** (35mm, 16mm) **and Videotapes;** 35 minutes maximum; limit 1 per organization; no commercials or former EBU festival winners. Purpose: to promote international exchange of programs; stimulate wider interest in traditional cultures. Sponsored by Radio Telefis Eireann. Recognized by EBU. Average statistics: 35 entries, 60 entrants, 27 countries, 3 awards. Held in Galway, Ireland. Event, May.

86

Ondas Awards
Radio Barcelona
Joaquin Pelaez, Executive Secretary
Calle de Caspe, No. 6
Barcelona 10, SPAIN
Tel: 343-302-22-66

October-November

International; entry open to all; annual; established 1954. Purpose: to exalt artistic, cultural values of radio, television; reward outstanding international programs, professionals. Sponsored by Radio Barcelona (Manuel G. Teran, President). Supported by Sociedad Espanola de Radiofusion (SER). Average statistics: 160 entries, 40 entrants, 24 countries. Held in Barcelona. Also sponsor PREMIO HOLANDA EUROPEAN PHILIPS CONTEST for young scientists, inventors. Second contact: Jean Michel Banberger, General Executive Secretary, Gran Via, No. 32 (9), Madrid 13, Spain; tel: 341-232-80-00.

VIDEOTAPE CONTEST: Artistic,

Cultural, News Television Broadcast (625-line PAL system; U-matic, VCR cassette).

AUDIOTAPE CONTEST: Artistic, Cultural, News Radio Broadcast (15 or 7 1/2 ips) full-track magnetic tape; in original language.

ELIGIBILITY: Radio, television programs of special artistic quality, broadcast during previous calendar year. Require complete program file; 15 scripts in Spanish, French or English; 5 photographs of author, producer, or actors; biographical note. 2 maximum per entrant.

AWARDS: Ondas Award, Silver Winged Horse Trophies for outstanding work in artistic, news, cultural fields, event-broadcasting, or increased solidarity between peoples through communication: 10 to Spain for Radio; 5 to Spain, TV; 4 to other countries, Radio; 4 to other countries, TV; 5 to Latin America, Radio, TV.

JUDGING: All entries reviewed by minimum 5 international radio, TV professionals, each category. Radio winners kept in Awards Archives for 1 SER broadcast to promote competition.

ENTRY FEE: None.

DEADLINES: Entry, July. Judging, October. Event, November.

DOCUMENTARY, FEATURE, SHORT

Video and Film, including ADVERTISING, FOR CHILDREN, DRAMATIC, EDUCATIONAL, EXPERIMENTAL, INDEPENDENT, STUDENT. (Also see BROADCAST, BUSINESS-INDUSTRIAL, EDUCATIONAL, INDEPENDENT, TELEVISION FILMS.)

87

Athens Video Festival
Athens Center for Film and Video
David Burke, Director
P.O. Box 388
Athens, Ohio 45701 U.S.A. Tel: (614) 594-6888

October

International; entry open to all; annual; established 1976. Expanded to 3-day festival 1979. Purpose: to support awards to independent videomakers, distribute outstanding video works; provide forum for independents. Sponsored by 3M Corporation, Colorado Video, Midwest Corporation. Supported by NEA, Ohio Arts Council, Ohio University. Average statistics: 200 entries, 3 countries, 42 finalists, 15 awards, 250 attendance. Held at Video Space (Athens, Ohio). Tickets: $3.50. Publish *Frame Lines* (newsletter). Also sponsor ATHENS INTERNATIONAL FILM FESTIVAL, OHIO UNIVERSITY FILM CONFERENCE, ATHENS FESTIVAL ROADSHOW (touring exhibition), workshops, screenings, guest speakers. Second contact: Giulio Scalinger, Athens Center for Film and Video, 384 Lindley Hall, Ohio University Department of Film, Athens, Ohio 45701.

VIDEOTAPE CONTEST: Documentary, Drama, Art-Experimental, Educational, Performance (3/4-inch U-matic, 1/2-inch VHS) reel-to-reel, NTSC standard, single VTR monitor playback. No film transfers. Produced in previous year.

AWARDS: $1500 to winners in cash, services or supplies. Special Merit and Merit Awards.

JUDGING: Preliminary screening over cable TV by local judges. Final by guest judges and Festival staff (3 per category). Festival may broadcast winning entries. Not responsible for loss or damage.

ENTRY FEE: Under 20 minutes, $10; under 30, $20; under 60, $30; over 60 minutes, $45.

DEADLINES: Entry forms, September. Event, October. Materials returned, November.

88

Global Village Video and Television Documentary Festival
Global Village Video Study Center
Irving Vincent, Coordinator
454 Broome Street
New York, New York 10013 U.S.A.
Tel: (212) 966-7526

April-May

International; entry open to all; annual; established 1974. Purpose: to provide recognition, forum for video works. Sponsored by Global Village (Julie Gustafson, Associate Director) founded 1969 as first nonprofit alternate media center and production group in U.S. for creative study of portable video and videotape. Supported by NEA, NYSCA, CPB, Rockefeller Foundation, Sony Corporation of America. Average statstics: 100 entries, 50 shown. Held at Global Village Video Study Center and as miniseries on WNYC-31 New York City public television. Also sponsor FESTIVAL OF WORKS BY MINORITY VIDEO AND FILMMAKERS, held November-December for 3 weeks. Have seminars, symposia, workshops, film-video-book library. Publish *Airtime* (newsletter), *Videoscope Magazine.* Second contact: Charles Addotta.

VIDEOTAPE CONTEST: Documentary (1/2-inch reel, 3/4-inch cassette, no Betamax) any length. Require description, production information. Request press materials, pho-

togr

FILM CONTEST: Documentary Television (16mm). Requirements same as for Videotape.

AWARDS: Best Video Documentary; Best Documentary Television Film or Tape. Special Jury Recognition award. Money Awards.

JUDGING: By 4-member panel.

ENTRY FEE: None.

DEADLINES: Entry, March. Event, April-May.

89

Houston International Film Festival (Festival of the Americas)
Cinema America Inc.
J. Hunter Todd, President-Founder
P.O. Box 56566
Houston, Texas 77027 U.S.A.
Tel: (713) 757-0028

April

International; entry open to all; annual; established 1968. Formerly called ATLANTA INTERNATIONAL FILM FESTIVAL to 1974, VIRGIN ISLANDS INTERNATIONAL FILM FESTIVAL to 1977, GREATER MIAMI INTERNATIONAL FILM FESTIVAL to 1978. Purpose: to honor excellence in film and TV. Sponsored and supported by Cinema America, Houston Film Society. Recognized by IFFPA, IAIFD. Average statistics: 2100 entries, 900 entrants, 30 countries, 600 semifinalists, 150 winners, 50 exhibitions, 15,000 attendance. Held at Stouffers Hotel, Greenway Plaza, Houston, Texas, for 6 days. Tickets: $4 each premiere, $50 series. Second contact: Rikki Kipple, Assistant Director, 2100 Travis, Central Square, Suite 626, Houston, Texas 77002.

VIDEOTAPE CONTEST: Feature, Short, Documentary, Student, Experimental, Television, Television Commercials (compatible with 525-lines interlaced, color sync 59.99, hiband color, quad head systems or Sony Videocassette) completed in previous 2 years, unlimited entries. Require synopsis, photos. Foreign tapes include English subtitles.

AWARDS: Gold Venus, Best of Festival, each major category. Gold, Silver, Bronze Venus, Best of Festival and subcategory. Special Jury Prizes, entries of unusual merit. Grand Prize (Script, Feature) each category, assistance in possible production; (Script, Short) raw stock and cameras. Best Student Film.

JUDGING: International Blue Ribbon Committee of 100 selects top 3, each category. Final by International Grand Awards Jury of 7. May change categories. Sponsor insures to maximum of $200 or replacement cost, whichever is less.

ENTRY FEE: Feature $50. Documentary, Short, Experimental, Television (30 minutes and under $60, over 30 $80). TV Commercial (single $35, series $90). Student with ID, Super 8mm, $25. Videotape Market $50. Screenplay $75. Foreign (submitted by governments and delegations) free. Festival pays return postage.

DEADLINES: Entry, March. Event, April. Materials returned day after festival.

VIDEOTAPE SALES MARKET: Any type. Have 5 market theaters.

90

Ithaca Video Festival
Ithaca Video Projects, Inc.
Philip Mallory Jones, Director
328 East State Street
Ithaca, New York 14850 U.S.A.
Tel: (607) 272-1596

March

International; entry open to all; annual; established 1975. Originally shown in one location; video programs now selected for presentation at museums, galleries, libraries, schools throughout U.S., with audiences in the thousands. Purpose: to promote public appreciation of professional video artists and work. Sponsored by Ithaca Video Projects. Supported by NYSCA, NEA. Average statistics: 375 entries, 2 countries, 20 winners. Held in 30 locations around the U.S.

VIDEOTAPE CONTEST-EXHIBITION: Short Independent (1/2-inch open reel, 3/4-inch U-matic) 30 minutes maximum. Must originate on videotape, all genres.

AWARDS: $100 each tape selected for touring exhibition.

JUDGING: By 4 professional video artists, producers, critics, curators; based on creative use of medium, inventiveness, craftsmanship, execution. Festival may duplicate tape for festival tour only, shown on closed circuit.

ENTRY FEE: None. Entrant pays postage.

DEADLINES: Entry, February. Judging, March.

91

Video Shorts Festival
High Hopes Media
Mike Cady, Co-producer
233 Summit Avenue East
Seattle, Washington 98102 U.S.A.
Tel: (206) 322-9010

July

International; entry open to all; annual; established 1980. Purpose: to demonstrate variety of styles and approaches in video production; encourage public involvement. Sponsored by

Videospace Stores, High Hopes Media. Average statistics: 78 entries, 60 entrants, 2 countries, 10 winners, 10 showings. Held in Seattle for 3 days. Tickets: $2.

VIDEOTAPE CONTEST: Short (3/4-inch VHS, Beta I, Beta II) 5 minutes suggested length; excerpts from longer works, PSAs accepted; 3 tapes maximum per entrant. Categories: Experimental-Art, Documentary, Professional-Industrial.

AWARDS: 10 winners awarded $50 each for nonexclusive distribution rights, plus $50 Honorarium 6 months after Festival.

JUDGING: All entries viewed in entirety by 5 videographers of High Hopes Media. Festival may transfer selected highlights to composite tape for showing at Fair, broadcast on television to promote Videospace (consumer video show in Seattle); reserves nonexclusive distribution rights for nonbroadcast, noncommercial, home use purposes. Not responsible for loss or damage.

ENTRY FEE: $5 per entry. Entrant pays postage.

DEADLINES: Entry, Event, July. Awards, August, February. Materials returned, August.

92

Figueira da Foz International Cinema Festival

Centro de Estudos e Animacao Cultural (CEAC)
Jose Vieira Marques, Director
Rua Castilho 61-2, Dt.
1200 Lisbon, PORTUGAL
Tel: 576952

September

International; **entry restricted to independents, professionals;** annual; established 1972. Formerly called INTERNATIONAL CINEMA WEEK OF FIGUEIRA DA FOZ (noncompetitive film exhibition). Became competitive in 1974. Purpose: to promote young international progressive films. Sponsored and supported by CEAC; Ministries of Commerce and Tourism, Education and Science, Culture; Portuguese Institute of Film; Municipal Government of Figueira da Foz. Average statistics: 90 entries, 40 entrants, 25 countries, 30 finalists, 7 winners, 350 attendance per screening. Held at Figueira da Foz for 11 days. Tickets: $1. Have restrospectives, colloquia, seminars, workshops, exhibitions. Second contact: CEAC, Maria Cecilia Vieira Marques, Rua Luis de Camoes No. 106, 2600 Vila Franca de Xira, Portugal.

VIDEOTAPE CONTEST: **Feature Fiction, Long Documentary, For Children** (width not specified) 50 minutes minimum; produced in previous 3 years. Non-Portuguese entries must have subtitles in Portuguese, Spanish, French or English. Require publicity materials, biography, photographs, synopsis.

AWARDS: Grand Prizes, Fiction Films, Images and Documents. 3 Second Prize Silver Plates. Cidade da Figueira da Foz Prize, Best Portuguese. Jury Prize to Personality or Film Trend. Certificates.

JUDGING: By 30-member audience jury, including international film directors, critics, technicians, artists, general public. Not responsible for loss or damage.

ENTRY FEE: None. Entrant pays postage.

DEADLINES: Entry, August. Event, September. Materials returned, October.

93

Barcelona International Cinema Week

Association for the Promotion of
Cinema and Television (APROCIT)
Jose Luis Guarner, Director
Avenida Maria Christina s/N
Palacio No. 1
Barcelona 4, SPAIN Tel: 223-31-01

October

International; entry open to all; annual; established 1959. Began as specialized event in color films; has emphasized cinema-TV relations since 1978. Purpose: to promote cooperation between TV and cinema; publicize positive, stimulating new ideas in artistic, educational, social communication. Sponsored and supported by Minister of Culture, Madrid; Barcelona Town Hall; Catalonian Government. Average statistics: 35-40 entries, 10-20 countries. Held in Barcelona for 1 week. Tickets: 200 pesetas, $3. Also sponsor annual meetings and workshops.

VIDEOTAPE CONTEST: **Short, Documentary, Experimental, Dramatic, Television** (U-matic). Interested in movies by distinguished filmmakers for TV, movies for TV or cinema by TV directors, all TV initiatives for advancement of cinema.

AWARDS: First Prize, Gold Lady of the Umbrella. Second, Silver Medal. Third, Bronze Medal, each category. Honor Mention, all participants.

JUDGING: 5-member selection committee; Prizes by 3-member international jury. Preference to European premieres. May exclude entries likely to wound national feelings, encourage racial or national discrimination.

ENTRY FEE: None. Entrant pays postage.

DEADLINES: Entry, September. Event, October.

DRAMATIC, MUSICAL

TV-Radio Broadcasting (video, film, audio), including DOCUMENTARY, LIGHT ENTERTAINMENT, and NEWS. (Also see The ARTS, BROADCASTING, FOR CHILDREN, INDEPENDENT, TELEVISION FILMS.)

94

Golden Prague International Television Festival

Czechoslovak Television
Dr. Gennadij Codr, Director
29 Gorkeho Nam
11150 Prague 1, CZECHOSLOVAKIA

June

International; **entry restricted** (selection by official broadcasting organizations in each country); annual; established 1964. Golden Prague Awards, Special Prizes to **Dramatic, Musical Television Films** (35mm, 16mm) **and Videotapes** (2-inch SECAM, PAL); 90 minutes maximum (drama), 60 minutes maximum (musical); limit 2 per organization; produced in previous year; no former international festival entries. Purpose: to further international cooperation in television; provide platform for broad examination of creative work. Motto: "Television screen serves mutual knowledge, better understanding between nations." Average statistics: 50 entries, 37 countries, 14 awards, 1500 attendance. Sponsored by Czechoslovak Television. Held in Prague for 9 days. Have press conferences, Special Open Tribute (theme varies yearly). Event, June.

95

**Prix Italia International
Competition for Radio and
Television Programs**
RAI-Radiotelevisione Italiana
Alvise Zorzi, Secretary General
Vilale Mazzini 14
00195 Rome, ITALY Tel: 3878-4118

September

International; **entry restricted** (selection by national broadcasting member organizations in each country); annual; established 1948. Prix Italia (monetary) and Special Prize to **Dramatic, Documentary, Music Television Videotapes, and Radio Audiotapes;** 90 minutes maximum; limit 2 each (TV and Radio) per country; first broadcast in previous 2 years; no advertising, live reportage, music-hall or variety programs. Sponsor retains 1 copy for study and documentation. Purpose: to promote quality of radio, TV programs; encourage member organizations to broadcast entries. Sponsored by RAI. Recognized by EBU. Average statistics: 140 entries, 600 entrants, 33 countries, 12 awards. Held in various Italian cities for 13 days. Have meetings, seminars. Also sponsor Italian Press Association Prize to Best Radio Documentary. Event, September.

96

**Monte Carlo International
Television Festival**
Pierre Blanchy, President
Palais des Congres
Avenue d'Ostende
Monte Carlo, MONACO
Tel: 30-43-47, 30-49-44

February

International; **entry restricted to ITU-member country television producers, organizations;** annual; estab-lished 1961. Purpose: to promote development of international program exchange.

VIDEOTAPE CONTEST: Television **Drama, News** (3/4-inch cassette, standard U-matic, 625 lines 50 Hz; 1-inch IVC or Ampex, 625 lines 50 Hz or 819 lines 50 Hz; 2-inch 625 lines 50 Hz; all standard French recordings or CCIR 50 Hz; standard SECAM or PAL 625 lines 50 periods). Video-Film categories: (1 entry each): News Reports (10 minutes maximum), News Features (50 Minutes maximum), News Broadcasts (Video only) (50 minutes maximum), Drama (100 minutes maximum). 60 minutes total in news categories.

FILM CONTEST: Television **Drama, News** (35mm) optical, (16mm) optical, composite or separate magnetic. Categories same as for Videotape.

ELIGIBILITY: First publicly viewed in previous year; produced by TV producers, organizations of ITU-member countries. Editing permitted using original broadcast. Require typewritten dialog, commentary, screenplay in original language and in French (30 copies), English (10 copies); English and French synopsis, technical and artistic information, still photos, additional information. No advertising or previous award winners.

AWARDS: Nymph Awards to Best in News Categories; in Drama for Best Screenplay, Direction, Actor, Actress. AMADE-UNESCO Prize, 10,000 francs to nonviolent solution to human relations problem. Cino del Duca Prize, Best Young Director. UNDA Silver Dove Prize, film reflecting ideals or activities of International Catholic Association for Radio and Television. International Critics Prizes, Best News and Drama.

JUDGING: By international juries. News judged on picture quality, intensity as witness of event. May reject on moral, political, religious grounds; withhold awards. AMADE may use 1 copy free (AMADE-UNESCO winner) for 10 months after festival at 3 charity events per country for benefit of underprivileged children. Not responsible for loss or damage.

ENTRY FEE: None. Entrant pays postage.

DEADLINES: Entry, November. Materials, December. Event, February.

SALES MARKET: Television Video, Film. Technical regulations same as for competition. 300 francs per 90-minute entry. Require typed script in original language, English (19 copies), French (30 copies); English and French synopsis or resume, still photos, other materials. Entry, December.

97

Golden Rose of Montreux International Contest for Television Light Entertainment Programs
Swiss Broadcasting Corporation (SBC)
Frank R. Tappolet, Secretary General
1 Giacomettistrasse
CH-3000 Berne 15, SWITZERLAND
Tel: 031-43-91-11

May

International; **entry restricted** (selection by official broadcasting organizations in each country); annual; established 1960. Rose of Montreux Awards (monetary), Special Mentions and Prizes to **Light Entertainment Television Films** (35mm, 16mm) **and Videotapes** (Sony U-matic BVU 200 625-line PAL); 30-52 minutes maximum (depending on category); limit 2 per category; produced in previous 14 months. Purpose: to promote knowledge of light entertainment programs; encourage creation of original works. Sponsored by City of Montreux, SBC. Recognized by EBU. Average statistics: 45 entries, 600 entrants, 35 countries, 4 awards. Held at Maison des Congres (Montreux) for 9 days. Have private screenings, symposia. Also sponsor International Television Symposium and Technical Exhibition (Hansruedi Probst, Chairman), EBU INTERNATIONAL SEMINAR FOR EDUCATIONAL TV, LAUSANNE GOLDEN RING COMPETITION FOR TV SPORTS PROGRAMS.

EDUCATIONAL

TV-Radio Broadcasting (video, film, audio) and Video, including ANIMATED, DOCUMENTARY, FEATURE, EXPERIMENTAL, INDEPENDENT, INFORMATIONAL, PUBLIC AFFAIRS, READING, EDUCATION, SHORT, STUDENT. (Also see ADVERTISING, BROADCASTING, BUSINESS-INDUSTRIAL, DOCUMENTARY, JOURNALISM.)

98

American Film Festival Video Competition
Educational Film Library Association (EFLA)
Nadine Covert, Director
43 West 61st Street
New York, New York 10023 U.S.A.
Tel: (212) 246-4533

June

International; entry open to all; annual; established 1981. Sponsored by

EFLA (Claire Monagahn, Coordinator) nonprofit corporation founded 1943 to promote production, distribution, utilization of films, audiovisual materials in education, community programs. Held in New York City for 6 days during AMERICAN FILM FESTIVAL, and as national traveling exhibition to Libraries, schools, universities. Have libary, workshops. Publish *Sightlines Magazine*, book, pamphlets, film evaluation guide.

VIDEOTAPE CONTEST: Educational all types, Documentary, Short, Entertainment (3/4-inch cassette) maximum 110 minutes, released for general distribution, purchase, rental, loan in U.S. during previous 2 years. Categories: Documentary, Education, Training, Health and Mental Health, Art, Entertainment, Public Service (30 or 60-second informational spots).

AWARDS: Blue Ribbon First Place, Red Ribbon Second Place, each category. Honorable Mentions. May withhold awards.

JUDGING: By screening committee. 6 persons per category judge entries on technical quality, presentation, accuracy of subject matter, programming potential for intended audience. All entries viewed in entirety.

ENTRY FEE: 30-60 seconds, $25; 2-11 minutes, $50; 12-25, $65; 26-49, $90; 50-110, $120.

DEADLINES: Entry, January. Materials, February. Event, June.

99

Birmingham International Educational Film Festival
Craig Battles
Box 78-SBD, University Station
Birmingham, Alabama 35294 U.S.A.
Tel: (205) 934-3884

March

International; entry open to all; annual; established 1973. Purpose: to recognize, encourage use of original, creative, instructive educational audiovisual media. Sponsored by University of Alabama (Birmingham), Alabama Education Association, Alabama Power Company, Interlock Film Studio. Held at University of Alabama for 5 days. Also sponsor SADIE AWARD to individual for outstanding contributions to education. Second contact: Alabama Education Association, P.O. Box 4177, Montgomery, Alabama 36195.

VIDEOTAPE CONTEST: Educational (VHS 1/2-inch, 3/4-inch cassette) 60 minutes maximum, released after January in previous 2 years, original production. Entries in English, with English subtitles, or accompanied by English script. Categories: Americana, Applied and Performing Arts, Corporate Communications, Early Childhood, Energy, Health and Physical Education, Human Relations, Language Arts, Mathematics and Science, Social Sciences, Specialized Programs, Student Productions (require proof of student status).

ELIGIBILITY: Closed to members of Festival Board of Directors, sponsors or organizations, agencies they represent.

AWARDS: Gold Electra Statuette, $600, Best of Festival. Silver Electra, $400. Electra Certificate, $150 Best of Category. Certificate of Recognition, each finalist. May withhold awards.

JUDGING: Prescreening by volunteer committees of teachers, writers, students, media, subject specialists. Final by 6 judges based on educational merit of work and technical quality. Not responsible for loss or damage.

ENTRY FEE: $25-$30, $15-$20

(student). Additional category over 2 entries, $5.

DEADLINES: Entry, February. Awards, March. Materials returned, June.

| 100 |

Columbus International Film Festival

Film Council of Greater Columbus
Mary A. Rupe, Secretary
257 South Brinker Avenue
Columbus, Ohio 43204 U.S.A.
Tel: (614) 274-1826

October

International; **entry restricted to college students, independents, professionals;** annual; established 1950. Purpose: to promote use of 16mm motion pictures and videotape throughout world. Sponsored by Film Council of Greater Columbus. Supported by Ohio Arts Council. Recognized by Columbus Chamber of Commerce. Average statistics: 550-600 entries. Held at Columbus Athletic Club, Ohio State University for 2 days. Have exhibit space (on written request). Tickets: $40, Chris Award Banquet. Second contact: Daniel F. Prugh, President of Council, Center of Science and Industry, 280 Broad Street, Columbus, Ohio 43215: tel: (614) 228-5613.

VIDEOTAPE CONTEST: Nontheatrical, **Feature, Short, Animated, Documentary, Experimental, Student, Television Announcements** (3/4-inch cassette) unlimited entry. Categories (and subject areas): Art, Culture (Animated, Experimental, Feature, Fiction, On Motion Pictures, Fine Arts, Performing Arts). Business, Industry (Animated, Civil Defense, Consumerism, Economics, Business and Labor, Employee Relations, Fund Raising, Industrial Safety, Job Orien-

tation, Labor Relations, Manufacturing and Technical Processes, Personnel and Sales Training, Public Relations, Sales Promotion, Shareholder and Public Information, TV Announcements). Education (Agriculture, Forestry, Mining, Classroom for Lower Grades, For High School and College, Driver Education, Child Care and Development, English and Language Arts, Guidance, Home Economics, Mathematics, Nature and Wildlife, Autobiography and Biography, Recreation, Crafts, Safety Education, Science, Sports and Games, Stories for Children). Health, Medicine (Dentistry and Dental Health, Diet and Nutrition, First Aid, Health Science Research for Professionals, Medical Sciences, Mental Health, Physical Health, Public Health). Religion, Ethics (Old and New Testament, Church at Work, Denominational and Doctrinal Materials, Ethical Problems, New Religions, World Religions, TV Announcements). Social Studies (Americana, Anthropology and Ethnography, Citizenship, Conservation of Energy, Conservation of Natural Resources, Customs and Folklore, Environment, Geography, History, International Relations, Public Services, Social Documentaries). Travel (Commercial, Outdoor and Wilderness, Travel for Classroom, Documentaries, Vacationing, TV Announcements).

AWARDS: President's Award for Originality, Photographic, Technical Excellence. Mayor's Chris Award for Most Innovative. Chris (Christopher Columbus) Statuette for Excellence or Approaching Perfection, each subject area. Chris Bronze Plaque, runners-up, each area. Honorable Mentions.

JUDGING: By selected professionals based on acting, clarity, technical proficiency, interest, truthfulness. May show winning entries on television. Not responsible for loss or damage.

ENTRY FEE: 12 minutes and under, $65; 13-25 minutes, $80; 26-48 minutes, $100; 49 minutes, not over 110 minutes, $120.

DEADLINES: Entry, July. Judging, September. Event, October.

[101]

International Reading Association (IRA) Broadcast Media Awards for Radio and Television
Drew Cassidy, Public Information Officer
800 Barksdale Road
P.O. Box 8139
Newark, Delaware 19711 U.S.A.
Tel: (302) 731-1600

April

International; **entry restricted to professionals;** annual. Purpose: to recognize outstanding reporting and programming on radio, TV, cable TV dealing with reading, literacy; recognize value of reading in society; promote reading as lifetime habit. Sponsored by IRA, nonprofit educational association. Held at annual IRA conventions in various U.S. cities. Also sponsor awards for contributions, research in reading field.

VIDEOTAPE CONTEST: Reading Education Television Broadcast (3/4-inch cassette) with transcript, other supporting information. Broadcast during previous calendar year; informational rather than instructional, oriented toward general public. Classes: Network, Local. Categories: Journalism on Reading (in school, home, including research and educational practices); School Reading Programs; Interview; Public Service-Entertainment.

AUDIOTAPE CONTEST: Reading

Education Radio Broadcast (monaural) Requirements, categories same as for Videotape.

AWARDS: Medals, Best Television, Best Radio. Certificates of Merit, each class. Limited travel allowance for winner to attend awards ceremony.

JUDGING: By IRA subcommittee. Not responsible for loss or damage.

ENTRY FEE: None.

DEADLINES: Entry, February. Awards, April-May.

[102]

Midwest Film Conference Exhibitions of Films and Video
Charles Boos, Director
P.O. Box 1665
Evanston, Illinois 60204 U.S.A.
Tel: (312) 869-0600

February

International; entry open to all; annual; established 1969 by educators, film distributors interested in exposing new and creative classroom film and video. Theme: Creative use of film. Sponsored by Midwest Film Conference and various film associations, producers, distributors. Average statistics: 400 entries, 10 countries, 150 shown, 1200 attendance. Held at Chicago O'Hare Marriott Hotel, Chicago, Illinois. Tickets: $30 (in advance), $35 (at door). Also have seminars, workshops, repeat screenings.

VIDEOTAPE EXHIBITION-MARKET: Educational, Independent (all widths and types) any length.

AWARDS: Selection of film for screening at conference.

JUDGING: By selection committee.

ENTRY FEE: Under 30 minutes, $20; over, $35.

DEADLINES: Entry, judging, October. Winners announced, January. Conference, February. Materials returned, December.

| 103 |

Ohio State Awards in Broadcasting

Institute for Education by Radio-Television
Dale K. Ouzts, Director
Ohio State University
2400 Olentangy River Road
Columbus, Ohio 43210 U.S.A.
Tel: (614) 422-9678

March

International; entry open to all; annual; established 1936. Considered oldest program competition in broadcasting. Purpose: to recognize meritorious achievements in educational, informational, public affairs broadcasting; encourage, stimulate excellence in production. Sponsored by Institute for Education by Radio-Televison (founded 1930 as Institute for Education by Radio), Ohio State University Telecommunications Center. Average statistics: 900 entries. Awards presented at National Press Club, Washington, D.C.

VIDEOTAPE CONTEST: Educational, Informational, Public Affairs Television Broadcast (3/4-inch U-matic cassette). Broadcast between July 1 previous year, June 30 year of entry, in English, intended primarily to educate. Categories: Performing Arts-Humanities, Natural-Physical Sciences, Social Sciences-Public Affairs. Divisions: Network-Major Producer, Metropolitan City, Local-Other. Type: Formal, Informal Instruction. Intended audience: Adults-General, Children.

FILM CONTEST: Educational, Informational, Public Affairs Television Broadcast (16mm) composite. Requirements, categories same as for video.

AUDIOTAPE CONTEST: Educational, Informational, Public Affairs Radio Broadcast (7-inch reels or cassetes, 7 1/2 ips) full-track. Categories, requirements same as for Videotape.

AWARDS: Award Certificates for excellence in educational, informational, public affairs broadcasting.

JUDGING: By 7 panels of judges (audition every entry), based on significance of subject-theme, content preparation-organization, presentation effectiveness, authenticity, audience suitability.

ENTRY FEE: $45 per reel, $50 per cassette. Audiotape, $25 per reel (no audiotapes returned).

DEADLINES: Entry, September. Awards, March.

| 104 |

Japan Prize International Educational Program Contest

NHK Japan Broadcasting Corporation
Hiroji Minour, General Secretary
2-2-1 Jinnan, Shibuya-ku
Tokyo 150, JAPAN Tel: 03-465-1111

October-November

International; entry restricted to radio, TV broadcasting organizations in ITU-member countries; biennial; established 1965. Alternates with PRIX JEUNESSE INTERNATIONAL. Purpose: to advance educational broadcast programs; contribute to promotion of understanding, cooperation among nations. Sponsored by Japan Broadcasting Corporation (NHK-Nippon Hoso Kyokai), founded 1925. Average statistics: 163

entries, 89 broadcasting organizations, 56 countries. Held at NHK Broadcasting Center, Tokyo, for 12 days. Have Japan Prize Circulating Library, symposia.

VIDEOTAPE CONTEST: Educational Television Series Broadcast (525 lines, 30 pictures per second, or 625 lines, 25 pictures per second) part of series, 60 minutes maximum per program. Require 30 script copies each in English, French; date-hour of broadcast, educational aims, synopsis, school system broadcasting information, educational-promotional materials, photos; dubbed, narrated, subtitles in English or French. Categories: Educational for Primary-Kindergarten-Nursery, Secondary Educational, Adult Educational.

FILM CONTEST: Educational Television Series Broadcast (35mm) optical, (16mm) optical, separate, composite magnetic; part of series, 60 minutes maximum per program. Requirements, categories same as for videotape.

AUDIOTAPE CONTEST: Educational Radio Series Broadcast (monaural, single-track tape) part of series, 60 minutes maximum per program. Categories, requirements same as for Videotape.

ELIGIBILITY: Broadcast for first time in previous 2 years by permanent producing broadcasting organization, union, association from ITU member or associate member country-territory. 2 radio and (or) TV program for independent regional broadcasting organizations. Produced by entrants. No advertising, closed circuit broadcast.

AWARDS: Japan Prize, $2000, trophy, certificate of honor, one each for Best Radio, TV Program. Minister of Education Prize, $1000, insignia, certificate of honor, Best Primary or Sec-ondary Education Radio Program. Governor of Tokyo Metropolis Prize, $1000, insignia, certificate of honor, Best Secondary or Adult Education Radio Program. Minister of Posts and Telecommunications Prize, $1000, insignia, certificate of honor, Best Primary or Secondary Education TV Program. Abe Prize, $1000, insignia, certificate of honor, Best Secondary or Adult Education TV Program. Special Prizes, $500, insignia, certificate of honor, Outstanding Programs by Organizations with Limited Means of Production, 3 each for Radio, TV. Maeda Prize, $1000, insignia, certificate of honor, Best Radio or TV Program Promoting World Understanding, Cooperation. Hoso Bunka Foundation Prize, $1000, insignia, certificate of honor, Best Preschool Education TV or Radio Program. UNICEF Prize, $1000, gold statuette, Best TV Program Dealing with Children in Developing Countries.

JUDGING: By 15-member international jury. All entries may be broadcast by participating organizations over their facilities, for pay, 2 times in 2 years following contest. Sponsors may withhold awards, use excerpts from entries for broadcast, publication.

ENTRY FEE: None. Entrant pays postage.

DEADLINES: Application, August. Entry, September. Event, October-November.

EXHIBITION, DISTRIBUTION, BROADCAST

Exhibition, Distribution, and Broadcast sources for Independent, Short, Documentary,

Noncommercial, Nontheatrical Videotapes and Films. Includes DISTRIBUTION INFORMATION SERVICES, PURCHASE PROGRAMS, TRAVEL-TOUR LISTINGS, and INTERN-TRAINING PROGRAMS.

105

Ampersand International Distribution Service
Athens Center for Film and Video
Christine Rath, Director
Box 388
Athens, Ohio 45701 U.S.A. Tel: (614) 594-6007

Continuous

International; entry open to all; continuous; established 1979. Purpose: to provide nonexclusive international distribution service for independent film, video makers. Sponsored by Athens Center for Film and Video (ACFV). Supported by Ohio Arts Council, NEA.

VIDEOTAPE DISTRIBUTION: **Independent** (3/4-inch) any length, unlimited entries. Foreign language entry with English subtitles.

JUDGING: By screening committee, including Ampersand Director, ACFV representative, film, videomakers. All entries viewed in entirety. Sponsor insures for replacement cost.

SALES TERMS: Nonexclusive distribution service (terms not specified).

ENTRY FEE: None. Entrant pays postage.

DEADLINES: Screenings twice yearly (dates not specified).

106

Boston Film-Video Foundation Open Screenings of Film and Video
Julie Levinson, Programmer
1126 Boylston Street
Boston, Massachusetts 02215 U.S.A.
Tel: (617) 536-1540

September-June

International; monthly screenings open to all (special screenings of independents and professionals by invitation); monthly; established 1977. Formerly called BOSTON VIDEO AND FILMMAKERS COLLECTIVE. Purpose: to support independent video and filmmakers through presentation of their works. Sponsored by 400-member Boston Film-Video Foundation. Supported by NEA, WGBH (public TV), membership fees. Average statistics: 80 exhibitions, 70-100 attendance per event. Held at 130-seat BFVF theater. Tickets: open screenings free; $2-$3 individual; $15-$20 (series) invitation screenings. Publish *Visions* newsletter. Also sponsor education programs, information

VIDEOTAPE EXHIBITION: **Independent** (3/4-inch cassette, 1/2-inch reel and cassette). Invited artist should send background and publicity material.

AWARDS: Honorarium for invited artist present at screenings.

ENTRY FEE: None.

DEADLINES: Entry, June (Fall program), October (Spring program).

107

Brief Encounters Film and Video Broadcasts
Center Screen
18 Vassar Street, 20B-126

Cambridge, Massachusetts 02139
U.S.A. Tel: (617) 494-0201

Various

National; **entry open to U.S.;** various. Sponsored by Center Screen. Supported by NEA, WGBH (Public TV) Educational Foundation. Average Statistics: 500 entries.

VIDEOTAPE BROADCAST-DISTRIBUTION: Short Television Broadcasts (2-inch 1-inch, 3/4-inch, 1/2-inch) 30 seconds to 7 minutes; sound; for consideration as intermission spots on public TV. Must meet or be correctable to FCC technical speculations.

FILM BROADCAST-DISTRIBUTION: Short Television Broadcasts. (16mm) for consideration as intermission spots on public TV. Other requirements same as for Videotape.

JUDGING: By Center Screen Director and WGBH Executive Producer for Community Affairs.

SALES TERMS: Rates for local broadcast (on unlimited basis): $100 per minute for 30 seconds to 4 minutes; $95 per minute, 4-5 minutes; $90 per minute, 5-6 minutes; $85 per minute, 6-7 minutes. Will be packaged on 2-hour maximum, 2-inch videotape, offered to regional, national PBS systems for acquisition. Additional rates paid if sold.

DEADLINES: Entry, April.

108

Chinsegut Film & Video Conference Exhibitions
Atlantic Productions
Stan Kozma
10002 Lola Street
Tampa, Florida 33612 U.S.A.
Tel: (813) 977-0590

May

International; entry open to all; annual; established 1976. Formerly called INDEPENDENT AMERICAN FILMMAKERS SOUTHERN CIRCUIT FILM EXHIBITIONS. Purpose: to exhibit films and video on noncompetitive basis. Sponsored by Atlantic Productions, South Carolina Arts Commission. Supported by University of South Florida Art Department, NEA. Average statistics: 200 entrants. Held in Reddington Beach, Florida, for 4 days. Tickets: $5. Second contact: 13710 N. 20th Street, Tampa, Florida 33612.

VIDEOTAPE EXHIBITION: Independent (widths not specified). Request videomaker attendance.

ENTRY FEE: None.

DEADLINES: Not specified.

109

Film and Video Makers Travel Sheet Listings
Carnegie Institute Museum of Art
(Film Section)
Margot Gloninger, Editor
4400 Forbes Avenue
Pittsburgh, Pennsylvania 15213
U.S.A. Tel: (412) 622-3212

Monthly

International; entry open to all; monthly. Purpose: to encourage, facilitate wider use of exhibition, lecture tours by film, videomakers. Sponsored by Carnegie Institute Museum of Art (Film Section). Supported by NEA, Pennsylvania Council on the Arts. Publish *Film and Videomakers Travel Sheet, Film and Videomakers Directory.*

TRAVEL-TOUR LISTING: Videomakers, listings in 15-page travel sheet (including tour information, exhibiting institutions, new film, video for rent or purchase, special announcements), distributed to interested organizations, institutions, individuals, other subscribers.

ENTRY FEE: $1.80, monthly listings. Annual subscription, $3.

DEADLINES: Entry, first week of previous month.

| 110 |

ICAP Cable and Broadcast Programming Service
Independent Cinema Artists & Producers (ICAP)
Susan Eeingenburg, Sandy Mandelberger, Katherine Morgan
625 Broadway
New York, New York 10012 U.S.A.
Tel: (212) 533-9180

Continuous

International; entry open to all; continuous; established 1975 as suppliers of independent film-video to cable markets; public television since 1979. Purpose: to serve as nonprofit distribution, programming service to independent film-video makers. Sponsored by ICAP. Supported by NYSCA, NEA, Markle Foundation. Recognized by AIVF. Publish quarterly newsletter for artists under contract.

VIDEOTAPE-FILM BROADCAST DISTRIBUTION: Independent (35mm, 16mm film; 3/4-inch U-matic video cassette) of broadcast quality. Require synopsis, promotional material, copyright information. Categories: Short Animation, Live Action (3-15 minutes), Children's, Sports, Leisure, Arts-Performance, Drama, Topical Issue-Oriented, Cultural or Personality Portrait.

VIDEOTAPE-FILM DISTRIBUTION INFORMATION SERVICE: Independent (35mm, 16mm film;

3/4-inch U-matic video cassette). Marketing, distribution information to independent film-video producers. Referral service to relevant foundations, government programs, monetary assistance, production studios, post production facilities.

JUDGING: Weekly by programming committee.

SALES TERMS: ICAP returns to entrant 75% of all payments received for cablecasting. Nonexclusive contract.

ENTRY FEE: None. Sponsor pays return postage.

DEADLINES: Open. Entries returned in 2-3 weeks.

| 111 |

Independent Film and Video Series for Public Television
Independent Film and Video Distribution Center
Douglas Cruickshank, Director
P.O. Box 6060
Boulder, Colorado 80306 U.S.A.
Tel: (303) 469-5234

Continuous

International; entry open to all; continuous; established 1980. Purpose: to increase distribution of independent work to public television. Sponsored by Independent Film and Video Distribution Center. Supported by NEA, Reginald A. Fessenden Educational Fund, KBDI-TV. Publish *The Sky's the Limit,* quarterly Newsletter.

VIDEOTAPE-FILM BROADCAST DISTRIBUTION: Independent (35mm, 16mm film; 2-inch, 1-inch, 3/4-inch, 1/2-inch video). Categories: Feature, Short, Fiction, Docudrama, Animation, Computer.

SALES TERMS: Producer receives 75% of gross revenues, based on length.

ENTRY FEE: None.

DEADLINES: Open.

| 112 |

Independent Focus and Video Showcase
WNET-13
Liz Oliver, Series Producer
356 West 58th Street
New York, New York 10019 U.S.A.

January

International; **entry restricted to independent producers;** annual. Sponsored by WNET-13 for *Independent Focus,* showcase for independent film-video.

VIDEOTAPE-FILM BROAD-CAST: **Independent** (16mm Film; 3/4-inch Video) over 20 minutes preferred, produced recently. Categories: Documentary, Fiction, Animation.

AWARDS: Acquisition fee, $40 per minute, for which station receives rights to two releases within 2 years from initial broadcast.

JUDGING: Series producer chooses 100 films for review by 7 independent producers-programmers, who recommend 30 for semifinal judging; final by panel, series producer.

ENTRY FEE: None.

DEADLINES: Entry, October. Initial screening, September-October. Judging, November. Winners announced, December.

| 113 |

INPUT International Public Television Screening Conference
International Film Seminars, Inc.
Barbara Van Dyke, Administrative Director
1860 Broadway

New York, New York 10023 U.S.A.
Tel: (212) 247-5536

March

International; entry open to all; annual; established 1977. Purpose: to activate increased international flow of quality cultural programs; recognize potential of television; promote better understanding among people. Sponsored by International Film Seminars. Supported by Rockefeller Foundation, CPB, PBS (U.S.), Societe Radio Canada (CBC-SRC), Agency for Tele-Education (ATEC) (Canada), CIRCOM (Europe). Held in various locations for 7 days. Also sponsor ROBERT FLAHERTY FILM SEMINAR EXHIBITIONS, PUBLIC TELEVISION AND INDEPENDENT FILM SEMINAR EXHIBITIONS.

VIDEOTAPE EXHIBITION: Non-commercial **Public Television** (3/4-inch Sony U-matic cassette) previously produced by public television (broadcast or not); independent productions aired or acquired for future broadcast.

AWARDS: None.

JUDGING: Preview by program directors; based on responsibility, service to audience, social understanding, educational and entertainment.

ENTRY FEE: None.

DEADLINES: Entry, January. Exhibition, March.

| 114 |

Lawson & Arts Film and Video Broadcasts
San Francisco Arts and Letters Foundation
Todd S. J. Lawson, Director
P.O. Box 99394
San Francisco, California 94109

U.S.A. Tel: (415) 771-3431,
771-6711

Weekly

International; entry open to all; continuous (weekly); established 1978. Purpose: to bring arts to the hearing and hearing-impaired. Motto: "International arts for all." Sponsored and supported by San Francisco Arts and Letters Foundation (formerly called Peace and Pieces Foundation; nonprofit grass-roots arts agency), California Arts Council, NEA. Shown at Channel 25 cable TV studio (1855 Folsom Street, San Francisco). Have display facilities. Also sponsor Bay Area Small Press Bookfair.

VIDEOTAPE-FILM BROADCAST: Independent (16mm, Super 8mm film; 1/2-inch VHS video). Send background, biographical information. Equipment and facility available to volunteer interpreters, deaf and hearing-impaired individuals and organizations.

ENTRY FEE: $20 interpreter's fee in advance (refundable). Not responsible for loss or damage. Entrant pays postage.

DEADLINES: Open.

115

Los Angeles Video Library Distribution Program
Lance Diskan, Curator
Box 467
Venice, California 90291 U.S.A.
Tel: (213) 396-6343

Continuous

International; entry open to all; continuous; established 1979. Purpose: to distribute popular and unusual video works; provide independent videographers with library, museum, institutional, cable TV marketing services.

Supported by private investors. Average statistics: 50 entries, 6 countries. Publish catalog.

VIDEOTAPE DISTRIBUTION: Independent (3/4-inch, VHS). Categories: Art, Dance, Music, Health, Science, Environment, Children, Social Action, Women's Programs, Native American, Humor, Nuclear Safety, Others. No pornography.

JUDGING: All entries viewed in entirety.

SALES TERMS: Tapes offered for sale only (no rentals). Cablecast contracts require individual negotiations. Income from tape divided between Library and videomaker.

ENTRY FEE: None. Library liable for replacement cost; pays return postage for unaccepted entries.

DEADLINES: Open.

116

Museum of Modern Art Video Exhibitions
Barbara London, Curator
Department of Video
11 West 53rd Street
New York, New York 10019 U.S.A.
Tel: (212) 956-6146, 956-6100

Continuous

International; entry open to all; continuous; established 1974 (Projects Video), 1978 (Video View Points). Sponsored by and held at Museum of Modern Art. Supported by NEA, NYSCA. Also sponsor film exhibitions, NEW DIRECTORS, NEW FILMS in conjunction with Film Society of Lincoln Center.

VIDEOTAPE EXHIBITION: Independent (3/4-inch cassette for exhibition; accept 1/2-inch reel for judging) any length. Have *Projects Video* independent video exhibition with various themes, including documentary, artist works, video installations; *Video View Points* for videomakers with body of work who have not received commercial distribution (require director in attendance to lecture).

AWARDS: None.

ENTRY FEE: None.

DEADLINES: Open. Allow 2-3 weeks for judging.

117

Pacific Mountain Network Video Purchase and Distribution

Dana J. Rouse, Manager
Suite 170B
2480 West 26th Avenue
Denver, Colorado 80211 U.S.A.
Tel: (303) 455-7161

Continuous

National; **entry open to U.S.;** continuous; established 1975. Formerly called ROCKY MOUNTAIN PUBLIC BROADCASTING NETWORK, organization comprised of 32 public TV stations in western U.S. Purpose: to coordinate cooperative efforts between stations through program exchange, coproduction with outside producers, program purchase. Supported by Pacific Mountain Network member stations. Originates in Denver; program distribution possible to all PBS affiliates. Have satellite distribution, production facilities. Publish bimonthly newsletter.

VIDEOTAPE PURCHASE AND DISTRIBUTION: Public Television (3/4-inch cassette) suitable for public broadcast.

VIDEO INTERN TRAINING PROGRAM: Public Television Broadcasting. Occasional opportuni-

ties for placement with network office or member station.

AWARDS: Purchase and distribution.

JUDGING: Network coordinates member stations who select material purchased. Each purchase individually negotiated.

ENTRY FEE: None.

DEADLINES: Open.

118

Pittsburgh Film-Makers Public Exhibition-Screening Program

Marilyn Levin, Executive Director
P.O. Box 7467
Pittsburgh, Pennsylvania 15213
U.S.A. Tel: (412) 681-5449

Continuous

International; entry open to all; continuous; established 1971 as a membership organization for filmmakers, photographers. Purpose: to provide center for production, exhibition, understanding, study of film, photography, video as art forms. Supported by Pennsylvania Council of the Arts, NEA, Howard Heinz Endowment. Recognized by National Association of Media Arts Centers, Ohio Valley Regional Media Arts Coalition. Average statistics: 15,000 attendance, 12 exhibitions, 156 performances. Located at 205 Oakland Avenue, Pittsburgh, Pennsylvania 15213. Have 55-seat screening room. Tickets: $2.-50. Publish *Field of Vision,* quarterly journal. Second contact: Margaret Ahwesh.

VIDEOTAPE EXHIBITION: Independent (width not specified).

AWARDS: Not specified.

ENTRY FEE: Not specified.

DEADLINES: Not specified.

119

Public Television and Independent Film Seminar Exhibitions
International Film Seminars, Inc.
Barbara Van Dyke, Administrative Director
1860 Broadway
New York, New York 10023 U.S.A.
Tel: (212) 247-5536

June

International; entry open to all; annual; established 1971. Purpose: to provide opportunity for nontheatrical film and video makers to meet those responsible for programs on public TV stations. Theme varies. Sponsored by International Film Seminars Inc., non-profit corporation devoted to art of film. Supported by NEA, CPB. Held at Arden House, Harriman, New York for 5 days. Also sponsor ROBERT FLAHERTY FILM SEMINAR EXHIBITION, INPUT INTERNATIONAL PUBLIC TELEVISION SCREENING CONFERENCE.

VIDEOTAPE EXHIBITION: Nontheatrical (width not specified).

ENTRY FEE: None.

DEADLINES: Entry, March. Event, June.

120

Synapse Film and Video Distribution
Synapse Video Center
Henry Baker, Director
103 College Place
Syracuse, New York 13210 U.S.A.
Tel: (315) 423-3100

Continuous

International; **entry restricted to independents, artists;** continuous; established 1970. Purpose: to cultivate, develop all aspects of independent media work with emphasis on relationship to broadcast television. Sponsored by Syracuse University (Synapse Video Center). Supported by NYSCA, NEA. Recognized by New York State Media Alliance, National Alliance of Media Arts Centers. Average statistics: 50 entries, 2 countries, 15 winners, sales over $5000, 69 exhibitions. Held in Syracuse, New York, throughout year. Have VIDEOTAPE EDITING EQUIPMENT ACCESS (2-inch videotape post production studio rental available to independents, non-profit organizations; require proposal, rough edit of final tape); TV BROADCAST WORKSHOPS. Publish *Telecast,* monthly newsletter.

VIDEOTAPE DISTRIBUTION: Documentary, Aesthetic for Television (3/4-inch U-matic, 2-inch) of broadcast quality. Require synopsis, format, rights restrictions. No commercial projects.

FILM DISTRIBUTION: Documentary, Aesthetic for Television (16mm) optical, magnetic. Require synopsis, format, rights restrictions. No commercial projects.

JUDGING: By staff. Nonexclusive rights to distribute for 3 years. Not responsible for loss or damage.

ENTRY FEE: None. Sponsor pays return postage.

DEADLINES: Open throughout year.

121

Tele-Vision Ideas Film and Video Broadcasts
Laird Brooks Schmidt, Director
2710 West 110th Street
Bloomington, Minnesota 55431
U.S.A. Tel: (612) 884-7262

Continuous

International; entry open to all; continuous; established 1955. Purpose: nationwide recognition on network television; to promote programs that help manage, give new sense of worth to our lives. Theme: Input for the Future Output of Television. Presented on any television vehicle (cable, commercial, satellite, network, local stations). Average statistics: 25 entries, 100 entrants.

FILM-VIDEOTAPE BROADCAST: **Independent** (gauges not specified).

AWARDS: Broadcast is its own reward. Possible career start for entrant.

JUDGING: Based on suitability for television audience, production feasibility, originator ability to discuss work, originality. Sponsor has right to produce material for first time.

ENTRY FEE: None. Entrant pays postage.

DEADLINES: Open.

122

Visualizations Gallery Video Showcase of Independent Artists' Works
Borgers Audio Gallery of Video Art
Diane Smith, Rhonda Ronan
130 West 72nd Street
New York, New York 10023 U.S.A.
Tel: (212) 873-4009

March

International; entry open to all; annual; established 1981. Purpose: to demonstrate possibilities of video medium; exemplify state of the art; showcase, sell, distribute work. Sponsored by Borgers Audio Gallery of Video Art. Held at Visualizations Gallery in New York City for 1 week.

VIDEOTAPE EXHIBITION: **Independent.** Need not be originally created on video format to qualify. Categories: Performance, Animation, Documentary, Instruction, Crafts, Film, Computer Imagery, Theater, Dance, General.

AWARDS: Not specified.

ENTRY FEE: None.

DEADLINES: Entry, February. Event, March.

123

Whitney Museum of American Art New American Filmmakers Series
Callie Angell, Curatorial Assistant
Film and Video Department
945 Madison Avenue
New York, New York 10021 U.S.A.
Tel: (212) 570-3617

September-June

National; **entry restricted to independent noncommercial;** continuous; established 1970. Purpose: to exhibit works in film, video by independent American artists, which might otherwise not be shown. Sponsored by NYSCA, NEA. Held at Whitney Museum (Madison at 75th Street, New York, New York). Programs are usually week-long with regularly scheduled screenings during daily museum hours. Also sponsor circulating film program, gallery talks with artist of current exhibition. Also accept performance exhibitions using both film and video in museum gallery context.

VIDEOTAPE EXHIBITION: **Independent Noncommercial** (3/4-inch, 1/4-inch cassette) any length; sound, silent. Any number of works per person; all produced in U.S. Require biography, still, statement about work.

AWARDS: Artist's fee (per length

of work, length of exhibition), advertising (major New York newspapers), publicity, exposure.

JUDGING: By curator.

ENTRY FEE: None.

DEADLINES: Open.

| 124 |

Grierson Film Seminars Film and Video Exhibitions
Ontario Film Association (OFA)
Liz Avison, President
P.O. Box 366, Station Q
Toronto, Ontario M4T 2M5 CANADA
Tel: (416) 978-6522

November

National; entry open to Canada; annual; established 1975. Named after John Grierson, first Film Commissioner, NFB. Purpose: to provide forum for young videomakers to discuss current trends in documentary videomaking with colleagues, international guests. Theme: Sharing Ideas and Information about Videotapes. Sponsored by OFA (founded 1949), nonprofit organization interested in all aspects of nontheatrical 3/4-inch videotape. Supported by Canada Council, Arts Council of Ontario, Film Festivals Bureau. Average statistics: 40 entries, 60-90 entrants. Held at Niagara-on-the-Lake, Ontario, Canada for 5-6 days. Registration fee: $50-$75, plus accommodations. Have seminars, screenings, discussions. Publish *A Newsletter Called Fred*. Also sponsor film showcase, distributor's marketplace.

VIDEOTAPE EXHIBITION: Documentary (3/4-inch cassette). Works in progress considered. Require synopsis, distribution information, running time, credits.

AWARDS: Artists with works in

program are guests of Exhibition, expenses paid.

JUDGING: Programmer previews, selects for Seminar based on significant trends, developments in recent production (emphasis on documentary techniques). Not responsible for loss or damage.

ENTRY FEE: None. Sponsor pays return postage.

DEADLINES: Entry, April-June. Materials, May-August. Acceptance, September. Event, November.

GRANTS (General)

Primarily for PRODUCTION, POST-PRODUCTION, DEVELOPMENT, and AID. Includes TV-Radio Broadcasting, Video, Film, Audio, Multimedia. (Also see INTERN-TRAINING-APPENTICE PROGRAMS, RESIDENCE GRANTS-EQUIPMENT LOANS, SCHOLARSHIPS-FELLOWSHIPS.)

| 125 |

Alabama Film Makers Co-op
Regional Grants to Media Artists
L. Wade Black, Director
4333 Chickasaw Drive
Huntsville, Alabama 35801 U.S.A.
Tel: (205) 534-3247

Summer-Winter

Regional; **entry restricted to Southeastern U.S. independents;** semiannual; established 1978. Formerly called ALABAMA FILM & VIDEO PROJECT. Purpose: to support independent film, video, audio producers living and working in Southeast. Sponsored by ALabama Film Makers Co-op. Supported by NEA, Alabama

State Council on the Arts and Humanities. Average statistics: 100 entrants, 10-15 grants. Publish *The Reel World* bimonthly newsletter.

VIDEO GRANT: Video Production, maximum $5000 per grant to media artists for video production, any format and genre. Submit production and release format, length, genre, treatment or narrative (if dramatic, sample of script), budget, production schedule, distribution plans, resume. Require sample of previous work on 3/4-inch cassette.

AUDIO GRANT: Audio-Radio Production (1/4-inch audiotape). Same as for Video grant.

ELEGIBILITY: Residents of Southeast (Alabama, Florida, Georgia, Kentucky, Louisiana, Mississippi, North Carolina, South Carolina, Tennessee, Virginia) at entry and during grant period.

JUDGING: 3 judges. Short works viewed in entirety, longer works viewed minimum 10 minutes. One copy granted work kept by Co-op, 2 copies to NEA archives. Recipient retains all other rights.

ENTRY FEE: None. Entrant pays return postage.

DEADLINES: Entry, Spring, Fall. Judging, Summer, Winter. Materials returned within 2 months.

126

American Film Institute (AFI) Directing Workshop for Women
Jan Haag, Director
501 Doheny Road
Beverly Hills, California 90210 U.S.A.
Tel: (213) 278-8777

September-March

National; **entry restricted to U.S. women;** annual; established 1974.

Sponsored by AFI (Jean Firstenberg, Director, John F. Kennedy Center for the Performing Arts, Washington D.C. 20566), founded 1967 as independent nonprofit organization to preserve heritage, advance art of film and TV in U.S. Supported by Ford Foundation, Sony Corporation, McMurray-Gihon Foundation. Held at AFI Center for Advanced Film Studies (Greystone Mansion, Beverly Hills, California). Also sponsor ARTS ENDOWMENT FILM ARCHIVAL PROGRAM, CURRICULUM PROGRAM TUITION LOANS, INDEPENDENT FILMMAKER PROGRAM GRANTS, ACADEMY INTERNSHIP PROGRAM.

VIDEO GRANT: Video Directing by Women, $1000 each for 2 videotape projects (each 30 minutes maximum, 6 days maximum shooting, 2 weeks editing), including volunteer crew and Screen Actors Guild cast, screening, discussion after completion, to professional women experienced in feature TV films (who have not directed). Require professional background, Los Angeles residence during individual projects.

ENTRY FEE: $10.

DEADLINES: Open. Academic year September-March.

127

American Film Institute (AFI) Independent Filmmaker Program
Jan Haag, Production Program Director
501 Doheny Road
Beverly Hills, California 90210 U.S.A.
Tel: (213) 278-8777

September-February

National; **entry restricted to U.S. permanent residents;** annual; established 1968. Purpose: to nurture new talent in film and videomaking field; aid established artists to explore new directions in their work. Sponsored by AFI, founded 1967 as independent nonprofit organization to preserve heritage, advance art of film and TV in U.S. Supported by NEA. Average statistics: 1500 entrants, 35-40 winners. Administered at AFI, Beverly Hills. Also sponsor ACADEMY INTERN-SHIP PROGRAM, DIRECTING WORKSHOP FOR WOMEN, ARTS ENDOWMENT FILM ARCHIVAL PROGRAM, CURRICULUM PROGRAM TUITION LOANS. Second contact: Willa Robertson, Coordinator, Production Programs.

VIDEO GRANT: Independent Video Production, $500-$10,000 for total or partial production or completion of videotape (widths not specified) to be produced in U.S. (beginning within 90 days after grant awarded, completed within 18 months). 1 project per grant cycle. Payment in steps (3 weeks prior to start date, each phase of production; final payment after delivery of 3 prints to AFI). Require synopsis of project, complete script (for dramatic), career summary, budget, work samples, rights and releases if applicable.

ELIGIBILITY: U.S. citizens or permanent residents. AFI employees, fellows of Center for Advanced Film Studies not eligible until conclusion of affiliation.

JUDGING: Initial by preselection committee; final by review committee based on potential, technical competence, creative ability. Not responsible for loss or damage.

ENTRY FEE: None. Sponsor pays return postage.

DEADLINES: Entry, September. Materials on request. Judging, January. Grants, February. Materials returned, March.

128

Arthur Vining Davis Foundation Grants
Marilyn C. Kahn, Administrative Officer
255 Alhambra Circle, Suite 520
Coral Gables, Florida 33134 U.S.A.
Tel: (305) 448-7712

Continuous

National; **entry restricted to U.S. organizations;** continuous: established 1952 and 1965 by Arthur Vining Davis, Chairman of the Board of Alcoa (Aluminum Company of America). William R. Wright, Executive Director. **Grants to Public Television,** education, religion and medicine. Require proposal letter, budget, additional materials; possible personal interview; report 1 year after receipt of grant. Purpose: to recognize, support public television and audience needs-interests; promote public TV as educational medium.

129

Artists Foundation Artists Fellowship Program
Dale Stewart, Manager
100 Boylston Street
Boston, Massachusetts 02116 U.S.A.
Tel: (617) 482-8100

October

State; **entry restricted to Massachusetts independents, professionals;** annual; established 1975. Purpose: to recognize outstanding creative artists in Massachusetts; support future work of high merit; make vital place for artists to live and work. Sponsored and supported by Massachusetts Council on the Arts and Humanities. Average statistics: 4000 entries, 3500 entrants, 160 finalists, 75 winners (in 12 fields). Have photography, dance, music, craft divisions; workshops.

VIDEO FELLOWSHIP GRANT: Video Production, $3500 each grant. Submit 2 tapes, 1 hour maximum.

ELIGIBILITY: Massachusetts residents, over 18, no students.

JUDGING: By practicing out-of-state artists, anonymously. Not responsible for loss or damage.

ENTRY FEE: None. Entrant pays postage.

DEADLINES: Entry, October.

130

Atlantic Richfield Foundation Grants
Eugene R. Wilson, Executive Director
515 South Flower Street, Room 2306
Los Angeles, California 90071 U.S.A.
Tel: (213) 486-8312

Monthly

National; **entry open to U.S. non-profit, tax-exempt public charities;** continuous. **Grants to Humanities and the Arts, Public Information (including TV)**, education, community programs, health and medical, environment. Sponsored by Atlantic Richfield Company. Require proposal letter, supporting data, budget, audited financial statement, tax-exemption proof; written reports from recipients. Requests reviewed monthly by Foundation, quarterly by Board of Directors.

131

Bush Foundation Fellowships for Artists
E-900 First National Bank Building
Saint Paul, Minnesota 55101 U.S.A.
Tel: (612) 227-0891

March

State; **entry open to Minnesota;** annual; established 1975. Purpose: to assist selected artists to work full-time in their chosen art forms. Sponsored by Bush Foundation. Also have art, sculpture, photography categories.

VIDEO FELLOWSHIP GRANT: Video Work, up to 10 grants ($12,000 maximum for 12-18 months, or $1000 per month for 6-12 months), up to $2000 program, travel expenses, for specific project or career, goal advancement, to 1-year minimum Minnesota resident visual artists, 25 or older. Require evidence of professional accomplishment through exhibition, recent work samples. No students.

JUDGING: Preselection by panels. Final by interdisciplinary judges, based on demonstrated artistic quality, fellowship importance to creative growth.

ENTRY FEE: None.

DEADLINES: Application, October. Preliminary selection, January. Notification, March.

132

California Public Broadcasting Commission (CPBC) Public Television and Radio Programming Grants
Joel Kugelmass, Executive Director
921 Eleventh Street, Suite 1200
Sacramento, California 95814 U.S.A.
Tel: (916) 322-3727

Continuous

State; **entry restricted to California public broadcast TV and radio stations, independent producers;** annual; established 1976. Purpose: to support, encourage orderly growth and development of public broadcasting service responsive to California informational, cultural, educational needs. Sponsored by CPBC. Average statistics: 50 applications, 10 awards.

BROADCASTING GRANTS: Public Television, Radio Program Production, various yearly grants of $5,000-$70,000 (Television), $300-$1000 (Radio) for program scripting, production, post production. Emphasize statewide news, public affairs, humanities programming. Requests for proposals announced through CPBC mailing list (free to all applicants).

ELIGIBILITY: California public broadcast TV and radio stations and independent producers working through and in cooperation with public stations. Programming produced under grant must be available at cost to California nonprofit educational institutions. Subcontracts subject to approval.

JUDGING: Reviewed by CPBC Advisory Committees. Final recommendations by Grants Committee. Ability to bring matching funds into project is important factor in judging.

DEADLINES: Various throughout year.

133

Change Inc. Emergency Assistance Grants
Susan Lewis, Secretary
Box 705, Cooper Station
New York, New York 10276 U.S.A.
Tel: (212) 473-3742

Continuous

National; **entry open to U.S.;** continuous throughout year; established 1970. Purpose: to award emergency grants to professional artists in all fields. Sponsored by Change Inc., tax-exempt foundation assisting artists in

emergency need. Second contact: Change Inc., P.O. Box 480027, Los Angeles, California 90048.

VIDEO GRANT: Emergency Assistance (amounts not specified). To professional artists in need of emergency assistance resulting from utility turn-off, eviction, unpaid medical bills, fire, illness. Require detailed letter, proof of professional artist status, recommendation letters (2 people in applicant's field), outstanding bills substantiating amount needed.

JUDGING: By Board of Directors.

DEADLINES: Open throughout year.

134

Corporation for Public Broadcasting (CPB) Instructional Television Series Grants
Mary Sceiford, Assistant Director
Instructional Television Project
1111 Sixteenth Street N.W.
Washington, District of Columbia
20036 U.S.A. Tel: (202) 293-6160

Winter, Spring

National; **entry restricted to U.S. independent producers, public TV stations;** semiannual. Purpose: to assist project showing promise of excellence, providing options to learners, significantly advancing education. Sponsored by CPB, private, nonprofit corporation founded 1967 by Public Broadcasting Act. Supported by NEA, federal, private funds. Also sponsor Production and Residence Grants, Women's and Minority Training Grant Programs, Minorities' and Women's Telecommunications Feasibility Project Grants, Radio Expansion Grants.

TELEVISION PRODUCTION GRANT: Instructional Public Tele-

vision, unspecified amounts on 50% matching basis for live, taped, or filmed series primarily for elementary-secondary instructional use. Content unrestricted. Preference to projects aimed at underserved groups (grades 1-3, 10-12).

ELIGIBILITY: Independent producers or agencies, public broadcasting licensees, state departments of education, LEAs, SEAs, consortia of such agencies. Require projects with single educational purpose; previous completion of planning, research, development; assurance of 50% matching funds. Submit 12 copies proposal (40 typed, double-spaced pages maximum) including fact sheet; justification of content, audience grade level; activities completed to date; description of content and format (including script-treatment, preferably 1 pilot cassette tape or example of other program produced by key staff); plans for series adoption, utilization, distribution; description of all rights; research plans; production personnel, facilities; project timeline; budget (including documented amount of matching support). Applicant warrants rights to proposal materials; pays postage; grants to CPB (for 3 years) unlimited public broadcasting rights, unlimited off-air record and reuse rights for school use.

JUDGING: Reviewer Advisory Committee (television production, instructional programming, education experts) recommends to CPB staff. Based on proposal quality, justification of need, valid design, feasibility, personnel qualifications, quality of pilot tape, suitability to audience. Final selection by Office of Educational Activities. Not responsible for loss, damage, third-party use or misuse.

DEADLINES: Application, March, December (multiple rounds).

135

Corporation for Public Broadcasting (CPB) Program Fund
Lewis Freedman, Director, Program Fund
1111 Sixteenth Street N.W.
Washington, District of Columbia
20036 U.S.A. Tel: (202) 293-6160

Various

National; entry open to U.S. independent producers and public TV stations; annual and quarterly; established 1980. Purpose: to present best American television programming to wide audience; develop new forms for exploring vital issues. Sponsored by CPB, private, nonprofit corporation founded 1967 by Public Broadcasting Act (1978 Public Telecommunications Financing Act offers expanded opportunities for public, minority, women's involvement). Supported by NEA, federal, private funds. Average statistics (*Crisis to Crisis* only): 363 entrants, 4 awards. Also sponsor INDEPENDENT ANTHOLOGY (for shorts dealing with urgent issues in American society); Women's, Minority Training Grant Programs; In-Service Training Grant Program; Minorities' and Women's Telecommunications Feasibility Project Grants; Instructional TV Series Grants; Radio Expansion Grants; RALPH LOWELL AWARD (founded 1971) for outstanding contributions to public broadcasting; EDWARD R. MURROW AWARD (founded 1977) for contributions to public radio (both open to nominations by members); and membership-only awards for local TV, radio programming, fund-raising, promotion-public information. Second contact (for proposal admission procedures): Eloise Payne.

TELEVISION   PRODUCTION GRANT: Public Television Production, Script Development, to public TV stations, independent producers for film, video, 60 minutes minimum. Divisions: Invited, Unsolicited.

Drama Production, for works 60-120 minutes, original or adaptation, self-contained. Nonbroadcast material preferred; American classics accepted. Deadlines: Proposal, January. Notification, April.

Crisis to Crisis Program Production, for single programs, 60-90 minutes, addressing controversial issues of critical importance to American public, to become part of series. Accept drama, live coverage, animation, documentary, responsible investigative reporting, other. Categories: Post-Production, In-Progress, Production Idea. Deadlines: Ongoing (quarterly) Rounds: Proposal, November, February, May, or August. Notification, December, March, June, September.

ELIGIBILITY: Public TV stations, independent producers. Require production experience; proposal including information sheet, script, production plan, budget, timeline, facilities, personnel biographies; synopsis. Samples on request (no videotapes or films with proposal). Require producer have full, complete rights. CPB may use, duplicate proposal for evaluation, review, research; have 4 national releases in 3-year period; clearance for exclusive use by all educational, public TV stations-facilities; rights to promotion. CPB may approve sale of rights and share income from ancillary uses. Require production completion 6 months after submission deadlines.

JUDGING: Program Fund staff checks for proposal completeness. Experts review, evaluate (deliberations confidential). Final selection by Program Fund Director. Based on research-writing quality, appropriateness to program purposes, television

as medium. Not responsible for loss, damage, third-party use or misuse of proposal.

ENTRY FEE: None. Entrant pays postage.

DEADLINES: Various (included above).

| 136 |

Corporation for Public Broadcasting (CPB) Radio Expansion Grants

Betsy Dirnberger, Radio Projects Manager
1111 Sixteenth Street N.W.
Washington, District of Columbia 20036 U.S.A. Tel: (202) 293-6160

Spring

National; entry restricted to U.S. organizations, radio stations; annual. Purpose: to aid activation of new noncommercial broadcast stations, expansion of established stations. Sponsored by CPB, private, nonprofit corporation founded 1967 by Public Broadcasting Act. Supported by NEA, federal, private funds. Also sponsor Production and Residence Grants, Women's and Minority Training Grant Programs, Minorities' and Women's Telecommunications Feasibility Project Grants, Instructional TV Series Grants.

RADIO GRANT: Radio Station Establishment and Expansion. Categories: Preoperation Grants, up to $200 per month for 18 months to those not already on the air. No local matching funds required. Operational Grants, on matching basis, for time beyond preoperational phase to total 30 months. Amounts based on staff size at start of grant period and projected nonfederal income (recipient not raising matching amount must refund unearned portion). Sponsor does not extend matching funds beyond applicant's projected income. Also have TELEVISION AND RADIO COMMUNITY SERVICE GRANTS FOR PUBLIC BROADCASTING STATIONS for support beyond 30-month Radio Expansion Grant period to on-the-air (UHF or VHF) public stations.

ELIGIBILITY: Preference to those seeking to reach unserved populations, provide rural multiple service. Applicant must have or propose FCC license; transmitter power sufficient to provide primary signal to community (1 mv-m for FM, 0.5 mv-m for AM); 5 full-time professional staff (at least 3 managerial or programming positions); sufficient office space, facilities; capability for simultaneous local production-organization; minimum 18-hour per day, 365-day per year operating schedule; educational-cultural-informational programming; origination of locally produced program service; minimum annual operating budget of $95,000 (adjusted upward annually by $5000).

JUDGING: Based on ability to extend public radio services to new audiences, status of proposed service area, financial base, community involvement, facilities, programming, planning.

DEADLINES: Application, December. Materials, March.

137

Creative Artists Public Service (CAPS) Program Fellowship Grants
Creative Artists Program Service
250 West 57th Street
New York, New York 10019 U.S.A.
Tel: (212) 247-6303

March

State; **entry restricted to New**

York; annual; established 1970. Purpose: to aid individual artists in creating new work, completing work-in-progress. Sponsored by CAPS, non-profit arts service organization. Supported by NEA, NYSCA. Average statistics: 200 awards (including art, painting, sculpture, graphics, choreography, music composition). Have community service program, visual arts referral service, playwrights referral service. Also sponsor other media fellowship grants.

VIDEO FELLOWSHIP GRANT: **Videomaking,** $3500-$5500 for 12 months to create new work or complete work-in-progress. Require (on request) 2 videotapes maximum (EIAJ) standard, 1/2-inch reel-to-reel, 3/4-inch) recent work preferred. Artists submitting work-in-progress must submit 1 other completed work. Applicant responsible for artistic direction of at least 1 work submitted. Require application form, budget.

MULTIMEDIA FELLOWSHIP GRANT: **Multimedia,** $3500-$6500 for 12 months to create new work or complete work-in-progress. Require audit or videotape (materials on request).

ELIGIBILITY: New York residents willing to perform community-related service. No matriculated graduate, undergraduate students. No proposals to travel, study, teach, publish-produce already completed work, purchase equipment.

JUDGING: By professionals (members change yearly). Work belongs to artists; CAPS requires 1 copy. Not responsible for loss or damage.

ENTRY FEE: None. Applicant pays postage.

DEADLINES: Application, June. Materials (on request), November. Notification, March.

138

Emerging Artist Grants Program
Oblate College of the Southwest
Adan Medrano
285 Oblate Drive
San Antonio, Texas 78216 U.S.A.
Tel: (512) 736-1685
August

International; entry open to all; annual; established 1980. Purpose: to assist emerging film and video artists in the production or completion of artistic work. Sponsored by Oblate College of the Southwest. Supported by NEA. Also sponsor SAN ANTONIO CINE FESTIVAL.

VIDEO GRANT: Hispanic Production, up to $2000 one-year grant to film-video producers interested in artistic and cinematic contributions in Hispanic production and programming. Require project description, biography, work examples (1/2-inch reel, 3/4-inch cassette), statement of intent.

ENTRY FEE: None. Not responsible for loss or damage.

DEADLINES: Entry, June. Grants awarded, August.

139

Film Fund Media Grants Program
The Film Fund
Terry Lawler, Director
80 East 11th Street, Suite 647
New York, New York 10003 U.S.A.
Tel: (212) 475-3720
April

National; **entry restricted to U.S. independents;** annual; established 1976, to bring new money to social issue video, filmmaking. Since inception, Film Fund has issued $235,000 in grants to 42 projects, served as agent for 51 independent media projects. Purpose: to encourage, support films, videotapes that take hard looks at pressing social issues, by providing resources for organizing social change, assisting in production and distribution of social issue media. Sponsored by The Film Fund, tax-exempt public foundation. Supported by foundations, individuals, government grants. Publish *News From The Film Fund,* quarterly newsletter (free on request). Second contact: The Film Fund, 309 Santa Monica Blvd., Santa Monica, California 90401; tel: (213) 394-6275.

VIDEO GRANT: Social Issue-Change Video Production and Distribution, $1000-$10,000 to individuals, organizations for preproduction, research, production, editing, completion of noncommercial artistic, educational, charitable videotapes on social issues, social change. Require project summary, table of contents, description, personnel, budget, verification of tax-exempt status. Suggested Categories: Racial, National Discrimination; Urban, Rural Issues (Health Care, Unemployment, Poverty, Consumer Rights); Energy, Environmental Issues; Labor Movement; Civil Liberties, Constitutional Rights; Economy. When projects generate income above cost, grants are returned to Fund at mutually agreeable rate.

JUDGING: Initial review by Film Fund staff, further by 9-person screening panel of film, videomakers; distributors; exhibitors; community activists. Final by Board of Directors based on importance, social relevance, ability, production aspects, potential audience.

DEADLINES: Entry, January. Grants, May.

| 140 |

Independent Documentary Fund
Television Laboratory at WNET
Thirteen
Kathy Kline, Coordinator
356 West 58th Street
New York, New York 10019 U.S.A.
Tel: (212) 560-3194

Fall

National; **entry restricted to U.S. independents;** annual; established 1977. Purpose: to support independent film and video makers in production of new and innovative documentaries for national public television. Sponsored by Television Laboratory at WNET-Thirteen. Supported by CPB, NEA, Ford Foundation, WNET-Thirteen. Average statistics: 650 entrants, 80 semifinalists, 10-15 finalists, 5-10 recipients. Have videotape postproduction facilities for rent. Publish *Vision News,* quarterly newsletter. Also sponsor WNET ARTISTS IN RESIDENCE PROGRAM.

VIDEOTAPE GRANT: **Independent Television Documentary Production,** one year, up to $90,000 for production, postproduction to 5-10 U.S. (citizen or permanent resident) independent film or video makers for work alone or at TV Lab on documentary project of own design (no docudrama) of standard broadcast length, meeting FCC requirements, any subject, 1 maximum per entrant.

ELIGIBILITY: Require written description of work or work-in-progress, schedule, estimated budget, resume, 1 completed sample work (film or videotape). Sample format: 3/4-inch video cassette, 1/2-inch reel-to-reel videotape.

JUDGING: Prescreening by independents, public television personalities. Final by 6-member Advisory Panel (including Project Director, Co-ordinator, public TV personalities, independents). Based on originality, talent, ability to complete work on budget, schedule. Public television given 3 years exclusive television, premiere rights in U.S. Projects intended for broadcast following year on the *Nonfiction Television* PBS series.

ENTRY FEE: None.

DEADLINES: Entry,   mid-Fall. Judging, December-January. Grants awarded, February.

| 141 |

National Endowment for the Arts (NEA) Video-Film-Audio Grants
2401 E Street N.W.
Washington, District of Columbia
20506 U.S.A.

Various

National; **entry open to U.S. individuals and nonprofit, tax-exempt organizations;** annual; established 1965. Sponsored by NEA (independent agency of federal government) to encourage and assist U.S. cultural resources, make arts widely available, strengthen cultural organizations, preserve cultural heritage, develop creative talent. Supported by annual appropriations from U.S. Congress, private donations. Address inquiries to program italicized in parentheses.

VIDEO-FILM-AUDIO GRANTS: **Arts Development** (*Challenge Arts Grants*) $30,000-$1,500,000   on matching basis to public television-radio stations, media arts centers, cultural groups, groups consortia, for fund-raising, other activities contributing to organization's long-term financial stability. Application, June. Notification, February.

Dance Film-Video Projects (*Dance Film-Video Program*) up to $15,000 on nonmatching basis to individuals, $10,000-$50,000 on matching basis to dance companies, other organizations; for film-video projects primarily involving dance, including extension of art, preservation, historical documentation. Application, May. Notification, January.

Design Communication (*Design Arts Program*) up to $50,000 on matching basis to audiovisual projects informing public about design issues, ideas. Deadlines: Open.

Folk Arts Presentation, Preservation (*Folk Arts Program*) up to $50,000 (usually $5000-$25,000) on matching basis to nonprofit, tax-exempt organizations, Native American tribes, media centers, educational institutions, state-local arts agencies for fees of technicians, artists, supplies other than major film-video equipment, to present, preserve traditional folk arts. Have limited grants, heritage awards, to nominated individuals, $1000 on one-time-only, nonmatching basis; apprenticeships, short-term advanced learning opportunities.

Museum Media Development (*Museum Program*) up to $50,000 for projects using film-video for communicating with audiences. Application, January. Notification, June.

Museum Media Purchase (*Museum Program*) $2500-$25,000 on matching basis to museums for purchase of video-film-audio by living, independent American artists. Application, January. Notification, June.

Museum Arts and Artifacts Indemnification (*Museum Program*) $15,000-$50,000 deductibles for exhibitions of $2-$10 million in value, by Federal Council on the Arts, for individuals, nonprofit agencies, institutions, governments, for exhibitions of artworks (including film, video, audio). Application, October.

Music (Folk-Ethnic) Preservation, Dissemination (*Music Program*) up to $15,000 on matching basis to individuals, organizations for documentation, preservation, dissemination of traditional musician techniques, lifestyles, repertories, historical recollections.

Orchestra-Opera Experimental Programming (*Music Program*) on matching basis to symphony orchestras, opera companies, with incomes in excess of $200,000 for 3 seasons minimum for commercial, educational public media experimental programming.

Special Arts Projects (*Special Projects*) to creative projects, artists' colonies, arts and service organizations (involving 2 or more arts, including video, film, audio), that are ineligible for funding under other NEA programs.

ELIGIBILITY: All programs require detailed proposal of activities, audiences; statement of organization's services, background; individual's biographical sketch, resume; samples, program notes, bibliographies; budget proposal; evidence of nonprofit, tax-exempt status; other documentation. Final reports usually required after project-program completion.

JUDGING: Application review by Program Panel. Recommendation by National Council on the Arts. Final by NEA Chair.

DEADLINES: Vary by program.

| 142 |

National Endowment for the Arts (NEA) Media and Visual Arts Program Grants
2401 E Street N.W.
Washington, District of Columbia
20506 U.S.A.

Various

National; **entry open to U.S. individuals and nonprofit, tax-exempt organizations;** annual; established 1965. Sponsored by NEA (independent agency of federal government) to encourage and assist U.S. cultural resources, make arts widely available, strengthen cultural organizations, preserve cultural heritage, develop creative talent. Supported by annual appropriations from U.S. Congress, private donations. Address inquiries to programs italicized in parentheses.

VIDEO-FILM-AUDIO GRANTS: Media Arts Centers Development (*Media Arts Program*) up to $50,000 on matching basis to nonprofit, tax-exempt organizations demonstrating excellence in exhibiting high-quality film-video; providing residencies, workshops, production facilities, study materials, information, distribution; independent or affiliated with tax-exempt cultural organization; with minimum $100,000 operating budget for previous year. Application, May. Notification, December.

Media Arts Education (*Expansion Arts Program*) $5000-$30,000 on matching basis to nonprofit, tax-exempt, community-based arts organizations for regional arts education programs, festivals. Includes Instruction-Training, Community Cultural Centers, Arts Exposure Programs, Summer Projects, Regional Tour-Events, Services to Neighborhood Arts Organizations. Application, November. Notification, June.

Radio Production (*Media Arts Program*) up to $15,000 on nonmatching basis to individuals, $50,000 on matching basis to organizations, for single or series radio productions (documentary, drama, audio art, children's programs, literature, music); 3 3/4, 7 1/2 ips cassette or reel. Application, September. Notification, March.

Video-Film Art in Public Places (*Visual Arts Program*) up to $50,000 for commissioned works, $25,000 for purchases, $10,000 for public site planning-design activities, on matching basis, to state-local governments,

nonprofit organizations, for making best contemporary art (including film-video) accessible in public places other than museums. Have planning-design grants for artists' fees. No exhibitions, museum acquisitions, historical-commemorative projects. Application, June, December. Notification, next June.

Video-Film Artists Spaces (*Visual Arts Program*) up to $20,000 on matching basis to organizations providing structure, atmosphere conducive to artistic dialog, experimentation, for exhibitions, screening, access to working facilities-equipment, visiting artists series (up to $10,000 on nonmatching basis for artist's honoraria). No amateurs, students, real estate, construction, maintenance, major equipment, creation of new organizations. Application, June. Notification, April.

Video-Film Exhibition (*Media Arts Program*) up to $30,000 on matching basis to organizations, independent or affiliated with tax-exempt organization, for exhibitions of high-quality film-video not available commercially. Requirements for Regular Exhibitions: one year previous programming (80 screenings minimum); no college film societies, media arts centers. Circulating Exhibitions: nonprofit, tax-exempt organizations, including media arts centers. Application, June. Notification, December.

Services to the Field (*Media Arts Program*) up to $10,000 on nonmatching basis to individuals, up to $25,000 on matching basis to organizations, for conferences, seminars, research, distribution, publications, facilities. Application, June. Notification, January.

Services to the Field (*Visual Arts Program*) up to $15,000 to individuals on nonmatching basis, to organizations on matching basis, for projects with direct, immediate effect on professional lives of visual artists, for financial-legal-technical assistance, information-resource-advisory services, publications. No students, amateurs, newsletters, major equipment, conferences, symposia, programs with restricted impact. Application, June (artists organizations, spaces), October (other). Notification, July.

ELIGIBILITY: All programs require detailed proposal of activities, audiences; statement of organization's services, background; individual's biographical sketch, resume; samples, program notes, bibliographies; budget proposal; evidence of nonprofit, tax-exempt status; other documentation. Final reports usually required after project-program completion.

JUDGING: Application review by Program Panel. Recommendation by National Council on the Arts. Final by NEA Chair.

DEADLINES: Vary by program.

143

National Endowment for the Arts (NEA) Fellowship and Residence Grants
2401 E Street N.W.
Washington, District of Columbia
20506 U.S.A.

Various

National; **entry open to U.S. individuals and nonprofit, tax-exempt organizations;** annual; established 1965. Sponsored by NEA (independent agency of federal government) to encourage and assist U.S. cultural resources, make arts widely available, strengthen cultural organizations, preserve cultural heritage, develop creative talent. Supported by annual appropriations from U.S. Congress, private donations. Address inquiries to programs italicized in parentheses.

VIDEO-FILM   FELLOWSHIP

GRANT: Video-Film Artists (*Visual Arts Program*) up to $12,500 to film-video artists ($4000 to emerging artists), for materials, general career advancement. Require sample film (16mm, Super 8mm, 8mm), videotape (3/4-inch, 1/2-inch cassette). No students, special projects, or awards for consecutive years. Application, August. Notification, April.

VIDEO-FILM-AUDIO   EXCHANGE FELLOWSHIP: Artist Exchange Between U.S. and England-Japan (*International Activities Program*), 6-9 month stipend and round-trip transportation to American mid-career artists for exchange with British or Japanese artists. Priority to those with specific purpose, who have not recently resided in chosen country.

VIDEO-FILM-AUDIO   RESIDENCE GRANTS: Artists In-Residence Workshop Programs (*Media Arts Program*) $1000-$10,000 on matching basis to organizations (including public and cable television, radio stations; colleges, universities, art schools, museums, municipal-county authorities, community arts organizations, artist's exhibition spaces), for honoraria, transportation, supplies to artists, producers, critics for varying length stays. Deadlines; Application, October. Notification, March.

Museum Visiting Specialists (*Museum Program*) up to $15,000 to museums for obtaining professionals for consultation on special projects increasing, improving museum use of nonprint media (film, video, radio, television). Deadlines: Open. Notification in 7 months.

Visual Artists Forums (*Visual Arts Program*) up to $5000 per institution on matching basis for lectures, residencies, artists' fees, symposia, conferences, seminars, workshops. No faculty positions, regular educational curricula, administrative salaries, equipment, exhibitions, receptions. Application, April, February. Notification, next September.

ELIGIBILITY: All programs require detailed proposal of activities, audiences; statement of organization's services, background; individual's biographical sketch, resume; samples, program notes, bibliographies; budget proposal; evidence of nonprofit, tax-exempt status; other documentation. Final reports usually required after project-program completion.

JUDGING: Application review by Program Panel. Recommendation by National Council on the Arts. Final by NEA Chair.

DEADLINES: Vary by Program.

144

National Endowment for the Humanities (NEH) Grants
806 15th Street N.W.
Washington, District of Columbia
20506 U.S.A.

Various

National; **entry open to U.S. individuals, nonprofit organizations;** semiannual; established 1965. Sponsored by NEH (independent federal grant-making agency) to support research, education, public activity in the humanities (modern, classical languages; linguistics; literature; history; jurisprudence; philosophy; archaeology; comparative religion; ethics; art history, criticism, theory, practice; historical, philosophical social sciences with humanistic content, methods; human environment, condition; national life). Supported by annual appropriations from U.S. Congress, private donations. Address inquiries to programs italicized in parentheses.

VIDEO-FILM-AUDIO GRANTS: Humanities Television-Radio Planning (*Division of Public Programs, Humanities Projects in the Media*) up to $15,000 on outright or gifts-and-matching basis to nonprofit professional groups, organizations, institutions, or individuals for television, radio programming in humanities areas where little has been presented to the public. **Humanities Television-Radio Production,** on outright or gifts-and-matching basis for production costs of innovative television, radio, single, pilot, series programs.

Humanities Television-Radio Station Development Grants (*Challenge Grants Program*) $2,000-$500,000 on 3 (private) to 1 (federal) matching basis to university or independent television, radio stations for development of humanities (fund-raising, community development activities, public promotion, outreach for humanities); encouraging cooperation with other humanities institutions; endowment. No general, nonhumanities operation support.

Youth Humanities Projects (*Division of Special Programs*) to youth (teens, 20s) or organizations to develop, conduct humanities projects. May include media programs exploring humanities topics.

ELIGIBILITY: Fresh approach to humanities subject, evidence of potential for new uses of humanities resources. Require proposal, work plan, script-treatment, resumes, recommnedations, third-party support for gifts-and-matching funding. Funds for approved budget only; NEH approves distribution and publicity. Grantee owns grant products (possibility of sharing income over $50,000 with Federal Treasury). No projects recording performances; advocating single viewpoint or social program; only describing current events or experimenting with electronic technology; presenting uninterpreted information; addressing regions or youth exclusively; requiring extensive preproduction research, permanent facilities, equipment, training.

JUDGING: By 4-stage review: NEH Panel (subject-area experts), Individual Review (external experts), National Council on the Humanities (26 presidential appointees), NCH Chair (makes final funding decisions). Based on proposal clarity, logic; use of humanities resources; interpretive nature; appeal to large audience (including English, Spanish speakers, blind, hearing-impaired); outreach potential to underserved social groups; feasibility, planning efficiency, budget.

DEADLINES: Vary by program.

145

Ohio Arts Council Aid to Individual Artists
Denny Griffith, Coordinator
727 East Main Street
Columbus, Ohio 43206 U.S.A.
Tel: (614) 466-2613

June

State; **entry restricted to Ohio residents;** annual; established 1978. Purpose: to provide direct, nonmatching grants to artists for creation of new work. Sponsored by Ohio Arts Council. Average statistics: 590 entries, 110 awards. Also have fellowships for visual artists, architects-designers, choreographers, composers, craftspersons, creative writers. Second contact: 50 West Broad Street, Columbus, Ohio 43215; tel: (614) 466-2613.

FILM-VIDEO GRANTS: **Film and Videomaking,** up to $8000 (minigrants to $500) to Ohio residents for planning, supplies, facilities-services rental, research, presentation, reproduction, documentation, publication expenses for creating new work. No grants for out-of-state travel or over $500 equipment. Submit up to 2 films or tapes (3/4-inch U-matic cassette). No originals, description of artist's relationship to production, 1-page history of project, other supporting materials. No students.

MULTIMEDIA GRANTS: Multidisciplinary Artists. Require letter of justification for work's conceptual basis. Other requirements same as for Film-Video, vary with disciplines involved.

JUDGING: Based on creative, technical excellence of work submitted for review. Preference to works advancing the arts.

ENTRY FEE: None.

DEADLINES: Application, January. Notification, June.

146

Public Telecommunications Facilities Program (PTFP) Grants
National Telecommunications and Information Administration
U.S. Department of Commerce
1800 G Street N.W., Suite 803
Washington, District of Columbia
20504 U.S.A. Tel: (202) 724-3307

Continuous

National; **entry restricted to U.S. public broadcast stations, nonprofit educational-cultural organizations, state and local governments;** continuous; established 1963. Purpose: to extend delivery of public telecommunications services to unserved, underserved citizens; increase ownership, operation of public telecommunications by minorities, women; strengthen capabilities, enhance services of existing broadcast services; activate new services. Average statistics: Brings public television to 90%, public radio to 70%, of U.S. population; awards $23 million yearly. Second contact: PTFP Program Officer or Administrator of applicant's state, territory.

BROADCASTING GRANT: Television, Radio Station Activation, Expansion, Construction Matching Grants, up to 75% total eligible project costs for activation, expansion, improvement of public broadcast stations, nonbroadcast service facilities, interconnect systems.
Television, Radio Planning Grants, up to 100% eligible costs for planning projects for which construction funds are eligible.

ELIGIBILITY: Public broadcast stations; nonprofit foundations; corporations, institutions, associations organized primarily for educational, cultural purposes; state, local governments or political, special subdivisions of state. For planning projects, preoperational costs for new facilities, electronic equipment, related installation. No land, major buildings, renovations, operational supplies-expenses, vehicles, scenery, office equipment will be funded. Require evidence of adequacy, continuity of financial resources; that eligible matching funding is available for construction; that applicant has proposed service designed to meet community needs, has coordinated with other local, state, regional telecommunications entities, has evaluated alternate technologies, has obtained or initiated timely request for FCC authorization.

JUDGING: Based on funding criteria for construction-planning applications outlined in Federal Regulations (Communications Act of 1934; Public Telecommunications Financing Act of 1978).

ENTRY FEE: None.

DEADLINES: Application, January. Grants throughout year.

| 147 |

Public Understanding of Science Grants
National Science Foundation (NSF)
G. Triml, Program Director
Science Education Directorate
1800 G Street N.W.
Washington, District of Columbia
20550 U.S.A.

Continuous

National; **entry restricted to U.S. organizations, academic institutions;** continuous. Purpose: to improve communication between scientific, nonscientific communities for increased public understanding of scientific, technological public policy issues, methods, activities of scientists, engineers. Sponsored by NSF Science Education Directorate, dedicated to understanding between scientific, technological communities and general society. Also sponsor TECHNOLOGICAL INNOVATION IN EDUCATION PROGRAM GRANTS to innovative educational television, communication technology in science education institutions; SCIENCE FOR CITIZENS PROGRAM GRANTS.

BROADCASTING GRANT: Science Communication Television, Radio. Require 5-page preliminary proposal (3 copies), formal proposal and budget (20 copies), quarterly activity-progress reports, final fiscal and technical report, summary of completed project from grant recipient. Categories: Projects Improving Public Understanding of Science, Technology; Projects Increasing Communication Between Scientists, Nonscientists; Research, Analysis on Scientific, Technological Information Flow to General Public.

ELIGIBILITY: Open to colleges, universities, laboratories, museums, government agencies, professional associations and societies, citizens' groups, profit and nonprofit organizations interested in improving public understanding of science. No long-term institutional support, communication among scientists, facility construction, equipment purchase, educational system course and curriculum development.

JUDGING: By scientists, engineers, professional and institutional leaders, based on innovative communication modes, rationale, project design, impact, cost-effectiveness, monitoring and evaluation, personnel and institutional resources, budget, quality. Sponsor has royalty-free irrevocable, worldwide, nonexclusive license in U.S. government to reproduce, perform, translate, use, authorize others to use for government purposes, and to sell any materials produced under grant.

DEADLINES: Entry, April, August, December. Preliminary proposal response within 8 weeks.

148

University Film Association (UFA) Grant Program

Richard M. Blumenberg, Associate Dean
College of Communications & Fine Arts
Southern Illinois University at Carbondale
Carbondale, Illinois 62901 U.S.A.

August

International; **entry restricted to college, university student UFA members, or UFA member schools;** annual. Sponsored by UFA. Held at UFA Conference.

VIDEO GRANT: Video Production and Studies. $500 grant for video production, historical, critical, theoretical or experimental studies. Require 1-page resume, description of production-project (including purpose, funds available for completion, summary of production, study), budget, script if narrative; treatment if documentary; treatment, script and-or story boards if experimental or animated. Proposals for study require methodology, relationship to previous research in field.

ELIGIBILITY: Must be undergraduate at time of application, sponsored and certified by UFA faculty member.

JUDGING: May withhold award.

ENTRY FEE: None.

DEADLINES: Materials, July. Awards announced, August.

149

Visual Arts Fellowship Program

Western States Arts Foundation
141 East Palace
Santa Fe, New Mexico 87501 U.S.A.
Tel: (505) 988-1166

Fall

Regional; **entry restricted to Western states professionals;** Periodic; established 1978. Sponsored by Western States Arts Foundation. Supported by NEA. Also sponsor grants in other media in various years.

VIDEO GRANT: Video Production, up to 9 fellowships of $5000 each for start-up production, finishing, equipment, promotion (including travel). Require sample on 1/2-inch, 3/4-inch videotape. No first film production.

ELIGIBILITY: U.S. citizen, 6-month resident of Arizona, Colorado, Idaho, Montana, Nevada, New Mexico, Oregon, Utah, Washington, Wyoming. No undergraduate students.

JUDGING: Based on past work, artistic excellence, not on project or proposal.

DEADLINES: Entry, July. Grants, Fall.

150

Canada Council Grants

Robert Kennedy, Head, Arts Award Service
P.O. Box 1047
255 Albert Street
Ottawa, Ontario K1P 5V8 CANADA
Tel: (613) 237-3400

September, March

National; **entry open to Canada;** semi-annual; established 1957. Sponsored by Canada Council, founded 1957 by Act of Parliament to foster and promote study, enjoyment, production of art in Canada. Have architecture, arts criticism, dance, music, theatre, visual arts, multidisciplinary and performance art sections. Also sponsor AID TO ARTS ORGANIZATIONS.

FILM-VIDEO GRANTS: **General** (Under *Aid to Artists Branch*) to Canadian citizens, landed immigrants with 5 years residence. Categories: **Arts Grants A:** up to $19,000 for living expenses, project, travel costs for 4-12 months to senior artists with record of significant contribution. **Arts Grants B:** up to $11,000 for living expenses, project costs (possible added travel allowance) for 4-12 months to professional artists. **Short-Term Grants:** $800 per month and travel allowance (up to $800 possible project allowance) for 3 months to artists for specific project. **Project Costs Grants:** up to $2700 for goods, services, travel (no living) for completion of project. **Travel Grants:** for travel (up to $100 possible living expenses). Discipline divisions follow:

Film Training, Research, Distribution to professional filmmakers who have directed 1 film minimum, for training, critical research, postcompletion, distribution preparation expenses.

Film-Video Production to independent film and videomakers and groups for production costs.

New Work (called *Explorations Program*) to individuals, organizations for first-time film and video production, new cultural expression, research, participation, diffusion, creativity.

Video Research, Experimentation, to professional videomakers with several noncommercial productions, for creative expression, research, experimentation. No pedagogical works. Require samples.

JUDGING: Preliminary by outside juries, based on artistic merit, potential, significance, project value, artistic quality, relevance. Secondary by 28-member Advisory Arts Panel. Final by 31-member Canada Council.

ENTRY FEE: None.

DEADLINES: Entry, April, October. Recipients announced, September, March.

GRANTS (Regional Arts Groups)

Regional Arts Groups in U.S. and territories. National Endowment for the Arts (NEA) funds Regional Arts Groups that continually develop various new artistic opportunity programs to be carried out on a multistate basis. Regional groups must first present plans for arts support that meet established

*requirements. (Also see STATE
ARTS AGENCIES, STATE
HUMANITIES COMMISSIONS, and
GRANTS.)*

151

**Affiliated State Arts Agencies of
the Upper Midwest**
430 Oak Grove Street, Suite 402
Minneapolis, Minnesota 55403
U.S.A. Tel: (612) 871-6392

For Iowa, Minnesota, North Dakota, South Dakota, Wisconsin.

152

**Consortium for Pacific Arts and
Culture**
P.O. Box 4263
Honolulu, Hawaii 96813 U.S.A.
Tel: (808) 524-7120

For Alaska, American Samoa, California, Guam, Hawaii, Northern Marianas.

153

Great Lakes Arts Alliance
11424 Bellflower Road
Cleveland, Ohio 44106 U.S.A.
Tel: (614) 444-1922

For Illinois, Indiana, Michigan, Ohio.

154

Mid-America Arts Alliance
20 West 9th Street, Suite 550
Kansas City, Missouri 64105 U.S.A.
Tel: (816) 421-1388

For Arkansas, Kansas, Missouri, Nebraska, Oklahoma.

155

**Mid-Atlantic States Arts
Consortium**
Maryland State Arts Council
15 West Mulberry Street
Baltimore, Maryland 21201 U.S.A.
Tel: (301) 685-6740

For Delaware, Maryland, New Jersey, New York, Pennsylvania, West Virginia.

156

**New England Foundation for the
Arts**
25 Mount Auburn Street
Cambridge, Massachusetts 02138
U.S.A. Tel: (617) 492-2914

For Connecticut, Maine, Massachusetts, New Hampshire, Rhode Island, Vermont.

157

Southern Arts Federation
225 Peachtree Street, Suite 712
Atlanta, Georgia 30303 U.S.A.
Tel: (404) 577-7244

For Alabama, Florida, Georgia, Kentucky, Louisiana, Mississippi, North Carolina, South Carolina, Tennessee, Virginia.

158

Western States Arts Foundation
141 East Palace Avenue
Santa Fe, New Mexico 87501 U.S.A.
Tel: (505) 988-1166

For Arizona, Colorado, Idaho, Montana, Nevada, New Mexico, Oregon, Utah, Washington, Wyoming.

GRANTS (State Arts Agencies)

State Arts Agencies in U.S. and territories. *National Endowment for the Arts (NEA) reserves 15% of its yearly funds for individual State Arts Agencies that continually develop new artistic opportunity programs for state residents, on competitive basis. Most states have ARTISTS-IN-SCHOOLS PROGRAMS for individual professional artists (matching grants for salary, studio space, facilities, equipment) for instruction, lectures, demonstrations, production of continuing or new projects in elementary-secondary schools, colleges, universities. Other RESIDENCY GRANTS available to communities, cultural-social institutions. GRANTS (usually on one-to-one matching basis, including both cash and in-kind contributions) and MINIGRANTS (up to $500) for various artistic projects to nonprofit, tax-exempt organizations. Some have FELLOWSHIP GRANTS to individuals for various state artistic projects (funding same as for Grants). SERVICES for policy, program planning-development to state, regional, local arts agencies, through Office for Partnership. (Also see REGIONAL ARTS GROUPS, STATE HUMANITIES COUNCILS, and GRANTS.)*

| 159 |

Alabama State Council on the Arts and Humanities
114 North Hull Street
Montgomery, Alabama 36130 U.S.A.
Tel: (205) 832-6758

| 160 |

Alaska State Council on the Arts
619 Warehouse Avenue, Suite 220
Anchorage, Alaska 99501 U.S.A.
Tel: (907) 279-1558

| 161 |

American Samoa Arts Council
P.O. Box 1540
Office of the Governor
Pago Pago, American Samoa 96799
Tel: 633-4347

| 162 |

Arizona Commission on the Arts and Humanities
6330 North 7th Street
Phoenix, Arizona 85014 U.S.A.
Tel: (602) 255-5884

| 163 |

Arkansas Arts Council
Continental Building, Suite 500
Little Rock, Arkansas 72201 U.S.A.
Tel: (501) 371-2539

| 164 |

California Arts Council
2022 J Street
Sacramento, California 95814 U.S.A.
Tel: (916) 445-1530

| 165 |

Colorado Council on the Arts and Humanities
770 Pennsylvania Street
Denver, Colorado 80203 U.S.A.
Tel: (303) 839-2617

| 166 |

Connecticut Commission on the Arts
340 Capitol Avenue
Hartford, Connecticut 06106 U.S.A.
Tel: (203) 566-4770

| 167 |

Delaware State Arts Council
Office of the Arts
State Office Building, 820 North
French Street
Wilmington, Delaware 19801 U.S.A.
Tel: (302) 571-3540

| 168 |

D.C. Commission on the Arts and Humanities
1012 14th Street N.W.
Suite 1203
Washington, District of Columbia
20005 U.S.A. Tel: (202) 724-5613

| 169 |

Fine Arts Council of Florida
Division of Cultural Affairs
Department of State, The Capitol
Tallahassee, Florida 32304 U.S.A.
Tel: (904) 487-2980

| 170 |

Georgia Council for the Arts and Humanities
1627 Peachtree Street N.E.
Suite 210
Atlanta, Georgia 30309 U.S.A.
Tel: (404) 656-3967

| 171 |

Insular Arts Council of Guam
P.O. Box 2950
Office of the Governor
Agana, Guam 96910 U.S.A.
Tel: 477-9845

| 172 |

Hawaii State Foundation on Culture and the Arts
250 South King Street, Room 310
Honolulu, Hawaii 96813 U.S.A.
Tel: (808) 548-4145

| 173 |

Idaho Commission on the Arts
c/o Statehouse
Boise, Idaho 83720 U.S.A. Tel: (208)
364-2119

| 174 |

Illinois Arts Council
111 North Wabash Avenue
Room 720
Chicago, Illinois 60602 U.S.A.
Tel: (312) 793-6750

| 175 |

Indiana Arts Commission
155 East Market Street, #614
Indianapolis, Indiana 46204 U.S.A.
Tel: (317) 232-1268

| 176 |

Iowa State Arts Council
State Capitol Building
Des Moines, Iowa 50319 U.S.A.
Tel: (515) 281-4451

| 177 |

Kansas Arts Commission
112 West 6th Street
Topeka, Kansas 66603 U.S.A.
Tel: (913) 296-3355

| 178 |

Kentucky Arts Commission
302 Wilkinson Street
Frankfort, Kentucky 40601 U.S.A.
Tel: (502) 564-3757

| 179 |

Louisiana State Arts Council
Division of the Arts
P.O. Box 44247
Baton Rouge, Louisiana 70804
U.S.A. Tel: (504) 342-6467

180

Maine State Commission on the Arts and Humanities
State House
Augusta, Maine 04330 U.S.A.
Tel: (207) 289-2724

181

Maryland Arts Council
15 West Mulberry
Baltimore, Maryland 21201 U.S.A.
Tel: (301) 685-6740

182

Massachusetts Council on the Arts and Humanities
1 Ashburton Place
Boston, Massachusetts 02108 U.S.A.
Tel: (617) 727-3668

183

Michigan Council for the Arts
1200 Sixth Avenue
Executive Plaza
Detroit, Michigan 48226 U.S.A.
Tel: (313) 256-3735

184

Minnesota State Arts Board
2500 Park Avenue, South
Minneapolis, Minnesota 55404
U.S.A. Tel: (612) 341-7170

185

Mississippi Arts Commission
P.O. Box 1341
Jackson, Mississippi 39205 U.S.A.
Tel: (601) 354-7336

186

Missouri State Council on the Arts
706 Chestnut, #925
St Louis, Missouri 63101 U.S.A.
Tel: (314) 241-7900

187

Montana Arts Council
1280 South 3rd Street, West
Missoula, Montana 59801 U.S.A.
Tel: (406) 543-8286

188

Nebraska Arts Council
8448 West Center Road
Omaha, Nebraska 68124 U.S.A.
Tel: (402) 554-2122

189

Nevada State Council on the Arts
329 Flint Street
Reno, Nevada 89501 U.S.A.
Tel: (702) 784-6231

190

New Hampshire Commission on the Arts
Phenix Hall
40 North Main Street
Concord, New Hampshire 03301
U.S.A. Tel: (603) 271-2789

191

New Jersey State Council on the Arts
109 West State Street
Trenton, New Jersey 08608 U.S.A.
Tel: (609) 292-6130

192

New Mexico Arts Division
113 Lincoln Avenue
Santa Fe, New Mexico 87503 U.S.A.
Tel: (505) 827-2061

193

New York State Council on the Arts
80 Centre Street
New York, New York 10013 U.S.A.
Tel: (212) 488-5222

194

North Carolina Arts Council
North Carolina Department of
Cultural Resources
Raleigh, North Carolina 27611
U.S.A. Tel: (919) 733-2821

195

North Dakota Council on the Arts
Box 5548
State University Station
Fargo, North Dakota 58105 U.S.A.
Tel: (701) 237-7674

196

Commonwealth Arts Council
(Northern Marianas)
Office of the Governor
Saipan, Northern Mariana Islands
96950

197

Ohio Arts Council
50 West Broad Street, #3600
Columbus, Ohio 43215 U.S.A.
Tel: (614) 466-2613

198

State Arts Council of Oklahoma
Jim Thorpe Building
2101 North Lincoln Boulevard
Oklahoma City, Oklahoma 72105
U.S.A. Tel: (405) 521-2931

199

Oregon Arts Commission
835 Summer Street N.E.
Salem, Oregon 97301 U.S.A.
Tel: (503) 378-3625

200

Pennsylvania Council on the Arts
3 Shore Drive Office Center
2001 North Front Street
Harrisburg, Pennsylvania 17102
U.S.A. Tel: (717) 787-6883

201

Institute of Puerto Rican Culture
Apartado Postal 4184
San Juan, Puerto Rico 00905 U.S.A.
Tel: (809) 723-2115

202

**Rhode Island State Council on
the Arts**
334 Westminster Mall
Providence, Rhode Island 02903
U.S.A. Tel: (401) 277-3880

203

South Carolina Arts Commission
1800 Gervais Street
Columbia, South Carolina 29201
U.S.A. Tel: (803) 758-3442

204

South Dakota Arts Council
108 West 11th Street
Sioux Falls, South Dakota 57102
U.S.A. Tel: (605) 339-6646

205

Tennessee Arts Commission
222 Capitol Hill Building
Nashville, Tennessee 37219 U.S.A.
Tel: (615) 741-6395

206

Texas Commission on the Arts
P.O. Box 13406
Capitol Station
Austin, Texas 78711 U.S.A.
Tel: (512) 475-6593

207

Utah Arts Council
617 East South Temple Street
Salt Lake City, Utah 84102 U.S.A.
Tel: (801) 533-5895

208

Vermont Council on the Arts, Incorporated
136 State Street
Montpelier, Vermont 05602 U.S.A.
Tel: (802) 828-3291

209

Virginia Commission for the Arts
400 East Grace Street, 1st Floor
Richmond, Virginia 23514 U.S.A.
Tel: (804) 786-4492

210

Virgin Islands Council on the Arts
Caravelle Arcade
Christiansted, St. Croix
U.S., Virgin Islands 00820 U.S.A.
Tel: (809) 773-3075, ext. 3

211

Washington State Arts Commission
9th and Columbia Building
(Mail Stop FU-12)
Olympia, Washington 98504 U.S.A.
Tel: (206) 753-3860

212

Arts and Humanities Division of West Virginia Department of Culture and History
Science and Culture Center
Capitol Complex
Charleston, West Virginia 25305
U.S.A. Tel: (304) 348-0240

213

Wisconsin Arts Board
123 West Washington Avenue
Madison, Wisconsin 53702 U.S.A.
Tel: (608) 266-0190

214

Wyoming Council on the Arts
122 West 25th Street
Cheyenne, Wyoming 82002 U.S.A.
Tel: (307) 777-7742

GRANTS (State Humanities Councils)

State Humanities Councils in U.S. and territories. National Endowment for the Humanities (NEH) reserves 20% of its yearly funds for individual State Humanities Commissions that continually develop new humanities public issue programs for state residents, on competitive basis. These include public forums, conferences, workshops, seminars, and MEDIA PROGRAM GRANTS for adult public communications projects involving humanities-human values, public policy issues, advanced humanities issues, and individual state themes. (Also see STATE and REGIONAL ARTS AGENCIES, and GRANTS.)

215

Committee for the Humanities in Alabama
Box 700
Birmingham-Southern College
Birmingham, Alabama 35204 U.S.A.
Tel: (205) 324-1314

216

Alaska Humanities Forum
429 D Street, Room 211
Loussac Sogn Building
Anchorage, Alaska 99501 U.S.A.
Tel: (907) 272-5341

217

Arizona Humanities Council
112 North Central Ave., Suite 304
Phoenix, Arizona 85004 U.S.A.
Tel: (602) 257-0335

218

Arkansas Endowment for the Humanities
University Tower Building
12th & University, Suite 1019
Little Rock, Arkansas 72204 U.S.A.
Tel: (501) 663-3451

219

California Council for the Humanities
312 Sutter Street, Suite 601
San Francisco, California 94108
U.S.A. Tel: (415) 391-1474

220

Colorado Humanities Program
855 Broadway
Boulder, Colorado 80302 U.S.A.
Tel: (303) 442-7298

221

Connecticut Humanities Council
195 Church Street
Wesleyan Station
Middletown, Connecticut 06457
U.S.A. Tel: (203) 347-6888,
347-3788

222

Delaware Humanities Forum
2600 Pennsylvania Avenue
Wilmington, Delaware 19806 U.S.A.
Tel: (302) 738-8491

223

D.C. Community Humanities Council
1341 G Street N.W.
Suite 620
Washington, District of Columbia
20005 U.S.A. Tel: (202) 347-1732

224

Florida Endowment for the Humanities
LET 360
University of South Florida
Tampa, Florida 33620 U.S.A.
Tel: (813) 974-4094

225

Committee for the Humanities in Georgia
1589 Clifton Road N.E.
Emory University
Atlanta, Georgia 30322 U.S.A.
Tel: (404) 329-7500

226

Hawaii Committee for the Humanities
2615 South King Street, Suite 211
Honolulu, Hawaii 96826 U.S.A.
Tel: (808) 947-5891

227

Association for the Humanities in Idaho
1403 W. Franklin Street
Boise, Idaho 83702 U.S.A. Tel: (208)
345-5346

228

Illinois Humanities Council
201 W. Springfield Avenue
Suite 205
Champaign, Illinois 61820 U.S.A.
Tel: (217) 333-7611

229

Indiana Committee for the Humanities
4200 Northwestern Avenue
Indianapolis, Indiana 46205 U.S.A.
Tel: (317) 925-5316

230

Iowa Board for Public Programs in the Humanities
Oakdale Campus
University of Iowa
Iowa City, Iowa 52242 U.S.A.
Tel: (319) 353-6754

231

Kansas Committee for the Humanities
112 West Sixth Street, Suite 509
Topeka, Kansas 66603 U.S.A.
Tel: (913) 357-0359

232

Kentucky Humanities Council
Ligon House
University of Kentucky
Lexington, Kentucky 40508 U.S.A.
Tel: (606) 258-5932

233

Louisiana Committee for the Humanities
4426 S. Robertson
New Orleans, Louisiana 70115
U.S.A. Tel: (504) 865-9404

234

Maine Council for the Humanities and Public Policy
P.O. Box 7202
Portland, Maine 04112 U.S.A.
Tel: (207) 773-5051

235

Maryland Committee for the Humanities
330 North Charles Street, Room 306
Baltimore, Maryland 21202 U.S.A.
Tel: (301) 837-1938

236

Massachusetts Foundation for the Humanities and Public Policy
237-E Whitmore Administration Bldg.
University of Massachusetts
Amherst, Massachusetts 01003
U.S.A. Tel: (413) 545-1936

237

Michigan Council for the Humanities
Nisbet Building, Suite 30
Michigan State University
East Lansing, Michigan 48824 U.S.A.
Tel: (517) 355-0160

238

Minnesota Humanities Commission
Metro Square, Suite 282
St Paul, Minnesòta 55101 U.S.A.
Tel: (612) 224-5739

239

Mississippi Committee for the Humanities
3825 Ridgewood Road, Room 111
Jackson, Mississippi 39211 U.S.A.
Tel: (601) 982-6752

240

Missouri State Committee for the Humanities
Loberg Building, Suite 202
1145 Dorsett Road
St Louis, Missouri 63043 U.S.A.
Tel: (314) 889-5940

241

Montana Committee for the Humanities
P.O. Box 8036
Hellgate Station
Missoula, Montana 59807 U.S.A.
Tel: (406) 243-6022

242

Nebraska Committee for the Humanities
Cooper Plaza, Suite 405
211 N. 12th Street
Lincoln, Nebraska 68508 U.S.A.
Tel: (308) 234-2110

243

Nevada Humanities Committee
P.O. Box 8065
Reno, Nevada 89507 U.S.A.
Tel: (702) 784-6587

244

New Hampshire Council for the Humanities
112 South State Street
Concord, New Hampshire 03301
U.S.A. Tel: (603) 224-4071

245

New Jersey Committee for the Humanities
Rutgers, The State University
CN 5062
New Brunswick, New Jersey 08903
U.S.A. Tel: (201) 932-7726

246

New Mexico Humanities Council
1805 Roma N.E.
The University of New Mexico
Albuquerque, New Mexico 87131
U.S.A. Tel: (505) 277-3705
(Albuquerque); (505) 646-1945 (Las Cruces)

247

New York Council for the Humanities
33 West 42nd Street
New York, New York 10036 U.S.A.
Tel: (212) 354-3040

248

North Carolina Humanities Committee
112 Foust Bldg.
UNC-Greensboro
Greensboro, North Carolina 27412
U.S.A. Tel: (919) 379-5325

249

North Dakota Committee for the Humanities and Public Issues
Box 2191
Bismarck, North Dakota 58501
U.S.A. Tel: (701) 663-1948

250

Ohio Program in the Humanities
760 Pleasant Ridge Avenue
Columbus, Ohio 43209 U.S.A.
Tel: (614) 236-6879

251

Oklahoma Humanities Committee
Executive Terrace Building
2809 Northwest Expressway, Suite 500
Oklahoma City, Oklahoma 73112
U.S.A. Tel: (405) 840-1721

252

Oregon Committee for the Humanities
418 S. W. Washington, Room 410
Portland, Oregon 97201 U.S.A.
Tel: (503) 241-0543

253

Public Committee for the Humanities in Pennsylvania
401 N. Broad Street
Philadelphia, Pennsylvania 19108
U.S.A. Tel: (215) 925-1005

254

Fundacion Puertorriquena des las Humanidades
Box 4307
Old San Juan, Puerto Rico 00904
U.S.A. Tel: (809) 723-2087

255

Rhode Island Committee for the Humanities
86 Weybosset Street, Room 307
Providence, Rhode Island 02903
U.S.A. Tel: (401) 521-6150

256

South Carolina Committee for the Humanities
17 Calendar Court
Columbia, South Carolina 29206
U.S.A. Tel: (803) 799-1704

257

South Dakota Committee on the Humanities
University Station, Box 35
Brookings, South Dakota 57006
U.S.A. Tel: (605) 688-4823

258

Tennessee Committee for the Humanities
1001 18th Avenue South
Nashville, Tennessee 37212 U.S.A.
Tel: (615) 320-7001

259

Texas Committee for the Humanities
1604 Nueces
Austin, Texas 78701 U.S.A.
Tel: (512) 473-8585

260

Utah Endowment for the Humanities
10 West Broadway
Broadway Building, Suite 900
Salt Lake City, Utah 84101 U.S.A.
Tel: (801) 531-7868

261

Vermont Council on the Humanities and Public Issues
Grant House, P.O. Box 58
Hyde Park, Vermont 05655 U.S.A.
Tel: (802) 888-5060

262

Virginia Foundation for the Humanities and Public Policy
One-B West Range
University of Virginia
Charlottesville, Virginia 22903 U.S.A.
Tel: (804) 924-3296

263

Washington Commission for the Humanities
Olympia, Washington 98505 U.S.A.
Tel: (206) 866-6510

264

Humanities Foundation of West Virginia
Box 204
Institute, West Virginia 25112 U.S.A.
Tel: (304) 768-8869

265

Wisconsin Humanities Committee
716 Langdon Street
Madison, Wisconsin 53706 U.S.A.
Tel: (608) 262-0706

266

Wyoming Council for the Humanities
Box 3274 - University Station
Laramie, Wyoming 82701 U.S.A.
Tel: (307) 766-6496

HEALTH, MEDICAL, PSYCHOLOGY

TV-Radio Broadcasting (video, film, audio), including ARTHRITIS, CYSTIC FIBROSIS, FAMILY RELATIONS, GUIDANCE-COUNSELING, HEART DISEASE, HUMANITARIAN, MENTAL HEALTH, OCCUPATIONAL SAFETY, OSTEOPATHIC, RED CROSS, REHABILITATION. (Also see BROADCASTING, BUSINESS-INDUSTRIAL, JOURNALISM, SCIENTIFIC-TECHNICAL.)

267

American Medical Writers Association (AMWA) Film Festival
Lillian Sablack, Administrator
5272 River Road, Suite 370
Bethesda, Maryland 20016 U.S.A.
Tel: (301) 986-9119

September-October

International; entry open to all; annual; established 1974. Purpose: to improve medical communication by review and recognition of outstanding medical film and videotapes. Sponsored by AMWA, international organization dedicated to advancement, improvement of medical communications. Held in varying cities at AMWA annual meeting. Have workshops, seminars. Publish *Medical Communication*. Second contact: Bill Fargie, Medigraphics, Inc., 1300 North Vermont Avenue, Suite 600, Hollywood, California 90027.

VIDEOTAPE CONTEST: Medical (3/4-inch) made in previous 5 years. Categories: Professional (Instructive, Public Relations); Lay (Instructive, Public Relations); Documentary; TV News or Editorial; Dramatic.

AWARDS: AMMIE Plaque, Best each category. Special Recognition to Best Script, Director, Technical Demonstration, Editing, Special Effects, Cinematography.

JUDGING: By professional filmmakers and medical educators. Not responsible for loss or damage.

ENTRY FEE: $35.

DEADLINES: Entry, June. Meeting, Fall.

268

American Personnel and Guidance Association (APGA) Film Festival
Nancy P. Kins, Promotion Director
Two Skyline Place, Suite 400
5203 Leesburg Pike
Falls Church, Virginia 22041 U.S.A.
Tel: (703) 820-4700, ext. 249

March-April

National; entry open to U.S.; annual. Purpose: to preview productions appropiate for showing in schools and colleges, to prospective users. Sponsored by APGA (40,000 members). Held at APGA Convention and exhibition (9000 attendance). Publish *Guidepost* (newspaper), in which award winners are featured.

VIDEOTAPE CONTEST: Guidance-Counseling (EIAJ 3/4-inch cassette). Categories: Guidance, Counseling, Careers, Psychology, Sociology,

Teacher Education, Rehabilitation, Human Rights.

AWARDS: Plaques to Best of Festival, Videotape. Special Recognitions of Merit. Winners reviewed in trade journals.

JUDGING: By committee based on revelance to APGA. Festival may withdraw production injurious to purposes of APGA. Not responsible for loss, damage, injury.

ENTRY FEE: Previewing $30. Additional $30 if accepted.

DEADLINES: Entry, November. Winners announced, January. Festival, March-April.

VIDEOTAPE REVIEW SERVICE: Guidance-Counseling. Free evaluations and reviews in career information publications, American Personnel and Guidance Association.

269

American Psychological Foundation (APF) National Media Awards

Kathleen Holmay, Public Information Officer
1200 Seventeenth Street, N.W.
Washington, District of Columbia
20036 U.S.A. Tel: (202) 833-7881

August

National; **entry open to U.S.;** annual; established 1956. Purpose: to recognize, honor, encourage outstanding, accurate psychology coverage to the public. Sponsored by APF, American Psychological Association (APA). Average statistics: 345 entries, 6 winners, 15,000 attendance. Held at annual APA convention.

VIDEOTAPE CONTEST: Psychology (3/4-inch cassette) 60 minutes minimum, aired in year prior to entry. Must include references to

psychology, psychologists, depict findings or applications of psychological science. No textbook-type videoaudio. Category: Film-Television.

AUDIOTAPE CONTEST: Psychology (7-inch reel) same as for Video. Category: Radio.

AWARDS: $1000 and citation, each category. Winner invited to 3-day convention, all expenses paid. Honorable Mentions. Special Citation.

ENTRY FEE: None. Entries returned upon request.

DEADLINES: Entry, May. Winners announced, July. Awards, August.

270

Anson Jones Award Competition

Texas Medical Association
Jon R. Hornaday
1801 North Lamar Blvd.
Austin, Texas 78701 U.S.A.
Tel: (512) 477-6704, ext. 120

May

State; **entry restricted to Texas media;** annual; established 1956. Named after Anson Jones, last president of Texas Republic. Purpose: to award Texas news media for communicating health information to public; recognize journalism contributing to public understanding of Texas medicine and health. Sponsored and supported by Texas Medical Association (TMA), founded 1853. Average statistics: 100 entries, 9 awards. Held at TMA annual meeting. Also sponsor awards for newspapers, magazines, newsletters. Second contact: Anne Shelnutt, Administrative Secretary.

VIDEOTAPE CONTEST: Health Television Broadcast (3/4-inch cassette), length not specified. Require script, summary, outline. Categories: Metro Markets (Dallas, Fort Worth,

Houston, San Antonio), Other Markets.

AUDIOTAPE CONTEST: Health Radio Broadcast (reel-to-reel non-stereo audiotape, cassette) length not specified. Require script, summary or outline. Categories same as for Videotape.

ELIGIBILITY: Broadcast in previous calendar year. No health information primarily for medical or allied professions. No entries from members of medical profession, associations, their employees, health-related organizations.

AWARDS: Anson Jones Plaque and $250 for Excellence in Communicating Health Information to Public, each category. Citations of Merit.

JUDGING: Preliminary by broadcast professionals, final by Texas physician panel, based on accuracy, significance, quality, public interest, impact. May withhold awards.

ENTRY FEE: None.

DEADLINES: Entry, January. Judging, February-March. Winners announced, April. Awards given, May.

271

Audio-Visual Resource Conference Screening Program
Labor Occupational Health Program, University of California
Ken Light
2521 Channing Way
Berkeley, California 94720 U.S.A.
Tel: (415) 642-5507

April

National; **entry open to U.S., Canada;** periodic; established 1981. Purpose: to show state of the art films, video, slide shows dealing with occupational health. Sponsored and supported by Labor Occupational Health

Program. Average statistics: 50 entries, 150 entrants. Held in San Francisco, California for 3 days. Tickets: $50. Have publications, audiovisual articles. Also sponsor screenings, workshops, conference programs.

VIDEOTAPE EXHIBITION: Occupational Safety and Health (requirements not specified).

AWARDS: None.

ENTRY FEE: None.

DEADLINES: Not stated.

272

Cystic Fibrosis Foundation Communications Awards Competition
Eric Bolton, Public Relations Director
6000 Executive Blvd., Suite 309
Rockville, Maryland 20852 U.S.A.
Tel: (301) 881-9130

February

National; **entry open to U.S.;** annual; established 1975. Formerly called LEROY WOLFE COMMUNICATIONS AWARDS. Purpose: to recognize news and feature reports on cystic fibrosis, the disease and its consequences. Theme: Cystic Fibrosis. Sponsored and supported by Cystic Fibrosis Foundation. Held at Spring Board of Trustees Meeting, Washington D.C.

VIDEOTAPE CONTEST: Cystic Fibrosis, Children's Lung Disease Television Broadcast (3/4-inch cassette) plus typewritten script; broadcast for U.S. general public January to December previous year; no CF Foundation personnel. Category: Broadcast.

AUDIOTAPE CONTEST: Cystic Fibrosis, Children's Lung Disease Radio Broadcast (standard audio cassette) plus typewritten script; broad-cast for U.S. general public January to December previous year. Category, restrictions same as for Videotape.

AWARDS: $1000 to top winners each category.

JUDGING: By professional communicators based on accuracy, quality, impact, ability to stimulate greater public knowledge and concern.

ENTRY FEE: None.

DEADLINES: Entry, February. Event, Spring.

273

Film Festival on the Exceptional Individual
Children's Hospital of Los Angeles, University Affiliated Program
Neil Goldstein, Co-Chairman
P.O. Box 54700, Terminal Annex
Los Angeles, California 90054 U.S.A.
Tel: (213) 669-2300

October

International; entry open to all; annual; established 1970. Purpose: to promote production of quality films about disabilities, handicapped persons; disseminate information about new films. Sponsored and supported by Children's Hospital, University Affiliated Program and Southern California Region American Association of Mental Deficiency. Average statistics: 100 entries, 12 countries, 1000 attendance. Held in Southern California, 5-hour event. Tickets: $3-$5.

VIDEOTAPE CONTEST: Medical-Mental Handicap (width not specified) produced within previous 18 months.

AWARDS: Trophy, Best of Festival; Certificates to Best Five. Winners broadcast on Southern California

Public Television. Certificate of Commendation to preview winners.

JUDGING: By preview committee of professionals, disabled; final by staff, students of University Affiliated Program.

ENTRY FEE: $5 donation. Entrant pays postage.

DEADLINES: Applications, June. Materials, July. Festival, October.

274

Health Education Media Association (HEMA) Media Festival
Marilyn Maple, Coordinator
J. Hillis Miller Health Center
University of Florida, Box J-16
Gainesville, Florida 32610 U.S.A.
Tel: (904) 392-4146

Various

International; **entry restricted to HEMA members;** annual; established 1975. Awards to **Health Education Videotapes** (3/4-inch cassette), **Audiotapes, Films** (16mm, Super 8mm) and **Filmstrips.** Purpose: to encourage professional production of educational audiovisual materials. Sponsored by HEMA. Recognized by NAUA, AECT. Average Statistics: 50 entries, 30 entrants, 2 countries, 5 awards. Held at annual HEMA conference.

275

Health Journalism Awards
American Chiropractic Association (ACA)
Joann Ozimak, Thomas E. Blackett, Public Affairs
220 Grand Avenue
Des Moines, Iowa 50312 U.S.A.
Tel: (515) 243-1121

Summer

International; **entry restricted to journalists;** annual; established 1976. Purpose: to recognize journalists who promote Public health, suggest problem solutions, motivate public health care, contribute to responsible reporting. Sponsored by ACA. Average statistics: 161 entries. Held at annual ACA conference.

VIDEOTAPE CONTEST: Health Television (3/4-inch cassette) kinescopes acceptable. Produced during previous calendar year, public oriented. No chiropractic professionals, associations, employees. Category: Television.

AUDIOTAPE CONTEST: Health Radio (1/4-inch reel). Restrictions same as for Videotape. Category: Radio.

AWARDS: First Place Distinguished Journalism Gold Award and $200. Runners-Up Bronze Medallions each category. Special Recognition Plaques.

JUDGING: By media professionals. Sponsor may withhold awards; display or broadcast entries to public.

ENTRY FEE: None.

DEADLINES: Entry, March. Event, Summer.

276

Howard W. Blakeslee Awards
American Heart Association (AHA)
Howard L. Lewis, Chairman
7320 Greenville Avenue
Dallas, Texas 75231 U.S.A.
Tel: (214) 750-5340

December

National; **entry open to U.S.;** annual; established 1952. Named for Howard W. Blakeslee, founder of National Association of Science Writers. Purpose: to encourage mass communication reporting on heart and circulatory diseases. Sponsored by AHA. Held at annual AHA meeting.

VIDEOTAPE CONTEST: Heart Disease Television Broadcast. Require objectives, audience. Categories: Film, Television.

AUDIOTAPE CONTEST: Heart Disease Radio Broadcast, tape or transcription. Require objectives, audience, script if available. Category: Radio.

ELIGIBILITY: Broadcast in U.S. or territories from March previous year to February current year. No employees or materials of American Heart Association affiliates, local heart organizations.

AWARDS: Plaque and $500 for outstanding public reporting on heart and blood vessel diseases, each winner.

JUDGING: Based on accuracy, significance, skill, originality, achievements.

ENTRY FEE: None.

DEADLINES: Entry, May. Awards, December.

277

International Rehabilitation Film Festival
Rehabfilm
John F. Moses, Director
20 West 40th Street
New York, New York 10018 U.S.A.
Tel: (212) 869-0460

Month varies

International; entry open to all; annual; established 1977. Began in Washington, D.C.; moved to New York, 1979. Purpose: to select and reward best films and tapes relating to disability. Theme: Mental or physical disability. Sponsored by Rehabfilm, division of Rehabilitation International USA. Average statistics: 250 entries, 150 entrants, 12 countries, 22 winners, 300 attendance. Have seminars, screening rooms. Held in New York for 2-3 days. Tickets: $10 per day. Publish *Rehabfilm* quarterly newsletter.

VIDEOTAPE CONTEST: Rehabilitation (3/4-inch NTSC only). English transcript required for non-English films. Categories: Physical Rehabilitation, Medical, Nonmedical, Allied Medical and Paramedical Disciplines, Programs and Facilities, Disabled Person in Society, Mental Health (General Audience, Professional Audience), Mental Retardation, Recreation, Employment, Special Education, Prevention of Disability, Technical Aids, Best Series.

AWARDS: Grand Prize Best of Festival. First, Second Prizes, each category (5 entries required). Certificates of Merit, all entries shown. Programs derived from events become reference guides.

JUDGING: Preliminary by subject and media specialist, consumer, based on point system. Final by 3 specialists. All entries viewed in entirety. Sponsor insures entries for full value.

ENTRY FEE: $10-$75 dependent on length. Sponsor pays return postage.

DEADLINES: Not specified.

278

Mental Health Media Awards
National Mental Health Association (NMHA)
Lynn Schultz-Writsel, Coordinator
1800 North Kent Street
Arlington, Virginia 22209 U.S.A.
Tel: (703) 528-6405

November

National; **entry restricted to U.S.;** annual; established 1977. Purpose: to honor media representatives for outstanding contributions in fight against mental illness and for promotion of mental health. Sponsored by NMHA. Held at NMHA annual meeting. Also sponsor NMHA FILM FESTIVAL.

VIDEOTAPE CONTEST: Mental Health Television Broadcast (preferably cassette) aired in previous year. Categories: Station, Individual Reporter, Public Service Announcement.

AUDIOTAPE CONTEST: Mental Health Radio Broadcast, aired in previous year. Require tape of announcement program or segments of program. Categories same as for Videotape.

AWARDS: Mental Health Media Awards.

JUDGING: Sponsor keeps all entries.

ENTRY FEE: None.

DEADLINES: Entry, July. Awards given, November.

279

National Council of Family Relations (NCFR) Film, Videotape, and Filmstrip Awards Competition
Betty Morrison, Coordinator
1219 University Avenue Southeast
Minneapolis, Minnesota 55414
U.S.A. Tel: (612) 331-2774

October

International; entry open to all; annual; established 1969. Purpose: to recognize, encourage excellence in production; promote effective use of film, videotapes, filmstrips in family field. Theme: Quality of Family Life; Integrating Theory, Research, Application. Sponsored by NCFR. Held at 4-day meeting of NCFR, attended by

1000 professionals. Second contact: T. Scott Lane, Department of Child and Family Development, School of Home Economics, University of Georgia, Athens, Georgia 30602.

VIDEOTAPE CONTEST: Family Relations (3/4-inch cassette), 3 maximum per entrant; nationally distributed, available for rental, free loan, purchase, or lease. Categories: Adolescence and Youth, Child Development and Parenthood, Family Crisis and Disorganization, Family: History and Cross-Culture, Human Reproduction and Family Planning, Male-Female Roles, Marital Interaction and Family Process, Marriage-Family Counseling, Sexuality-Sex Education, Social Issues and Family.

AWARDS: First, Second, Third Place. Best in Category to top-scoring entries in each format.

JUDGING: By committee not connected with production of entries. Each format judged separately.

ENTRY FEE: 1-15 minutes, $30 per entry; 16-30 minutes, $40; over 30 minutes, $50. Sponsor pays return postage.

DEADLINES: Entry, March. Event, October. Materials returned, May.

VIDEOTAPE EXHIBITION: Family Relations, shown out-of-competition; 3 maximum per entrant; produced in previous year. Request promotional literature. Categories same as for Videotape. Projection fee: 3/4-inch videotape, $2 per minute. Reservations by September. Contact: Deryck and Martha Calderwood, Co-Chairpersons, 27 Harvey Drive, Summit, New Jersey 07901.

| 280 |

Osteopathic Journalism Awards Competition
American Osteopathic Association (AOA)
Monica E. Lynch, Audio-Visual Coordinator
212 East Ohio Street
Chicago, Illinois 60611 U.S.A.
Tel: (312) 280-5857

Spring

International; **entry restricted to journalists;** annual; established 1956. Oldest journalism competition sponsored by a professional association. Purpose: to recognize journalists who report, interpret osteopathic medicine to scientific community, general public. Sponsored by AOA. Supported by Ross Laboratories (division of Abbott Laboratories).

VIDEOTAPE CONTEST: Osteopathic Medicine Journalism Television Broadcast (tape or cassette) 3 programs maximum (series may be submitted as single program). Submit script if available.

AUDIOTAPE CONTEST: Osteopathic Medicine Journalism Radio Broadcast. Requirements same as for Videotape.

ELIGIBILITY: Broadcast during previous calendar year. No members of osteopathic profession, spouses, employees, AOA employees.

AWARDS: $1000 to most outstanding broadcast; 2 supplemental awards, $500 each.

JUDGING: By professional journalists, based on good journalism, contribution to fuller understanding of osteopathic profession. AOA keeps all entries, may print winners in AOA publications.

ENTRY FEE: None.

DEADLINES: Entry, March. Event, Spring.

| 281 |

Russell L. Cecil Arthritis Writing Awards
Arthritis Foundation
Roy Scott, Communications Specialist
3400 Peachtree Road
Atlanta, Georgia 30326 U.S.A.
Tel: (404) 266-0795

Fall

National; **entry open to U.S.;** annual; established 1956. named after R. L. Cecil, pioneer rheumatologist, former medical director of Foundation. Purpose: to recognize, encourage writing on arthritis, related diseases. Sponsored by Arthritis Foundation. Average statistics: 75-100 entries, 75-100 entrants, 9 semifinalists, 4 winners, 150 attendance. Held for 1 day at site selected by Foundation. Free admission.

VIDEOTAPE CONTEST: **Arthritis Television Broadcast** (3/4-inch cassette) single broadcast or series. Require 5 copies script, date and place of broadcast. Category: Television.

AUDIOTAPE CONTEST: **Arthritis Radio Broadcast** (cassette or reel) single broadcast or series. Require 5 copies script, date and place of broadcast. Category: Radio.

ELIGIBILITY: Broadcast in U.S. general public media during previous calendar year.

AWARDS: Cecil Medallions.

JUDGING: By at least 2 journalism professionals, 1 rheumatologist selected by Foundation; based on accuracy, concern for arthritic problems. No entries returned.

ENTRY FEE: None.

DEADLINES: Entry, January. Judging, Spring. Winners announced, Spring-Fall. Event, Fall.

| 282 |

Varna International Festival of Red Cross and Health Films
Alexander Marinov
1 Biruzov
Sofia 1527, BULGARIA
Tel: 441-14-43, 441-14-45

June

International; entry open to all; biennial (odd years); established 1963. Purpose: to assemble, screen best films and videotapes on topical Red Cross, health, humanitarian subjects. Motto: Through Humanity to Peace and Friendship. Sponsored by Central Committee of the Bulgarian Red Cross; League of Red Cross Societies; International Federation of National Red Cross; Red Crescent, Red Lion, Sun Societies. Supported by Ministries of Public Health and Education, Committee for Art and Culture, Television and Radio, Recreation and Tourism; Bulgarian Cinematography, Bulgarian Film Producers Union. Recognized by IFFPA. Held in Varna, Bulgaria, for 10 days. Have Film Sales Market. Second contact: League of Red Cross Societies, P.O.B. 276, 1211 Geneva 19, Switzerland.

VIDEOTAPE CONTEST: **Health, Humanitarian, Red Cross Feature, Short, Television** (3/4-inch standard U-matic, 625 lines 50HZ; 1/2-inch VCR; 1-inch magnetic tape I.V.C. 625 lines 50HZ; 2-inch magnetic tape, 625 lines 50HZ) produced in previous 2 years; maximum 2 entries per country. Require full text (dialog, commentary in Bulgarian, Russian, English, French, Spanish), text of subtitles, publicity materials, biography, photos, synopsis (obligatory for features). Categories: Red Cross, Short and Medium Length

(Popular Science on Health, Cartoons, Prevention Problems in Environment Protection and Pollution); Features, Television (Popular Science, Documentary, Educational, Cartoons).

AWARDS: Golden Ship Grand Prize, Best Red Cross Film-Videotape. Grand Prize, each category. First Prize Gold, Second Silver Medals, each category. Prizes for best feature, actor, actress, feature with humanitarian character, feature reflecting humanity and heroism in medical worker activity. Participation Diplomas.

JUDGING: Preselection by National Red Cross, Red Crescent, Red Lion, Sun Society Commissions. Final by 4 international juries, each category. Not responsible for loss or damage.

ENTRY FEE: None. Sponsor pays return postage.

DEADLINES: Entry, February. Materials, April. Judging, May. Event, June. Materials returned 15 days after festival.

283

Medikinale Marburg International Competition for Medical Films
German Green Cross
Dr. H. Schreiner, Director
Schuhmarkt 4
D-3550 Marburg-Lahn, WEST
GERMANY (FRG) Tel: 6421-24044

July

International; entry open to all; biennial (odd years); established 1971. Purpose: to project recent documentaries on medicine, medical research and teaching, physician and public health education. Sponsored by German Green Cross Marburg ou Lahn, Federal Center for Health Information, Phillips University of Marburg Medical Faculty, International Green

Cross in Geneva. Average statistics: 130 entries, 20 countries, 40 winners, 300 attendance. Held in Marburg ou Lahn at City Hall for 5 days. Tickets: 30DM.

VIDEOTAPE CONTEST: Medical (VHS, U-matic, Beta) released in previous 3 years. Require German translation, summary (20 lines maximum, German or English), stills, explanatory brochures. No advertisements, advertising films. Categories: Medical Amateur, General Information, Particular Information, Medical and Scientific for Laypersons, Veterinary.

AWARDS: Grand Prix, Best Videotape. Grosser Preis, Major Prize, best popular medicine tape. Medikinale Medallions, Certificates, each category. Special Awards for post-graduate physician training, public health education. Special Prizes for script writing, direction, camera technique (Michael von Tobien Prize), trick films. Special Prize, outstanding videotape by young author (to 25 years).

JUDGING: By physician, specialist, medical journalist, film director, medical student, lay judges. Not responsible for loss or damage.

ENTRY FEE: 100DM registration plus 5DM per film minute (50DM minimum).

DEADLINES: Entry, May. Materials, June. Event, July. Materials returned, August.

INDEPENDENT VIDEO
Includes AMATEUR, STUDENT, MINORITY, SHORT. (Also see ANIMATED-EXPERIMENTAL, DOCUMENTARY, EDUCATIONAL, EXHIBITION-DISTRIBUTION,

STUDENT-AMATEUR.)

284

Atlanta Independent Film & Video Festival
IMAGE Film-Video Center
Linda S. Dubler
972 Peachtree Street, Suite 213
Atlanta, Georgia 30309 U.S.A.
Tel: (404) 874-4756

April

International; entry open to all; annual; established 1977. Only national festival jurying film and video in Southeast U.S. Purpose: to promote awareness and support of independent media activity. Sponsored by and held at IMAGE FILM-Media Center, High Museum of Art. Supported by NEA, Southern Arts Foundation, Atlanta Department of Cultural Affairs. Average statistics: 250 entries, 5000 attendance. Have technical workshops, seminars, special presentations by visiting artists at Festival. Publish *IMAGE Newsletter.* Also sponsor screenings, equipment access, information referral. Second contact: Terry Lambert.

VIDEOTAPE CONTEST: Independent (1/2-inch, 3/4-inch cassettes).

AWARDS: Over $2000 in cash and prizes available. AIFVF Touring Program of winners (national).

JUDGING: 5-member panel.

ENTRY FEES: $7, under 30 minutes; $10, over 30 minutes; $20, submissions of distributors.

DEADLINES: Entry, March. Event, April.

285

Hometown U.S.A. Video Festival
National Federation of Local Cable Programmers (NFLCP)
Greg Vawter, Coordinator
3700 Far Hills Avenue, Room 109
Kettering, Ohio 45429 U.S.A.
Tel: (513) 298-7890

Spring

International; **entry restricted to independents;** annual; established 1978. Formerly called HOMETOWN USA VIDEO AND FILM FESTIVAL. Purpose: to promote, ensure continued public access to community cable television; discover, assist users of local channels. Sponsored by NFLCP, nonprofit corporation organized to foster citizen participation in community television programming. Average statistics: 95 entries, 65 entrants, 2 countries, 10 winners, 20 rentals each winner. Have workshops, seminars, speakers bureau. Publish *Community Television Review,* bimonthly magazine.

VIDEOTAPE CONTEST: Independent (3/4-inch U-matic, 1/2-inch reel, 1/2-inch Beta I) 60 minutes or less; in English. Categories: Public Affairs, Documentary, Education, Video Art-Experimental, Performance, Special Audiences (Minorities, Senior Citizens, Children, Women), Fun.

AWARDS: Winners tour U.S. cable TV channels, convention showings, nonprofit rentals (called *Hometown USA Bicycle Tour).* Revenues shared with entrants.

JUDGING: By 2-member panel of community access programmers, video artists, instructors; based on importance, local community involvement, use of medium to convey message. Have nonexclusive distribution rights to winners for 2 years as part of

Tour. Not responsible for loss or damage.

ENTRY FEE: $5. Festival pays return postage.

DEADLINES: Entry, Spring. Winners announced, Summer.

286

JVC Tokyo Video Festival
Burson-Marsteller Public Relations
Tim McGowan
866 Third Avenue
New York, New York 10022 U.S.A.
Tel: (212) 752-6500, ext. 3430

December-January

International; entry open to all; annual; established 1978. Purpose: to create forum for exchange of video ideas throughout world. Sponsored by U.S. JVC Corporation (Victor Company of Japan), video equipment manufacturer. Average statistics: 700 entries, 7 countries, 75 finalists, 25-35 awards. Held in Tokyo, Japan. Also sponsor JVC STUDENT VIDEO FESTIVAL, JVC BUSINESS AND INDUSTRY VIDEO FESTIVAL. Second contact: John Bailey.

VIDEOTAPE CONTEST: **Independent** (1/2-inch EIAJ, VHS, Beta or 3/4-inch U-matic) 20 minutes maximum, produced with video camera. Require producer biography. No JVC employees or relatives.

AWARDS: Grand Prize, $1200 and trip to Tokyo awards ceremony. 25-35 other awards.

JUDGING: By Japanese producers, directors, critics. Sponsor keeps all entries. Not responsible for loss or damage.

ENTRY FEE: None.

DEADLINES: Entry, August. Judging, November. Event, December.

287

Mill Valley Film Festival
Mark Fishkin, Director
131 D Camino Alto
Mill Valley, California 94941 U.S.A.
Tel: (415) 383-5256, 383-1416

August

International; **entry open to all (video), by invitation of Festival (film)**; annual; established 1978, nonprofit organization. Focuses on Bay Area film-video makers. Purpose: to provide community service, education, cultural enrichment to audiences and artists. Supported by San Francisco Foundation, California Arts Council, Mill Valley Art Commission. Recognized by Mill Valley City Council, Mill Valley Center for the Performing Arts, Marin SummerFest. Average statistics: 100 entries, 50 entrants, 10 countries, 6000-8000 attendance, 35 screenings. Held at Sequoia Theatre, Outdoor Art Club, Mill Valley. Tickets $2 (video), $3-$3.50 (film). Also sponsor filmmaking, screenwriting, cinematography, directing, editing workshops-conferences. Second contacts: Rita Cahill, Managing Director; Richard Jett, Video Coordinator.

VIDEOTAPE CONTEST: **Independent** (3/4-inch cassette) any length, any subject. Require photographs, promotional material, English subtitles.

AWARDS: None.

JUDGING: By Video Coordinator and Bay Area video makers. All entries viewed in entirety. Not responsible for loss or damage.

ENTRY FEE: None. Entrant pays postage.

DEADLINES: Entry, May. Event, August.

288

Museroom
Center for Internationalising the
Study of English (CIE)
Mike Hazard, Director
628 Grand Avenue, #307
St Paul, Minnesota 55105 U.S.A.
Tel: (612) 222-2096

Periodic

International; entry open to all; periodic; established 1974. Formerly called WALT WHITMAN INTERNATIONAL MEDIA COMPETITION to 1976. Purpose: to promote, encourage literature and media from postcards to broadcasts. Sponsored by CIE.

VIDEOTAPE CONTEST: Various themes.

AWARDS: Not specified.

ENTRY FEE: Not specified.

DEADLINES: Not specified.

289

New River Mixed Media Gathering
Appalachian State University
Joseph R. Murphy, Associate
Professor
Educational Media Department
Boone, North Carolina 28608 U.S.A.
Tel: (704) 262-2243

October

International; **entry restricted to independents, students;** annual; established 1978. Purpose: to heighten awareness in region by bringing film-video people together, encourage student-independent production. Sponsored and supported by Appalachian State University, North Carolina Independent Film and Video Association (NCIFVA), NEA, North Carolina Arts Council. Average statistics: 30 entries, 6 winners, 300 attendance.

Held at Appalachian State University for 3 days. Tickets: $5 students, $10 nonstudents.

VIDEOTAPE CONTEST: Independent, Student (EIAJ 1/2-inch reel-to-reel or cassette; 3/4-inch cassette) 60 minutes maximum. Categories: 17 and below, 18 and above.

AWARDS: First, Second, cash awards, each category. Top 2 (audience selected) receive Certificates.

JUDGING: By 3 film-video professionals. May retain work selected (entrant receives $50 honorarium) for showing at 4-6 sites and cable TV in North Carolina. Not responsible for loss or damage.

ENTRY FEE: $5. Sponsor pays return postage.

DEADLINES: Entry and Event, October. Materials returned 2 weeks after.

290

Philafilm: The Philadelphia International Film Festival
International Association of Motion Picture and Television Producers (IAMPTP)
Lawrence L. Smallwood, Jr.,
Executive Director
1315 Walnut Street, Suite 320
Philadelphia, Pennsylvania 19107
U.S.A. Tel: (215) 732-9222

July

International; entry open to all; annual; established 1978 as major program of IAMPTP. Purpose: to provide forum for exhibition, critique of film and video works produced by minorities, independents; provide for distribution systems, financing, exhibition, training; create international marketplace for producers. Sponsored by IAMPTP. Recognized by City of Philadelphia, Greater Philadelphia Partnership, Philadelphia Council for Progress. Average statistics: 30 entries, 3 countries, 3 awards, 5000 attendance, 16 screenings. Held in Philadelphia for 4-7 days. Have auditorium for screenings. Tickets: $2-$3. Also sponsor internship and work-study programs, education program, job-listing service in communications; IAMPTP Producer of the Year Award.

VIDEOTAPE CONTEST: Independent, Minority (3/4-inch reel-to-reel or cassette) length unlimited; produced within 2 years of submission; works near completion considered. Require screen credits, biography, production data. Categories: Competition (with various subcategories; e.g., Animation, Documentary, Short), Market.

AWARDS: Leigh Whipper Award, Best each competition category; Silver Awards to Runners-up. Best Cinematography Award. Honorable Mentions to competition and market entries. Plaques, Certificates. Competition winners and selected market entries receive promotion, marketing support.

JUDGING: Screened in entirety by 6 judges from local press, independent producers, TV station promotion and program directors. If works are rented or sold by IAMPTP, producer pays 10% sales commission.

ENTRY FEE: $25-$100; average, $50. Sponsor pays return postage for most works.

DEADLINES: Entry, May. Acceptance, June. Event, July. Materials returned, August.

291

River City Arts Festival
Arts Assembly of Jacksonville
632 May Street
Jacksonville, Florida 32204 U.S.A.
Tel: (904) 633-3748

April

National; entry open to U.S.; annual; established 1972. Administered in 1973 by Jacksonville Public Library Film Department; no festival held 1974-1976. Formerly called JACKSONVILLE FILM FESTIVAL, JACKSONVILLE ARTS FESTIVAL. Purpose: to award excellence in filmmaking. Sponsored by Arts Assembly of Jacksonville, Fine Arts Council of Florida. Supported by community businesses and organizations, City of Jacksonville. Average statistics: 100 entries, 85 entrants, 7 awards, 400 attendance. Held in Jacksonville for 2 days. Second contact: Jeff Driggers, Jacksonville Public Library, 122 North Ocean Street, Jacksonville, Florida 32202.

VIDEOTAPE CONTEST: Independent (3/4-inch cassette) 30 minutes maximum. In original format, completed since January previous year. Request stills, synopsis of objectives. Categories: Entertainment, Contemporary-Human Concerns, Instructional-Informational, Innovations (technique, subject content), Children's.

AWARDS: Grand Prize $200. Second Prize $125. Best of Category $75.

JUDGING: By educators, filmmakers, critics, film programmers; final by 3. Festival may use entry or portion of for pre-Festival publicity, promotion. Sponsor insures for cost of unprocessed film, tape.

ENTRY FEE: $10 each.

DEADLINES: Entry, February. Judging, March. Event, April. Materials returned within 2 weeks.

292

San Francisco International Video Festival

Stephen Agetstein, Director
229 Cortland Street
San Francisco, California 94110
U.S.A. Tel: (415) 641-9207

September

International; entry open to all; annual; established 1980. Formerly called MOEBIUS VIDEO SHOW, established 1973. Purpose: to encourage production of quality video. Theme: Video of the Eighties. Sponsored by *Video 80 Magazine.* Average statistics: 230 entries, 212 entrants, 4 countries, 52 winners, 32 exhibitions, 3000 attendance. Held in various locations including University Art Museum, Goethe Institute, for 10 days. Have conferences, seminars, retrospectives. Tickets: half, $2; other half free. Second contact: Wendy Garfield, Publisher.

VIDEOTAPE CONTEST: **Independent** (3/4-inch).

AWARDS: Cash Prizes. $100 rental fee per tape exhibited.

JUDGING: By panel of respected curators, critics, producers, artists. Festival claims exhibition rights.

ENTRY FEE: $10. Sponsor pays return postage.

DEADLINES: Entry, August. Event, September.

293

San Mateo County Fair Video Cassette Competition

San Mateo County Fair Arts Committee
Lois Kelley, Administrator
171 Flying Cloud Isle
Foster City, California 94404 U.S.A.
Tel: (415) 349-2787

July-August

International; entry open to all; annual; established 1957. Purpose: to provide showcase for emerging trends in arts. Sponsored by and supported by San Mateo County Fair Arts Committee. Held at San Mateo County Fair (2495 S. Delaware, San Mateo, California), for 13 days, 200,000 attendance. Tickets: $3. Also sponsor SAN MATEO COUNTY FAIR FILM FESTIVAL, poetry competition, playwriting competition. Second contact: San Mateo County Fair Association, P.O. Box 1027, San Mateo, California 94403.

VIDEOTAPE CONTEST: **Noncommercial, Commercial** (3/4-inch U-matic cassette, 1/2-inch Sony EIAJ) 1 entry per tape, of good technical quality; no special edited versions. Categories: Public Affairs, Documentary, Industry-Instruction (includes Education, Entertainment).

AWARDS: $1000, Best of Show; First Prizes, 4 categories, $800. Second Prize, Merit Ribbon Awards. Ribbons, all categories. Special Subject Awards $100 (Thoroughbred Race Horse Interpretation, Floral Interpretation, Marine World Africa USA).

JUDGING: By distinguished members of video field. Not responsible for loss or damage.

ENTRY FEE: $5 per entry.

DEADLINES: Entry, July. Event, July-August.

294

Santa Cruz Video Festival
Open Channel
Peter Brown, Greg Becker, Coordinators
P.O. Box 1273
Santa Cruz, California 95061 U.S.A.
Tel: (408) 475-8210

February

International; entry open to all; annual; established 1981. Purpose: to provide wide audience for works of independent videographers, community access groups. Theme: varies yearly. Sponsored by Open Channel, Capitola Community Channel 8. Supported by Santa Cruz Arts Commission. Average statistics: 30 entries, 45 entrants, 6 winners, 200 nightly attendance. Held at Louden Nelson Center, Santa Cruz, for 2 days. Publish *CCC8,* monthly. Also sponsor monthly workshops, telemarathon. Second contact: Capitola Community Channel 8, P.O. Box 42, Capitola, California 95010.

VIDEOTAPE CONTEST: Independent (3/4-inch VHS) with entertainment, enrichment value. No instructional, promotional tapes. Categories: Santa Cruz In-County, Out-of-County entries.

AWARDS: First, Second, Third Place, cash awards dependent on financial support of festival. Possible PBS broadcast.

JUDGING: Prescreening, final selection by 3 media professionals, based on originality, technical execution, script, approach to Festival theme. Not responsible for loss or damage.

ENTRY FEE: $5. Entrant pays return postage.

DEADLINES: Entry, December. Materials, January. Judging, Event, February. Materials returned, March.

295

Toronto Super 8 Film Festival
Photo-Electric Arts Foundation
Sheila Hill, Director
P.O. Box 7109, Station A
Toronto, Ontario M4E 3B8 CANADA
Tel: (416) 367-0590

June

International; entry open to all; annual; established 1976. Purpose: to provide forum for and demonstrate capability of Super 8 in electronic media; display latest in techniques and equipment. Motto: "A celebration for and by Super 8 filmmakers." Sponsored by Photo-Electric Arts Foundation. Supported by Toronto and Ontario Arts Councils, Ministries of Trade and Industry, Culture and Recreation. Average statistics: 400 entries, 7 winners, 1200 attendance. Held at Medical Sciences Building, University of Toronto. Tickets: $6 per day, $15 for 3 days. Have workshops, seminars, trade shows, demonstrations, screenings. Second contact: Connie Filletti.

VIDEOTAPE CONTEST: Independent, Student, Amateur, Professional (3/4-inch cassette of original Super 8mm film). Categories: Fiction-Narrative, Fact-Documentary, Animation.

AWARDS: $500, Best each category. $300, James Blue Award to winner by audience ballot. Equipment prizes.

JUDGING: By 9-member panel. All entries screened in entirety. Sponsor insures for loss or damage.

ENTRY FEE: $10 first, $5 subsequent entries. Sponsor pays return postage.

DEADLINES: Entry, May. Event, June.

INDEPENDENT (Regional-State)

Includes AMATEUR, STUDENT. (Also see DOCUMENTARY-SHORT, EDUCATIONAL, EXHIBITION-DISTRIBUTION, STUDENT-AMATEUR.)

296

Cottonpix Mississippi Film Festival
University of Southern Mississippi, School of Library Service
Jeannine Laughlin, Assistant Professor
P.O. Box 5146, Southern Station
Hattiesburg, Mississippi 39401
U.S.A. Tel: (601) 266-7167

November-December

Regional; **entry restricted to southeast U.S. independent film and videomakers, Mississippi students;** annual; established 1973. Formerly called MISSISSIPPI FILM FESTIVAL to 1975. Purpose: to provide forum for student made films and videotapes; recognition of independent film and videomakers. Sponsored by University of Southern Mississippi, Mississippi Authority for Educational Television, Mississippi Arts Commission. Supported by NEA. Average statistics: 35 entries, 200 attendance. Held at University of Mississippi for 2 days.

VIDEOTAPE CONTEST: Independent, Mississippi Student (width not specified) completed in previous year. Categories: K-6, 7-12, College, Independent.

AWARDS: Certificate to entrants. Award to represented school. Individual awards to independents.

JUDGING: By 4 judges. All entries viewed in entirety.

ENTRY FEE: $6 per tape.

DEADLINES: Entry, November. Awards given, December. Materials returned, January.

297

Florida Independent Film and Video Festival
Arts Council of Tampa-Hillsborough County
Diane Howe Eberly, Director
512 North Florida Avenue, Suite 256
Tampa, Florida 33602 U.S.A.
Tel: (813) 223-8286

March

Regional; **entry restricted to Southeastern U.S.;** annual; established 1979. Purpose: to encourage independent film and video artists in Florida; make work available to public. Sponsored by Arts Council of Tampa-Hillsborough County. Supported by Fine Arts Council of Florida, Department of State, City of Tampa. Average statistics: 80 entries, 30 winners, 600 attendance. Held at Tampa Theater for 3 days. Tickets: $1 per night. Have workshop and showcase.

VIDEOTAPE CONTEST: **Independent Noncommercial** (3/4-inch cassette) 60 minutes maximum; any number of entries.

ELIGIBILITY: Produced in Southeastern U.S. by residents.

AWARDS: 20 $150 Individual

Honoraria. 10 $75 Individual Honoraria. $1500 Lab Expense Awards.

JUDGING: By 3 media professionals. Not responsible for loss or damage.

ENTRY FEE: $5 per entry, under 30 minutes; $7, over 30 minutes. Festival pays return postage.

DEADLINES: Entry, January. Event, March.

| 298 |

New Orleans Triennial
New Orleans Museum of Art
William A. Fagaly, Curator
P.O. Box 19123
New Orleans, Louisiana 70179
U.S.A. Tel: (504) 488-2631

Spring

Regional; **entry restricted to 12 southeastern states;** triennial; established 1887. Until 1960 sponsored annually by Art Association of New Orleans; 1969 changed to biennial, 1980 triennial. Formerly called ARTISTS BIENNIAL. Purpose: to give southeastern U.S. artists opportunity for review by outstanding specialists in contemporary art; introduction to collectors, gallery directors, museum professionals, news media, fellow artists, general public. Sponsored by New Orleans Museum of Art (established 1911). Average statistics: 3700 entries, 1300 entrants. Also have painting, sculpture, print, drawing, ceramic, photography, fiber categories.

VIDEOTAPE CONTEST: **Independent** (3/4-inch cassette) 3 entries maximum. Only copies of master tapes accepted.

ELIGIBILITY: Artists living, working in Kentucky, Tennessee, West Virginia, Virginia, North Carolina, South Carolina, Georgia, Florida, Alabama, Mississippi, Arkansas, Louisiana, Texas.

AWARDS: One-person exhibitions at Museum. Purchases by Museum for permanent collection.

JUDGING: By nationally prominent authority in contemporary art field.

ENTRY FEE: None.

DEADLINES: Entry and Event, Spring.

| 299 |

Northwest Film and Video Festival
Northwest Film Study Center
Bill Foster, Associate Director
Portland Art Museum
1219 Southwest Park
Portland, Oregon 97205 U.S.A.
Tel: (503) 221-1156

August

Regional; **entry restricted to northwest U.S. and Canada college students, independents, professionals;** annual; established 1973. Purpose: to survey new moving image art produced in Northwest. Sponsored by Northwest Film Study Center, Portland Art Museum. Supported by Portland Art Association. Average statistics: 125 entries, 6 winners, 2000 attendance. Held at Portland Art Museum. Also sponsor YOUNG FILMMAKERS FESTIVAL, PORTLAND FILM FESTIVAL.

VIDEOTAPE CONTEST: **Independent** (3/4-inch, 1/2-inch EIAJ standard) sound, silent.

ELIGIBILITY: Works produced in last year by Oregon, Washington, Alaska, Idaho, Montana, British Columbia residents.

AWARDS: $1600 total awards;

$200 each to six winning works, $50 to ten selected highlights, plus Honorable Mention. 7 cash and lab-processing prizes, $150 each.

JUDGING: 1-3 judges. Not responsible for loss or damage.

ENTRY FEE: None. Entrant pays return postage.

DEADLINES: Entry, July. Event, August.

300

Rochester Finger Lakes Film & Video Exhibition
Memorial Art Gallery
University of Rochester
490 University Avenue
Rochester, New York 14607 U.S.A.
Tel: (716) 275-3081

May-June

State; **entry restricted to New York residents age 18 or over;** biennial (even years). Alternates with FINGER LAKES CRAFT EXHIBITION. Sponsored by University of Rochester Memorial Art Gallery. Publish catalog of winners. Also sponsor art, photography, sculpture contests.

VIDEOTAPE CONTEST: **Independent Short** (1/2-inch EIAJ standard, VHS, or 3/4-inch cassette) 30 minutes maximum; completed within past two years. No reportage, documentary, commercial productions.

ELIGIBILITY: Open to 18 or older, residents of New York Counties: Allegany, Cayuga, Chemung, Cortland, Genese, Livingston, Monroe, Onondaga, Ontario, Orleans, Oswego, Schuyler, Seneca, Steuben, Tioga, Tompkins, Wayne, Wyoming, Yates.

AWARDS: $3500 in Cash and purchase awards. Invitation to present work at Gallery.

JUDGING: By 1 judge based on use of medium in visually creative manner. May refuse any entry; 20% commission on all sales. Not responsible for loss or damage.

ENTRY FEE: $10. Entrant pays postage.

DEADLINES: Entry, April. Event, May-June. Materials returned, June.

301

TEXPO Southwest Film and Video Festival
Southwest Alternate Media Project (SWAMP)
Ed Hugetz
1506 1/2 Branard
Houston, Texas 77006 U.S.A.
Tel: (713) 522-8592

March

Regional; **entry restricted to southwest U.S. independents, students, amateurs;** annual; established 1973. Purpose: to provide screening of new work by independent film and video makers. Sponsored by SWAMP, Houston Festival, Texas Commission on the Arts. Average statistics: 100 entries, 10 finalists, 500 attendance. Held at Rice University Media Center (during Houston Arts Festival) for 2 weekend days. Have auditorium screening facilities. Tickets: free admission. Publish *Southwest Media,* newsletter. Also sponsor *The Territory* (13-week PBS television series of independent film and video broadcast on KUHT-TV Houston, at minimal fee per minute), Summer Seminar in Film and Video Production.

VIDEOTAPE FESTIVAL: **Independent, Student, Amateur** (1/2-inch and 3/4-inch). Categories: Documentary, Fiction, Animation, Experimental.

AWARDS: Screening fees per minute for selected works.

JUDGING: By jury. Videomaker retains rights. Sponsor pays rental fees, insures for cost of replacement print.

ENTRY FEE: None. Sponsor pays return postage.

DEADLINES: Entry and Event, March.

INTERN, TRAINING, APPRENTICE PROGRAMS

Television, Radio, Video, and Film, including JOURNALISM, MINORITY, WOMEN. (Also see GRANTS, RESIDENCE GRANTS-EQUIPMENT LOANS, SCHOLARSHIPS-FELLOWSHIPS.)

302

AAAS Mass Media Intern Program
American Association for the
Advancement of Science (AAAS)
Gail Breslow, Program Administrator
1776 Massachusetts Avenue, N.W.
Washington, District of Columbia
20036 U.S.A. Tel: (202) 467-4310

Summer

National; **entry restricted to U.S. college students;** annual; established 1974. Purpose: to provide opportunity to observe, participate in news process, improve communication skills, increase understanding of editorial decision-making. Sponsored and supported by National Science Foundation; cosponsored by AAAS (112,000 member association, founded 1848), world's leading general scientific organization dedicated to increasing

public understanding, appreciation of science in human progress. Average statistics: 400 entrants, 20 finalists. Orientation in Washington, D.C.

BROADCASTING INTERNSHIP: Television, Radio. Paid 10-12 week internship, travel expenses for 20 advanced undergraduate, graduate, postdoctoral students in social or natural sciences as mass media reporters, researchers, production assistants at radio and TV stations. Require resume, writing examples, 2 faculty member recommendations, interim and final reports on internship.

JUDGING: Preliminary by experts in natural and social sciences, mass media. Final by AAAS staff, based on study area understanding, commitment to promoting human understanding and appreciation of science, scientific methods.

DEADLINES: Entry, February. Announcements, April. Internship begins, June.

303

American Dance Festival Dance Video Apprenticeships
Lisa Booth, Administrative Director
P.O. Box 6097, College Station
Durham, North Carolina 27708
U.S.A. Tel: (919) 684-6402

June-July

National; **entry restricted to U.S. students;** annual; established 1970. Sponsored by American Dance Festival. Supported by NEA. Held in Durham, North Carolina for 6 weeks. Have workshops, discussions, scholarships. Also sponsor DANCE CRITICS' CONFERENCE FELLOWSHIPS for professional working journalists; school for 250 dance students providing intensive dance training. Second contact: Judith Tolkow, ADF, 1860

Broadway, Room 1112, New York, New York 10023.

VIDEO   APPRENTICESHIP: Dance, full tuition and 4 semester credit hours to students for videotaping dance for 6 weeks. Not eligible to perform in faculty or repertory presentations during apprenticeship. Students responsible for room, board, living expenses. Require recommendation letter.

DEADLINES: Apprenticeship, June-July.

| 304 |

American Film Institute (AFI) Internship Program
Jan Haag, Director
501 Doheny Road
Beverly Hills, California 90210 U.S.A.
Tel: (213) 278-8777

Continuous

National; **entry restricted to U.S. permanent residents;** continuous; established 1967. Purpose: to provide opportunity for promising new film and videomakers to learn by observing established directors in making of feature or TV productions. Sponsored by AFI (Jean Firstenberg, Director, John F. Kennedy Center for the Performing Arts, Washington D.C. 20566), founded 1967 as independent nonprofit organization to preserve heritage, advance art of film and TV in U.S. Supported by Academy of Motion Picture Arts and Sciences. Also sponsor DIRECTING WORKSHOP FOR WOMEN, ARTS ENDOWMENT FILM ARCHIVAL PROGRAM, CURRICULUM PROGRAM TUITION LOANS, INDEPENDENT FILMMAKER PROGRAM GRANTS.

VIDEO INTERNSHIP: Television Direction, $3000 maximum; $125 stipend per week in Los Angeles ($175 on location); location travel cost during length of production. Require videotape (3/4-inch) work sample, biography, personal goals, list of 6 proposed directors; must submit report of experience, assessment of program effectiveness at end of internship (AFI will not publish). Internships based on availability and schedule of productions. No interns sent abroad.

ELIGIBILITY: U.S. citizens or permanent residents, age 21 or older.

JUDGING: Based on background, videotapes, interview. Sponsor may cancel, terminate at any time; limits right of intern to publish information gained from internship.

DEADLINES: Open.

| 305 |

Assistant Directors Training Program
Jane A. Klein, Administrator
8480 Beverly Blvd.
Hollywood, California 90048 U.S.A.

June

National; **entry open to U.S.;** annual; established 1965. Purpose: to train Second Assistant Directors in administrative-managerial functions of television film, motion picture production. Sponsored by Directors Guild of America, AMPTP.

TELEVISION FILM TRAINING PROGRAM: Assistant Director Television Film, Motion Picture Production. Production on-job training for 400 work days (4 periods, 100 cumulative days each) at Assistant Director Trainee pay scales (first 100 days, $242 per week; second 100, $261; third 100, $279; fourth 100, $297). No guarantee of continuous employment. Weekly evening training seminars in records maintenance, call sheets, production reports, requisitions, union-guild regulations, administrative procedures, actor-extra calls, background action staging, actor cuing, pay adjustments, equipment-facilities rental, script breakdown, scheduling, budgeting, film production techniques. No pay for seminars. Upon completion of program, trainee's name placed on Industry Experience Roster (eligible for hire as Second Assistant Director).

ELIGIBILITY: U.S. citizens or permanent residents graduated from accredited 4-year college or university, or have equivalent in college credits and-or motion picture industry work experience after age 18 (employment in theater, live television, allied arts not acceptable). Require proof of college, work, citizenship.

JUDGING: By committee based on education, job experience, results of 8-hour aptitude test at University of Southern California (Los Angeles), personal interviews of finalists in Hollywood, physical examination.

ENTRY FEE: None.

DEADLINES: Application, February. College, work, citizenship documents, March (July for June graduates). Aptitude test, April. Personal interviews, May. Judges' results, employment eligibility, June.

| 306 |

Camera Assistant Training Program
Eileen Vensel, Joey Whang,
Co-Administrators
8480 Beverly Blvd.
Hollywood, California 90048 U.S.A.
Tel: (213) 655-4200

Various

National; **entry open to U.S.;** periodic; established 1974. Purpose: to train assistant cameramen and special photographic effects assistants in television film, motion picture production. Sponsored by International Alliance of Theatrical and Stage Employees (IATSE) International Photographers' Local 659, Contract Services Administration Trust Fund. Average statistics: 1500 entrants, 10 awards.

TELEVISION FILM TRAINING PROGRAM: **Production Camera Assistant and Special Photographic Effects Assistant in Television Film, Motion Picture.** On-job training for 200 workdays within 1 year, at Cameraman Trainee pay scale. Cameraman Training Seminars in hand tests, placemarks, running tapes, photo logs-reports, slates, reloading magazines; setting up, dismantling, moving, and use of motion picture photographic equipment. Photographic Effects Seminars in opticals, miniature photography, insert stage work, electronic equipment, animation cranes, blue screen, matte painting, background projection. No pay for seminars. Upon completion of program, trainee's name placed on Industry Experience Roster (eligible for hire as Group I Second Assistant Cameraperson).

ELIGIBILITY: U.S. citizen or permanent resident, 18 or older, physically fit, with high school or General Education Development Diploma. Require proof of education, citizenship (resident status).

JUDGING: By committee based on education, photographic knowledge, experience, results of 8-hour screening test at University of Southern California in Los Angeles, personal interviews of finalists in Hollywood, physical examination.

ENTRY FEE: None.

DEADLINES: Various

307

Congressional Fellowship Program
American Political Science Association (APSA)
1527 New Hampshire Avenue, N.W.
Washington, District of Columbia
20036 U.S.A. Tel: (202) 483-2512

November-August

National; **entry restricted to U.S. professional journalists;** annual; established 1953. Purpose: to afford young journalists, political or social scientists, federal agency executives, medical faculty opportunity for understanding of national legislative process. Sponsored by APSA. Supported by Edgar Stern Family Fund of New Orleans, Ford Foundation, IBM, EXXON, Andreas Foundation, Johnson Wax Fund, Merck. Average statistics: 15 per year.

BROADCAST TRAINING PROGRAM: **Congressional Journalism Television, Radio.** $12,000 and travel expenses to journalists with BA degree, 2-10 years professional radio, television reporting experience for training as congressional staff members with duties of legislative assistant or press secretary (no cost to Congress). Have 1 month orientation; congressional conferences; seminars with legislators, administrators, lobbyists, reporters, scholars; 9 months as full-time aide to House, Senate members or Congressional Committee (including legislation drafting, lobbying coordination, briefing, strategy, speech writing, arranging congressional hearings, campaign problems, international conferences abroad, travel to congressional district, state, research opportunities). Require detailed curriculum vitae, resume; professional goal statement; 3 professional refer-

ence letters; clips or radio, TV scripts of best work. Preference to candidates without extensive Washington experience.

JUDGING: By journalist political scientist advisory committee, based on quality training, professional competence, maturity, responsibility, relevance to career goals, advancement potential.

ENTRY FEE: None.

DEADLINES: Application, December. Winners announced, March. Fellowship, November-August.

308

Corporation for Public Broadcasting (CPB) Women's and Minority Training Grant Program
Marlene Thorn, Director Training and Development Services
1111 Sixteenth Street N.W.
Washington, District of Columbia
20036 U.S.A. Tel: (202) 293-6160

Various

National; **entry restricted to women, minorities through public broadcast, TV, radio stations;** semi-annual; established 1973 (minority), 1976 (women). Purpose: to upgrade, improve skills of women and minorities as public broadcasting officials, managers, and in technical, professional positions. Sponsored by CPB, private, nonprofit corporation founded 1967 by Public Broadcasting Act. Supported by NEA, federal, private funds. Average statistics: 12 awards (7 TV, 5 radio) totalling $119,-488 for women; 27 awards (16 TV, 11 radio) totalling $465,000 for minorities. Also sponsor Production and Residence Grants, Minorities' and Women's Telecommunications Feasibility Project Grants, Instructional TV Series Grants, Radio Expansion Grants and IN-SERVICE TRAINING

GRANT PROGRAM for educational assistance, internships, exchanges to individuals employed in public broadcasting.

BROADCASTING TRAINING GRANT: Women and Minorities in Television, Radio, up to 50% cost of 1-2 year training plan, on matching basis, to public radio, television, telecommunications entities for training (not employment subsidy) of women, minorities through workshops, conferences, courses, seminars, observations, varied tasks, participation in station projects-productions. Applicants may submit more than 1 proposal. Have Candidate categories (for internal upgrading of staff members), and Position categories (employee-trainee selected after grant awarded).

ELIGIBILITY: Radio, Television, Public Telecommunications entities must meet legal, operational, noncommercial, public service standards of sponsor. No current CPB-funded trainees. Trainees must be women, minorities (Blacks; Indians including Aleuts, Eskimos; Hispanics; Asian-Pacific Americans). Require application sheet, proposal abstract, budget, 6-page (or less) proposal narrative, other documentation (resumes, job descriptions, justification of need); postprogram trainer financial reports, trainer-trainee evaluation reports. Funds must be expended by one year from grant effectiveness date (no carry-overs); funds not expended or left over revert to sponsor.

JUDGING: Proposal screened by panel committees for completeness of information, adherence to guidelines, appropriateness, merits, suitability of candidate (if candidate grant), previous track record with training grants, eligibility, competence to implement training. Panel committee recommendations reviewed, final selection by broadcasting experts.

DEADLINES: Multiple yearly rounds, semiannual application. Open Enrollment Program for Minority Training Grants, monthly.

309

International Association of Motion Picture and Television Producers (IAMPTP) Internship and Work-Study Programs
Lawrence L. Smallwood, Jr.,
Executive Director
1315 Walnut Street, Suite 320
Philadelphia, Pennsylvania 19107
U.S.A. Tel: (215) 732-9222

Continuous

International; entry open to all; continuous. Purpose: to provide opportunities to students of film and video. Sponsored by IAMPTP. Recognized by City of Philadelphia, Greater Philadelphia Partnership, Philadelphia Council for Progress. Also sponsor EDUCATION PROGRAM providing media advocacy information, technical assistance in mass communications; JOB LISTING SERVICE in communications; PHILAFILM: PHILADELPHIA INTERNATIONAL FILM FESTIVAL.

VIDEOTAPE INTERNSHIP: Video Project. Assignment to project staff person for high school and college students, nonmatriculating adults.

VIDEOTAPE WORK-STUDY PROGRAM: Video Project. For matriculating students or government, social service designates.

ENTRY FEE: None.

DEADLINES: Open.

310
Visnews Fellowships in International Television Journalism
Visnews Limited
Jill Belt, Marketing Services Manager
London NW10 7EH, ENGLAND
Tel: 01-965-7733

September

International; **entry restricted to developing countries with national-regional TV systems;** annual; established 1977. Purpose: to provide young broadcast journalists with education, training, experience in television news. Sponsored and supported by Visnews Limited. Average statistics: 2-3 awards. Held in Europe and North America for 12 weeks. Have all aspects of television news gathering facilities, particularly electronic.

TELEVISION TRAINING PROGRAM: **Television Journalism,** up to 3 fellowships per year to individuals with some broadcast journalism experience for travel, accommodation, subsistence, training costs during 12-week program. Require knowledge of English; report on "Development of Television News in My Country" (written to 2000 words; audiotape, 16mm film or videotape to 10 minutes if preferred); 2 references.

JUDGING: By Fellowships Trustees.

ENTRY FEE: None. Sponsor pays return postage.

DEADLINES: Entry, February. Judging, March. Notification, June.

JOURNALISM, NEWS
TV-Radio Broadcast Journalism (video, film, audio), including

CONSUMER, DOCUMENTARY, FASHION, INTERNATIONAL-FOREIGN AFFAIRS, JOURNALISM IMPROVEMENT, DIPLOMATIC and WASHINGTON CORRESPONDENTS. (Also see BROADCASTING, DOCUMENTARY, TELEVISION FILMS.)

311
Alfred I. DuPont Awards in Broadcast Journalism
Columbia University
Graduate School of Journalism
New York, New York 10027 U.S.A.

Fall

International; entry open to all; annual; established 1942. Sponsored by Columbia University since 1969. Supported by Alfred I. DuPont Foundation. Average statistics: 800 entries. Televised by Public Broadcasting System. Also sponsor other media awards.

VIDEOTAPE AWARD: **Journalism Television Broadcast** (width not specified). Require reasons for submission.

FILM AWARD: **Journalism Television Broadcast** (gauge not specified). Require reasons for submission.

AUDIOTAPE AWARD: **Journalism Radio Broadcast** (width not specified). Require reasons for submission.

ELIGIBILITY: Performance in broadcast news-public affairs aired between July 1 of previous, June 30 of current year by local or network station, and syndicated material.

AWARDS: For singular achievement in Broadcast Journalism.

JUDGING: By jury, based on outstanding performance in news-public affairs through research done in annual DuPont-Columbia Survey of Broadcast Journalism. Columbia University keeps all entries.

ENTRY FEE: None.

DEADLINES: Entry, July. Awards, Fall.

| 312 |

By-Line Awards
Marquette University
College of Journalism
1131 West Wisconsin Avenue
Milwaukee, Wisconsin 53233 U.S.A.
Tel: (414) 224-7132

February

International; **entry restricted to Marquette Journalism College alumni;** annual; established 1946. By-Line copper plaques to **Broadcasting and Film Journalists.** Purpose: to honor alumni who have attained distinction in journalism field for competence, acceptance and fulfillment of professional responsiblity. Sponsored by and held at College of Journalism, Marquette University. Event, February.

| 313 |

Deadline Club Journalism Awards Competition
Steven Osborne, President
P.O. Box 2503, Grand Central Station
New York, New York 10017 U.S.A.
Tel: (212) 644-2151

April

City; **entry restricted to New York City journalists;** annual. Held at and sponsored by Deadline Club, New York City Chapter of Sigma Delta Chi Society of Professional Journalists.

Also sponsor $250 scholarships at New York City journalism schools.

VIDEOTAPE CONTEST: Journalism Television Broadcast (3/4-inch cassette), aired in New York metropolitan area in previous year. Require descriptive material. Unlimited entries. Categories: Television News, Business, Financial.

AUDIOTAPE CONTEST: Journalism Radio Broadcasting (cassette, reel-to-reel) aired in New York metropolitan area in previous year. Require script. Unlimited entries. Categories: Radio News, Business, Financial.

AWARDS: Deadliner Statuette, top winners each category. Special Achievement Plaques, 2 finalists, each category.

ENTRY FEE: $10 per entry. Only video cassettes returned.

DEADLINES: Entry, March. Awards given, April.

| 314 |

Fashion Journalism "Lulu" Awards
Men's Fashion Association of America (MFA)
Norman Karr, Executive Director
1290 Avenue of the Americas
New York, New York 10019 U.S.A.
Tel: (212) 581-8210

January-February

National; **entry open to U.S.;** annual; established 1960. Purpose: to award excellence in coverage of men's and boys' fashions. Sponsored by MFA, Menswear Retailers of America. Held during 4-day MFA Spring-Summer Press Preview.

VIDEOTAPE CONTEST: **Men's and Boys' Fashion Television Broadcast** (3/4-inch cassette). Categories:

Local (up to 500,000 homes; over 500,-000); Network, Nationally Syndicated.

FILM CONTEST: Men's and Boys' Fashion Television Broadcast (16mm). Categories same as for video.

AUDIOTAPE CONTEST: Men's and Boys' Fashion Radio Broadcast (reel) 1 minute minimum, 5 minutes maximum. Categories: Local (up to 250,000 homes; 250,000-500,000; over 500,000). No paid syndicated services.

ELIGIBILITY: Editorial (nonadvertising) aired during previous calendar year.

AWARDS: Lulu and Runner-Up Awards for outstanding coverage of men's and boys' fashion, each category.

JUDGING: By panels of professionals, based on creativity, interest value, listener-viewer service.

ENTRY FEE: None.

DEADLINES: Entry, December. Event, January-February. Materials returned, April.

| 315 |

George Polk Awards in Journalism
Long Island University
Sidney Offit, Curator
The Brooklyn Center
University Plaza
Brooklyn, New York 11201 U.S.A.
Tel: (212) 834-6170

March

International; entry open to all; annual; established 1949. Formerly called GEORGE POLK MEMORIAL AWARDS. Purpose: to recognize distinguished reporting, writing, editing, photography, production, in newspaper, magazine, book, radio and TV lo-

cal, national, foreign coverage, community service, criticism. Sponsored by Long Island University, Department of Journalism. Average statistics: 200 entrants, 20 awards.

VIDEOTAPE CONTEST: Journalism, Documentary Television (3/4-inch cassette) 2 copies, with cover letter explaining, justifying entry. Include corresponding manuscripts.

FILM CONTEST: Journalism, Documentary Television (16mm). Requirements same as for Video.

AUDIOTAPE CONTEST: Journalism Radio, 2 copies, with cover letter explaining, justifying entry. Include corresponding manuscripts.

AWARDS: George Polk Awards for Outstanding Achievement in Journalism.

JUDGING: By journalism faculty of Long Island University, based on initiative, coverage, perception, style, courage, resourcefulness, skill. No entries returned.

ENTRY FEE: None.

DEADLINES: Entry, January. Winners announced, February. Awards, March.

| 316 |

Headliner Achievement Awards in Journalism
Press Club of Atlantic City
Herb Brown, Director
Devins Lane
Pleasantville, New Jersey 08232
U.S.A. Tel: (609) 645-1234

Spring

International; **entry restricted to journalists;** annual; established 1934. Purpose: to recognize men and women who uphold responsibilities, traditions of journalism profession. Sponsored by Press Club of Atlantic City (membership in Headliners Club limited to Headliner winners, consultants, judges). Statistics: over 1000 awards to date. Held during 3-day National Headliners weekend in Atlantic City.

VIDEOTAPE CONTEST: Journalism Television Broadcast (3/4-inch U-matic cassette or kinescope). Require biography, photo, printed resume of entry. TV station categories: TV Reporting (Cities Over 500,-000 Population, Under 500,000), Public Service, Documentary. TV network categories: TV Reporting, Public Service, Documentary.

FILM CONTEST: Journalism Television Broadcast (16mm). Requirements, Categories same as for Videotape.

AUDIOTAPE CONTEST: Journalism Radio Broadcast (7-1/2 ips, fulltrack, separate reel; campaign may be same reel, 7-inch only). Requirements same as for Videotape. Radio station categories: Radio Reporting (Cities Over 250,000 Population, Under 250,-000), Public Service, Documentary. Radio network categories: Public Service, Documentary.

ELIGIBILITY: Published, broadcast during previous 2 calendar years. Any number of entries, one per category only. Public Service, Investigative Reporting entries require background, accomplishments, results. Entries become property of Headliners Club.

AWARDS: Headliner Medallions for Outstanding Achievements in Journalism. Winners are guest at National Headliners Club.

ENTRY FEE: $10 per entry.

DEADLINES: Entry, February. Awards, Spring.

| 317 |

Lowell Mellett Award for Improving Journalism Through Critical Evaluation
Mellett Fund for a Free and Responsible Press
Ellis T. Baker
Suite 835
1125 15th Street N.W.
Washington, District of Columbia
20005 U.S.A. Tel: (202) 296-2990

Spring

International; **entry restricted to U.S., Canada;** annual; established 1979. Named after Lowell Mellett, distinguished Scripps-Howard editor, syndicated Washington columnist. Purpose: to improve journalism through critical evaluation without impairing press freedom. Sponsored by Mellett Fund for a Free and Responsible Press. Supported by Philip L. Graham Fund. Recognized by The Newspaper Guild. Average statistics: 42 entries. Held in Washington, D.C.

VIDEOTAPE AWARD: Journalism Improvement Television Broadcast (width not specified) final scripts, summaries in triplicate. Include description letter, other documentation.

AUDIOTAPE AWARD: Journalism Improvement Radio Broadcast (width not specified) requirements same as for Videotape.

AWARDS: Mellett Citation and (or) Plaque for Outstanding Work of media monitoring, press performance evaluation; significant contributions, current or cumulative.

JUDGING: By 3-member panel of prominent, respected journalists. Not responsible for loss or damage.

ENTRY FEE: None. Sponsor pays return postage.

DEADLINES: Entry, March. Event, Spring.

318

National Press Club Consumer Journalism Awards
Rick Gordon, Vice Chairman
National Press Building
Washington, District of Columbia
20045 U.S.A. Tel: (202) 638-5300
September-October

National; **entry restricted to U.S. professional journalists;** annual; established 1973. Purpose: to recognize outstanding journalism on consumer topics. Sponsored by National Press Foundation (nonprofit, tax-exempt). Supported by National Press Club. Average statistics: 150 entries, 6 winners. Held in Washington D.C. Have scholarships. Also sponsor EDWIN M. HOOD AWARD FOR DIPLOMATIC CORRESPONDENTS, WASHINGTON CORRESPONDENT AWARDS.

VIDEOTAPE CONTEST: Consumer Journalism Television Broadcast (width not specified). Single entry or feature, broadcast in previous year. Require description letter, resources outline (including evidence of impact). Categories: TV Networks, Syndicates, Stations (top 25 markets; 26 and below markets).

AUDIOTAPE CONTEST: Consumer Journalism Radio Broadcast (width not specified). Requirements same as for Videotape. Categories: Radio Networks, Syndicates, Stations (top 25 markets; 26 and below markets).

ELGIBILITY: Professional journalists who receive no less than 50% of earned income from journalistic activity.

AWARDS: $1000 Best in Consumer Journalism. First Place Certificates in Media categories. Merit Certificates at judges' discretion.

JUDGING: By panels designated by Awards Committee. Not responsible for loss or damage.

ENTRY FEE: None. Entrant pays postage.

DEADLINES: Entry, May. Awards given, September-October.

319

National Press Club Edwin M. Hood Award for Diplomatic Correspondents
Rick Gordon, Vice Chairman
National Press Building
Washington, District of Columbia
20045 U.S.A. Tel: (202) 638-5300
March

National; **entry restricted to U.S. diplomatic news correspondents;** annual; established 1980. Named after Edwin M. Hood, distinguished diplomatic correspondent. Purpose: to recognize excellence in reporting on American foreign policy, related issues. Sponsored by National Press Foundation (nonprofit, tax-exempt). Held in Washington D.C. Also sponsor CONSUMER JOURNALISM AWARDS, WASHINGTON CORRESPONDENT AWARDS.

VIDEOTAPE CONTEST: Diplomatic correspondent Journalism Television Broadcast (width not specified). Single entry or feature; broadcast previous year. Require letter of works' merit, English translation. Categories: Foreign, American Broadcasting.

AUDIOTAPE CONTEST: Diplomatic Correspondent Journalism Radio Broadcast (width not specified).

Requirements, categories same as for Videotape.

AWARDS: $1000 each Best Reporting Broadcast to Foreign Audiences, American Audiences.

JUDGING: By panel; based on awareness, clarity, insight achieved.

ENTRY FEE: None. Entrant pays postage.

DEADLINES: Entry, March.

| 320 |

National Press Club Washington Correspondent Awards
Rick Gordon, Vice Chairman
National Press Building
Washington, District of Columbia
20045 U.S.A. Tel: (202) 638-5300

March

National; **entry restricted to Washington News Correspondents;** annual; established 1979. Purpose: to encourage excellence in reporting on events in Washington affecting a community or region. Sponsored by National Press Foundation (nonprofit, tax-exempt). Held in Washington D.C. Also sponsor CONSUMER JOURNALISM AWARDS, EDWIN M. HOOD AWARD FOR DIPLOMATIC CORRESPONDENTS.

VIDEOTAPE CONTEST: **Washington Correspondent Journalism Television Broadcast** (width not specified). Single entry or feature. Require descriptive letter of work's merit. Categories: Congressional, Justice (including courts, Department of Justice, FBI, issues of law), Executive Branch (including departments, agencies, White House), Commentary.

AUDIOTAPE CONTEST: **Washington Correspondent Journalism Radio Broadcast** (width not speci-

fied). Requirements, categories same as for Videotape.

ELIGIBILITY: Normally, accredited resident Washington correspondents.

AWARDS: $100 Best Each Category. Additional $100 Best Overall Entry.

ENTRY FEE: None.

DEADLINES: Entry, Event, March.

| 321 |

National Press Photographers Association (NPPA) Television News Photography Competition
Sheila Keyes, Chairperson
23918 Via Copeta
Valencia, California 91355 U.S.A.
Tel: (805) 259-1136

July

National; **entry restricted to U.S. television news camerapersons;** annual; established 1946. Purpose: to recognize outstanding contribution to photojournalism. Sponsored by 7000-member NPPA (organized to represent, advance art, ensure legal rights of photojournalists), Eastman Kodak Company, Cinema Products Corporation. Average statistics: 690 entries, 340 entrants. Held at NPPA Business and Education Seminar. Have critique service. Also sponsor print PICTURES OF THE YEAR COMPETITIONS in Columbia, Missouri; membership QUARTERLY TV COMPETITIONS. Second contact: NPPA, Arizona State University, Department of Journalism and Telecommunications, Tempe, Arizona 85281.

VIDEOTAPE CONTEST: **News Journalism Television Broadcast** (3/4-inch cassette) maximum 2 per entrant per category. Categories: Spot News (5 minutes maximum), General News (5 minutes), Sports (5 minutes),

Feature (8 minutes), Minidocumentary (30 minutes), Documentary (60 minutes). For TV News Photographer of the Year (who best exemplifies skill, professionalism, talent, ability, honesty) one representative example in any 4 categories (except documentary), 30 minutes total maximum, complete newscast with commercials deleted; content list, biography required. For TV News Photography Station of the Year (which best uses news photography in local community coverage) 30 minutes maximum, complete newscast with commercials deleted; content list required.

FILM CONTEST: News Journalism Television Broadcast (16mm) silent, optical, magnetic, 2 maximum per entrant per category. Categories same as for Videotape.

ELIGIBILITY: First broadcast, January-December previous year by television news cameraperson.

AWARDS: Kodak Ernie Crisp Award (TV Photographer of the Year). Kodak NPPA Award (Television Photography Station of the Year). Plaques to first 3 winners. Lighting Kit, First Place, in Minidocumentary. Editing Awards to entries showing outstanding editing qualities.

JUDGING: By 6 broadcast industry specialists, based on individual merit. All entries viewed in entirety. Not responsible for loss, damage, non-receipt.

ENTRY FEE: NPPA members, free; others, $25. Entrant pays return postage.

DEADLINES: Entry, January. Event, July.

322

Overseas Press Club Awards
Overseas Press Club of America
Norman A. Schorr, Chairman
52 East 41st Street
New York, New York 10017 U.S.A.
Tel: (212) 679-9650

April

International; entry open to all; annual; established 1941. Purpose: to recognize outstanding journalism by newspeople who report overseas developments to American audiences. Sponsored by Overseas Press Club of America. Held at Biltmore Hotel Awards Dinner, New York City.

VIDEOTAPE CONTEST: International Journalism Television Broadcast (gauge not specified) broadcast in U.S. in previous calendar year. Require 3 copies 200-word biography, 3 nominee photos, contents description. Categories: TV Spot News from Abroad, Foreign Affairs Interpretation or Documentary, Business News from Abroad, International Humanity Reporting, Human Rights Editorial or Editorial Series from Abroad.

FILM CONTEST: International Journalism Television Broadcast (gauges not specified). Requirements and categories same as for Videotape.

AUDIOTAPE CONTEST: International Journalism Radio Broadcast (widths not specified). Requirements same as for Videotape. Categories: Radio Spot News from Foreign News Interpretation, Business News from Abroad, International Humanity Reporting, Human Rights Editorial or Editorial Series from Abroad.

AWARDS: Illuminated Scrolls for outstanding accomplishment in world journalism, each category. Humanity Reporting, $400.

JUDGING: By panel of newspeople.

ENTRY FEE: $20 per entry.

DEADLINES: Entry, February. Awards, April.

| 323 |

Radio-Television News Directors Association (RTNDA) International Awards Competition
Len Allen, Managing Director
1735 DeSales Street N.W.
Washington, District of Columbia
20036 U.S.A. Tel: (202) 737-8657

Fall

International; **entry restricted to U.S., Canadian Professionals**; annual; established 1946. Sponsored by RTNDA (Rob Downey, Executive Secretary, WKAR, Michigan State University, East Lansing, Michigan 48824), formerly called National Association of Radio News Directors (NARND). Publish *RTNDA Communicator*.

VIDEOTAPE CONTEST: News Television Broadcast (3/4-inch cassette) 1 maximum per station per category; U.S. and Canadian TV station programs broadcast during previous calendar year. Categories: Spot News Coverage, Continuing Coverage of Running Story, Investigative Reporting, Overall Performance by Broadcast News Organization.

FILM CONTEST: News Television Broadcast (16mm). Requirements, categories same as for Videotape.

AUDIOTAPE CONTEST: News Radio Broadcast (1/2-inch tape) 1 maximum per station per category; U.S. and Canadian Radio station programs broadcast during previous calendar year; typewritten presentation

optional. Categories same as for Videotape.

AWARDS: Edward R. Murrow Award. Regional and International Awards, each category.

JUDGING: Regional Competition in 5 U.S., Canadian regions. Winners go to International Competition. Murrow Award based on courage, enterprise, social awareness in documentation.

ENTRY FEE: $20 per entry.

DEADLINES: Entries, March. Awards, Fall.

BROADCASTING SCHOLARSHIP: Broadcast Journalism Television or Radio. Five $1000 undergraduate scholarships, one $1000 graduate scholarship, one $1000 to minority personnel for study of broadcast journalism. Must be nominated by professor or department head. Entries by March.

| 324 |

Sigma Delta Chi Distinguished Service Journalism Awards
Society of Professional Journalists
Kathy Lieberman, Information Director
35 East Wacker Drive, Suite 3108
Chicago, Illinois 60601 U.S.A.
Tel: (312) 236-6577

April-May

International; entry open to all; annual; established 1932. Purpose: to foster high ethics; safeguard flow of information; attract young people to journalism; raise prestige of journalists in community. Sponsored by Society of Professional journalists (Sigma Delta Chi), international nonprofit voluntary professional journalist society with 154 campus, 130 professional chapters; founded 1909 as fraternity at Depauw University, Greencastle, Indiana. Average Statistics: 1200 entries, 16 winners, 1000 attendance. Publish *The Quill,* monthly magazine.

VIDEOTAPE CONTEST: Journalism Television Broadcast (cassette or tape) produced in previous calendar year. Require typewritten summary, biography, photograph if nomination is for individual. Categories: Reporting, Public Service, Editorial. Submit script, statement of results for editorial.

FILM CONTEST: Journalism Television Broadcast (16mm) produced in previous calendar year. Requirements, categories same as for Videotape.

AUDIOTAPE CONTEST: Journalism Radio Broadcast (cassette or tape). Requirements, categories same as for Videotape.

AWARDS: Bronze Medallions, Plaques for Distinguished Service in Journalism.

JUDGING: All entries reviewed in entirety by journalist jury. May withhold awards. Entries become property of sponsor.

ENTRY FEE: $10 per entry for handling.

DEADLINES: Entry, January. Judging, February-March. Winners announced, April. Event, April-May.

RELIGIOUS, HUMANITARIAN, PUBLIC SERVICE

TV-Radio Broadcasting (video, film, audio) and Film including BROTHERHOOD, CHRISTIAN, CURRENT ISSUE, DISADVANTAGED, HUMAN RIGHTS

and VALUES. (Also see BROADCASTING, DOCUMENTARY, EDUCATIONAL, JOURNALISM.)

| **325** |

American Jewish Committee Mass Media Awards
Institute of Human Relations
Jonathan Schenker, Director
Radio-Television
165 East 56th Street
New York, New York 10022 U.S.A.

Various

National; **entry restricted** (selection by members); periodic. Occasional **Awards to Individuals in Television, Radio** for integrity, commitment to democratic free expression. Sponsored by Institute of Human Relations, American Jewish Committee.

| **326** |

Christopher Awards
The Christophers
Peggy Flanagan, Coordinator
12 East 48th Street
New York, New York 10017 U.S.A.
Tel: (212) 759-4050

January

International; **entry restricted** (invitation by sponsor); annual; established 1949. Christopher Bronze Medallions for **Human Value Television Network Specials, Films.** Purpose: to encourage individuals to use God-given talents to make world a better place for all. Motto: "Better to light one candle than to curse the darkness." Sponsored by The Christophers. Average statistics: 16 television awards. Held in New York City. Event, January.

327

Clarion Competition
Women in Communications, Inc.
(WICI)
Mary E. Utting, Executive Director
P.O. Box 9561
7719 Wood Hollow
Austin, Texas 78766 U.S.A.
Tel: (512) 345-8922

October

International; entry open to all; annual; established 1973. Named after Clarion, medieval trumpet noted for tonal clarity. Purpose: to recognize excellence in all areas of communications; provide incentive for achievement; demonstrate role of communications in current issues. Sponsored and supported by WICI. Average statistics: 680 entries. Also have public relations category, and sponsor VANGUARD AWARD.

VIDEOTAPE CONTEST: Current Issue Television Broadcast (3/4-inch cassette) script or outline, synopsis, at least two-thirds broadcast in previous year. Dramatizations not eligible. Divisions: Human Rights, World We Live In, Community We Serve. Categories: Documentary Program, Documentary Series.

AUDIOTAPE CONTEST: Current Issue Radio Broadcast (1/4-inch cassette). Requirements, divisions, categories same as for Videotape.

AWARDS: Clarion Award Plaques and Honorable Mentions each category, each division. Judges may withhold, duplicate awards.

JUDGING: By national communications professionals. Based on excellence, creativity, believability, effectiveness, thoroughness, depth of research, use of innovative techniques, achievement of stated objectives. May recategorize or disqualify entries. All entries except audiovisual become WICI property.

ENTRY FEE: $50 WICI nonmembers; $25 members.

DEADLINES: Entry, February. Winners announced, July. Awards, October.

328

Gabriel Awards for Excellence in Broadcasting
UNDA-USA (National Association of Catholic Broadcasters and Allied Communicators)
Charles J. Schisla, Chairman
136 West Georgia Street
Indianapolis, Indiana 46225 U.S.A.
Tel: (317) 635-3586

November

International; entry open to all U.S., Canada; annual; established 1965 by Catholic Broadcasters Association of North America. Taken over by UNDA-USA in 1972. Named after Archangel Gabriel, patron saint of communications. Purpose: to acknowledge broadcast works which creatively treat issues concerning human values. Sponsored by UNDA-USA, professional Catholic association for broadcasters and allied communicators. Average statistics: 570 entries, 400 entrants, 2 countries, 65 finalists, 29 award winners, 400 attendance. Held in various U.S. cities. Tickets: $25.

VIDEOTAPE CONTEST: Human Values Television Broadcast (3/4-inch cassette, 525-line U.S. system), any length (120-second maximum, spot entries). Initial broadcast July previous year to June current year. Include English Synopsis, production talent credits, script for non-English entries. Composite tape representative schedule for one week programming for station category, written summary for series. Categories: Entertainment, Informational, Educational, Religion, Youth Oriented (TV, National Release, Local Release Market 1-25, 26-100, 101-212), TV Station, Personal Achievement.

AUDIOTAPE CONTEST: Human Values Radio Broadcast (7-1/2 ips reel-to-reel). Same as for Video.

AWARDS: Gabriel Award. Merit Certificate each category and class at judges' discretion.

JUDGING: Preliminary by jury; final by 7-member Blue Ribbon Jury, based on creative treatment of issues, artistic, informational, educational, technical qualities. May withhold awards. Right to use segments of award entries in closed showing. Not responsible for loss or damage.

ENTRY FEE: Videotape $60; audiotape $35. Sponsor pays return postage. No fee for personal achievement category.

DEADLINES: Entry, September. Winners announced, October. Awards given, materials returned November.

| 329 |

Merit Awards for Religious Communication
Religious Public Relations Council (RPRC)
Arvin C. Wilbur, Executive Secretary
Room 1031
475 Riverside Drive
New York, New York 10115 U.S.A.
Tel: (212) 870-2013

April

International; entry open to all; annual; established 1929 (print media), 1959 (broadcasting). Purpose: to establish, raise, maintain high standards of religious public relations-com-

munications. Sponsored by RPRC. Statistics: 188 awards to date, 55 in broadcasting. Held at RPRC annual conventions. Also sponsor membership-only HINKHOUSE-DEROSE AWARDS.

VIDEOTAPE CONTEST: Religious Journalism Television (cassettes). Work in previous calendar year by secular journalists, radio-TV. Not open to RPRC members. Category: Television.

AUDIOTAPE CONTEST: Religious Journalism Radio (cassettes). Restrictions same as for Videotape. Category: Radio.

AWARDS: RPRC Merit Awards for outstanding communication in religion.

JUDGING: By 18 judges based on excellence, consistency, creativity.

ENTRY FEE: None.

DEADLINES: Entry, January. Exhibits, February. Winners announced, March.

| 330 |

National Mass Media Brotherhood Awards
National Conference of Christians and Jews
Harry A. Robinson, Vice President
43 West 57th Street
New York, New York 10019 U.S.A.
Tel: (212) 688-7530

Various

National; **entry open to U.S.;** various throughout year. Purpose: to foster brotherhood and better understanding among people; pay tribute to outstanding creative work on behalf of brotherhood in mass communications. Sponsored by National Conference of Christians and Jews (Robert M. Jones, Executive Director, 3460

Wilshire Boulevard, Suite 1012, Los Angeles, California 90010).

AUDIOTAPE AWARD: Brotherhood Radio Shows, includes network and local broadcasts. Categories: Documentary, Editorial, Drama, Interview Shows.

AWARDS: Gold Medallion and Recognition Certificates.

JUDGING: Executive Director reviews entries, submits finalists to New York committee, based on mass impact, originality, creativity, integrity.

ENTRY FEE: None.

DEADLINES: Open.

| 331 |

Robert F. Kennedy Journalism Awards
Coates Redmon, Executive Director
4014 49th Street N.W.
Washington, District of Columbia
20016 U.S.A. Tel: (202) 362-0515

June

National; **entry open to U.S.;** annual; established 1968 by journalists covering Robert F. Kennedy's presidential campaign. Purpose: to encourage, recognize outstanding reporting on problems of disadvantaged in U.S. Sponsored by RFK Journalism Awards Committee (Paul Duke, Chairman). Average statistics: 740 entries. Also sponsor ROBERT F. KENNEDY BOOK AWARDS.

VIDEOTAPE CONTEST: Disadvantaged Television Broadcast, single or series, 1 copy tape, 3 copies full transcript (students, 2 copies). Categories: Professional, Student.

FILM CONTEST: Disadvantaged Television Broadcast. Requirements, categories same as for Videotape.

AUDIOTAPE CONTEST: Disadvantaged Radio Broadcast. Requirements, categories same as for Videotape.

ELIGIBILITY: Accounts of lifestyles, handicaps, potential of disadvantaged in U.S.; insights into causes, conditions, remedies; analysis of public policies, programs, attitudes, private endeavors. Broadcast in U.S. first time during previous calendar year. Students eligible in all categories.

AWARDS: $1000 First Prize, each category. $2000 Grand Prize. 9 Honorable Mentions, 8 Citations.

JUDGING: By 24 judges. Materials returned on request.

ENTRY FEE: None.

DEADLINES: Entry, February. Awards, June.

| 332 |

Roy W. Howard Public Service Broadcasting Awards
Scripps-Howard Foundation
Station WEWS
3001 Euclid Avenue
Cleveland, Ohio 44115 U.S.A.

spring

National; **entry open to U.S.;** annual. Sponsored by Scripps-Howard Foundation, founded 1962 as charitable nonprofit corporation. Also sponsor SCRIPPS-HOWARD FOUNDATION SCHOLARSHIPS AND GRANTS, Robert Scripps Graphic Arts Grants, Ernie Pyle Memorial Awards, awards for conservation, Editorial Writing, First Amendment Awards.

VIDEO AWARD: Public Service Television Broadcasting. Require letter from station manager and history of endeaver.

AUDIO AWARD: Public Service Radio Broadcasting. Requirements same as for Video.

AWARDS: Roy W. Howard Public Service Awards, 1 Bronze Plaque to Television, Radio Station. $2500 to individual or individuals contributing most to public service. $1000 to television, $1000 to radio station.

JUDGING: Based on public service, defined as exposure of, contribution to alleviation of corruption, crime, health, other problems inimical to general welfare.

ENTRY FEE: None.

DEADLINES: Entry, February.

333

UNDA-WACC International Christian Television Week
Catholic Association for Radio and Televsion (UNDA)
Jacques Dessaucy, Assistant Secretary General
12 rue de l'Orme
1040 Brussels, BELGIUM Tel: (32) 2-734-6361

May

International; **entry restricted** (selection by official broadcasting organizations in each country); Biennial; established 1969. Awards to **Christian Television Videotapes** (Sony U-matic 625-line PAL, Philips VCR N 1500, 1700 625-line PAL Type C); 60 minutes maximum per organization (90 minutes maximum if single program); produced in previous 2 years. Purpose: to show TV dealing with man and God. Sponsored by UNDA, World Association for Christian Communication (WACC). Average statistics: 45 entries, 25 countries. Held in various European cities. Also sponsor attendance scholarships. Event, May.

RESIDENCE GRANTS, LOANS
Video, Audio Production and Postproduction-Editing, and TV-Radio Broadcasting, including DANCE, JOURNALISM, SCIENCE. (Also see GRANTS, INTERN-TRAINING-APPRENTICE PROGRAMS, SCHOLARSHIPS-FELLOWSHIPS.)

334

American Dance Festival Dance Critics' Conference Fellowships
Lisa Booth, Administrative Director
P.O. Box 6097, College Station
Durham, North Carolina 27708
U.S.A. Tel: (919) 684-6402

June-July

National; **entry restricted to U.S. Professional working journalists;** annual; established 1970. Purpose: to stimulate interest, expand knowledge, develop skills in technique of dance criticism. Sponsored by American Dance Festival. Supported by NEA. Average statistics: 10 awards. Held in Durham, North Carolina for 3 weeks. Have workshops, discussions, scholarhips. Also sponsor VIDEO APPRENTICESHIPS; school for 250 dance students providing intensive dance training. Second contact: Judith Tolkow, ADF, 1860 Broadway, Room 1112, New York, New York 10023; tel: (212) 586-1925.

BROADCAST RESIDENCE FELLOWSHIP: Dance Journalism, Radio, 10 fellowships, for 3-week workshop to professional working journalists. Includes transportation, room, board, attending dance performances on ADF program. Require explanatory letter, 2 samples broadcast criticism (preferably on dance), two references.

JUDGING: Review and selection by director.

ENTRY FEE: None. Entrant pays postage.

DEADLINES: Entry, April-May. Acceptance, May-June. Event, June-July.

335

Artist In Residence Program (AIR)
ZBS Foundation
Gregory Shifrin, Director
R.D. No. 1
Fort Edward, New York 12828
U.S.A. Tel: (518) 695-6406

December-August

National; **entry open to all U.S.;** annual; established 1974. Purpose: to encourage audio production and experimentation with technical facilities to develop potential of audio art. Sponsored and supported by New York State Council on the Arts, NEA, ZBS Foundation. Held at 45-acre farm near Saratoga Springs, New York.

AUDIO RESIDENCE GRANT: **Audio, Radio, Sound Production.** 20 artists spend 2-5 days in audio experimentation or sound development for mixed media project. Includes travel expenses, room, board, 24-hour access to studio, audiotape, fully equipped 8-track facility, 12-input mixdown capabilities, sound effects library, portable field equipment, engineer and production staff assistance; additional equipment on request. Require written project proposal, number of days requested, sample of work. Audio production experience not required.

JUDGING: By panel of producers and engineers, based on merit, suit-ability for facilities offered. All proposals judged in entirety.

DEADLINES: Proposals, November. Residence, December-August

336

Artists Videotape Resource Editing and Post-Production Facility Loan Program
Electronic Arts Intermix
Alan Klein, Distribution
84 Fifth Avenue
New York, New York 10011 U.S.A.

Continuous

International; entry open to all; continuous; established 1978. Purpose: to help educational institutions expose students to creative personalities and video work. Sponsored by Electronic Arts Intermix, nonprofit corporation assisting artists in personal expression, communication through electronic media, television. Supported by NEA, NYSCA, Rockefeller Foundation. Also distribute videotapes to art schools, museums, universities, educational-cultural institutions. Publish videotape catalog.

VIDEO EDITING FACILITY LOAN: **Independent Video.** Free use of editing and post-production facility to qualified video artists for production of aesthetic high technical quality mastertapes.

ENTRY FEE: None.

DEADLINES: Open.

337

Boston Film-Video Foundation Equipment and Facilities Loans
Tom Wylie, Director
1126 Boylston Street
Boston, Massachusetts 02215 U.S.A.
Tel: (617) 536-1540

August-June

International; entry open to all; continuous; established 1975. Formerly called BOSTON VIDEO-FILMMAKERS COLLECTIVE. Purpose: to provide resource center to promote production, exhibition of high-quality work. Sponsored by 400-member Boston Film-Video Foundation, local arts institutions. Supported by NEA, WGBH (public TV), membership fees. Publish *Visions* newsletter. Also sponsor information services, exhibitions, workshops, internships.

VIDEOTAPE EQUIPMENT-FACILITIES LOAN: Videotape Production, Post-Production (called *Work Volunteer Program*). Openings limited; need background in video, some skill to benefit Foundation. Six-hour volunteer work week; $15 membership. Also have INTERNSHIP-WORKSTUDY PROGRAM, limited openings to college-university students; EQUIPMENT and FACILITIES ACCESS PROGRAMS for fees for inexpensive rental and use of video equipment, facilities. Available: 3/4-inch production, post-production, color and B&W; screening facilities.

AUDIOTAPE EQUIPMENT-FACILITIES LOAN: Audiotape Production, Post-Production (called *Work Volunteer Program*). Requirements same as for Videotape. Available: 1/4-inch stereo, 4-track, 1/2-track, full-track (mono).

DEADLINES: None.

338

Cummington Community of the Arts Artist in Residence Scholarships
Molly Snyder, Director
Potash Hill Road
Cummington, Massachusetts 01026
U.S.A. Tel: (413) 634-2172

Continuous

International; entry open to all; continuous; established 1923. Purpose: to stimulate individual artistic growth, development while providing atmosphere for communication, interdisciplinary cooperation. Sponsored and supported by Cummington Community of the Arts, formerly called Cummington School of the Arts, 150-acre educational community of filmmakers, photographers, writers, musicians, painters, sculptors, other artists, in Massachusetts Berkshires. Supported by NEA; Massachusetts Council for the Arts. Average statistics: 10-30 artists. Have library, darkrooms, kiln, studios, individual living accommodations, kitchen, dining hall, garden. Tuition: $275 per month, includes room, board, studio space. Publish *Cummington Journal.* Also sponsor workshops, readings, shows at local galleries.

VIDEO RESIDENCE SCHOLARSHIP: Videomaking, several partial tuition abatements per month, based on financial need. Require work samples, resume, work plan, complete financial statement (including past 2 years' income, tax forms, savings, holdings, projected income, expenses), interview.

JUDGING: By Admission Committee, on basis of work, interview. All entries reviewed in entirety.

ENTRY FEE: None.

DEADLINES: Applications, 2 months before desired residency.

339

Edward R. Murrow Fellowship for American Foreign Correspondents
Council on Foreign Relations (CFR)
Margaret Osmer, Secretary
58 East 68th Street

New York, New York 10021 U.S.A.

Tel: (212) 734-0400

September-June

National; **entry open to U.S. foreign correspondents;** annual; established 1949. Named after Edward R. Murrow, foreign correspondent. Purpose: to promote quality foreign events journalism that characterized career of Edward R. Murrow. Sponsored by CFR, nonprofit 1700-member organization for international relations study, research, meetings, publishing. Supported by CBS Foundation. Publish *Foreign Affairs,* quarterly journal.

BROADCASTING-RESIDENCE FELLOWSHIP: **Foreign Affairs Journalism Television, Radio,** stipend equal to salary, for office space and 9-month study-analysis-writing-research of international relations at CFR Harold Pratt House headquarters in New York City, and at a university, by U.S. citizen, television or radio correspondents-editors-producers serving abroad, or recently served and planning to return. Prefer under age 40. Require detailed study-writing plan, leave-of-absence grant from employer, 5 journalism examples, 8x10-inch glossy photo, 5 references, biographical essay.

JUDGING: By 7 judges, based on performance, experience, education, program proposal, achievement prospects.

ENTRY FEE: None.

DEADLINES: Entry, March. Selection, June. Fellowship, September for academic year.

| 340 |

Fulbright Awards for University Teaching and Advanced Research Abroad

Council for International Exchange of Scholars (CIES)
Suite 300
Eleven Dupont Circle
Washington, District of Columbia
20036 U.S.A. Tel: (202) 833-4950

Spring

National; **entry open to U.S.;** annual; established 1946 by legislation authorizing use of foreign currencies accruing to U.S. abroad for educational exchanges (1961 *Fulbright-Hays Mutual Educational and Cultural Exchange Act* authorizes congressional appropriations for these exchanges). Named after Senator J. William Fulbright. Purpose: to increase mutual understanding between U.S. and other nations through foreign study. Sponsored by CIES, U.S. International Communications Agency (USICA). Supported by annual appropriations from U.S. Congress, other governments. Average statistics: 2500 entrants, 1000 semifinalists, 500 awards. Have other grants for teacher-scholar exchanges, research abroad. Also sponsor FULBRIGHT-HAYS GRANTS.

VIDEO-AUDIO RESIDENCE GRANT: **University Teaching, Advanced Research,** stipend, round-trip transportation, other allowances for 1 academic year or less of university teaching and (or) postdoctoral research abroad.

ELIGIBILITY: U.S. citizens, scholars, creative artists, professionals. Require host-country language proficiency if needed; university teaching experience; doctorate, if specified by host country (for teaching); doctorate or recognized professional standing (for research); project presentation, other documentation.

JUDGING: 50 discipline, area committees, Binational Commissions, assist CIES in preparing nominations to Fulbright agencies abroad and U.S. Board of Foreign Scholarship. All entries reviewed.

DEADLINES: Application, June (American Republics, Australia, New Zealand), July (Africa, Asia, Europe). Judging, September-December. Notification, January-April. Awards given 12-18 months following notification.

| 341 |

Fulbright-Hays Grants
Institute of International Education (IIE)
Theresa Granza, Manager
809 United Nations Plaza
New York, New York 10017 U.S.A.
Tel: (212) 883-8265

Spring

National; **entry open to U.S.;** annual; established 1946 by legislation authorizing use of foreign currencies accruing to U.S. abroad for educational exchanges (1961 *Fulbright-Hays Mutual Educational and Cultural Exchange Act* authorizes congressional appropriations for these exchanges). Named after Senator J. William Fulbright. Purpose: to increase mutual understanding between U.S. and other nations through foreign study. Sponsored by IIE, founded to promote peace, understanding through educational, cultural exchanges in all academic fields; U.S. International Communication Agency (USICA). Supported by annual appropriations from U.S. Congress, other governments. Average statistics: 3000 entrants. Have grants to visiting scholars, American scholars-professionals, predoctoral fellowships,

teacher exchanges, Hubert H. Humphrey North-South Fellowship Program (study-internships), Faculty Research Abroad Program, Doctoral Dissertation Research Abroad Program, Group Projects Abroad. Fulbright-Hays booklets available from USICA, 1776 Pennsylvania Avenue N.W., Washington, D.C. 20547. Also sponsor FULBRIGHT AWARDS FOR UNIVERSITY TEACHING AND ADVANCED RESEARCH ABROAD.

VIDEO-AUDIO RESIDENCE GRANT: Creative Arts Foreign Study, round-trip transportation, language and orientation course, tuition, books, health-accident insurance, single-person maintenance for 6-12 months study in 1 foreign country (doctoral candidates may receive higher stipends).

ELIGIBILITY: U.S. citizens with majority of high school, college education in U.S., B.A. or equivalent (or 4 years professional experience, study in proposed creative art field). Require host-country language proficiency, certificate of good health, study plan, project proposal, reasons for choosing particular country, statement of contribution of foreign experience to professional development, work samples, possible interview.

JUDGING: Professional juries, Binational Commissions in fields of expertise prepare nominations to Fulbright agencies abroad, U.S. Board of Foreign Scholarship.

DEADLINES: Application, November. Judging, November-December. Preliminary notification, January. Awards, April-June.

342

Helene Wurlitzer Foundation of New Mexico Residencies

Henry A. Sauerwein, Jr., Executive Director
P.O. Box 545
Taos, New Mexico 87571 U.S.A.
Tel: (505) 758-2413

Continuous

International; entry open to all; continuous. Sponsored by Helene Wurlitzer Foundation of New Mexico. Have 12 studio apartments in Taos, New Mexico. Also accept painting, sculpture, choreography, allied fields.

VIDEO RESIDENCE GRANT: **Videomaking,** furnished studio apartment (including linen, utilities) for 3 months to 1 year. Residents purchase, cook, serve own meals, clean apartments. No families, transportation, living expenses, materials.

ENTRY FEE: $150 refundable damage deposit.

DEADLINES: Open.

343

Jefferson Fellowship Program

East-West Communication Institute (EWCI)
1777 East-West Road
Honolulu, Hawaii 96822 U.S.A.
Tel: (808) 944-7333

September-December

Regional; **entry restricted to Asian Pacific, U.S. journalists;** annual; established 1967. Coordinated by East-West Communication Institute since 1971. Named after U.S. President Thomas Jefferson. Purpose: to encourage exchange of professional experience, promote learning of international news operations, expand knowledge related to current year's theme (which varies yearly). Sponsored by EWCI, national education institution founded 1960 to promote relations, understanding among U.S., Asian, Pacific nations through study, training, research. Supported by U.S. Congress, Asian and Pacific governments. Average statistics: 40 countries, 8-10 awards. Held in Honolulu for 3 1/2 months. Have on-campus housing, office space. Also sponsor graduate educational, research grants to Senior Fellows, scholarships, internships, other awards.

BROADCASTING RESIDENCE FELLOWSHIP: **East-West Journalism Television, Radio,** 8-10 monthly stipends of $1500, round-trip fare to Honolulu.

ELIGIBILITY: Require resume, statement of reasons for interest in year's theme, study and intended projects proposal, letter of support from employer, 3 recommendation letters, 4 samples of professional work.

JUDGING: Final by East-West Center Selection Committee.

ENTRY FEE: None.

DEADLINES: Entry, May. Acceptance, June. Fellowships, January-May.

344

Nieman Fellowships for Journalists

Nieman Foundation for Journalism
Daphne B. Noyes, Program Officer
Walter Lippmann House
One Francis Avenue
Cambridge, Massachusetts 02138
U.S.A. Tel: (617) 495-2237

September-June

National; **entry open to U.S.;** annual; established 1938 by Agnes Wahl

Nieman, wife of Lucius W. Nieman, founder of *Milwaukee Journal* newspaper. Purpose: to promote, evaluate standards of journalism in U.S. by providing mid-career opportunity to TV and radio journalism broadcasters to study, broaden intellectual horizons. Sponsored by Nieman Foundation for Journalism. Supported by Ford Foundation, U.S. and Canadian newspapers, magazines. Average statistics: 150 entries, 40 finalists, 12 fellows. Held at Harvard University. Have non-U.S. citizen fellowships. Publish *Nieman Reports,* quarterly journal. Also sponsor LOUIS STARK MEMORIAL FUND (established 1961) to support labor reporting fellows; ROBERT WALDO RUHL FUND (established 1973) to support Associate Fellows from abroad. Occasional funding for other journalism fields.

BROADCASTING RESIDENCE FELLOWSHIP: Journalism Television, Radio. Approximately 12 fellowships (includes $300 weekly stipend, partially tax-exempt; tuition for classroom, library, faculty club costs; athletic, child care expenses) to full-time TV, radio journalists with at least 3 years professional experience in media, for 9-month nondegree academic study at Harvard University in any subject (including 1 complete required course, 2-4 audit courses per term, independent and supervised reading, independent research seminars, consultations, travel in New England and abroad). Require for TV, 1/2-inch videotape; for radio, reel or cassette tape, 30 minutes maximum, with transcript or synopsis, 2 1000-word essays (journalistic background, proposed study at Harvard), 4 recommendation letters, letter from immediate supervisor, agreement to return to former job, employer verification of leave of absence. Spouses may attend classes, libraries, seminars. No professional

broadcast during fellowship or formal credit for studies.

JUDGING: By 7-member selection committee, based on promise as contributors to craft. Finalist invited to Cambridge for interview.

ENTRY FEE: None.

DEADLINES: Entry, February. Judging, February-May. Winners announced, June. Fellowships, September-June.

345

Northwood Institute Creativity Fellowships
Alden B. Dow Creativity Center
Judith O'Dell, Director
3225 Cook Road
P.O. Box 1406
Midland, Michigan 48640 U.S.A.
Tel: (517) 631-1600, ext. 208

Summer

International; **entry restricted to English-speaking persons;** annual; established 1979. Named after Alden B. Dow, AIA. Purpose: to encourage creative thought; provide time, work facilities for creative persons to concentrate on ideas without financial worries; establish internationally recognized center for creativity technology. Sponsored by Northwood Institute, Alden B. Dow. Average statistics: 6 awards. Held at Northwood Institute, Midland, Michigan.

VIDEO RESIDENCE FELLOW-SHIP: **Creative Project,** for study, creation, innovation, appreciation. 3-month study at Northwood Institute; includes room, board, professional counsel. Considered applicants flown to personal interview. Applicants welcomed from all disciplines, areas of interest (e.g., Architecture, Science, Education, Food, Health Care, Literature, Performing or Visual Arts, Publishing). Require description of proposed project, resume, budget projection. College credit arranged upon request. Special certificates, recognition upon successful completion.

AUDIO RESIDENCE FELLOW-SHIP: Creative Project. Requirements same as for Video.

JUDGING: By Board of Directors, Advisory Panel, Northwood Institute Alden B. Dow Creativity Center. All entries viewed in entirety. Project ideas remain property of applicant. Not responsible for loss or damage.

ENTRY FEE: None. Entrant pays postage.

DEADLINES: Entry, December. Judging, December-March. Winners announced, April. Award, June-August.

346

Science for Citizens Program Grants
National Science Foundation (NSF)
G. Triml, Program Director
Science Education Directorate
1800 G Street N.W.
Washington, District of Columbia
20550 U.S.A.

Various

National; **entry restricted to U.S. organizations;** periodic. Purpose: to encourage scientists to participate in public policy related activities; provide scientific, technical expertise to citizen groups. Sponsored by NSF Science Education Directorate, dedicated to understanding between scientific, technological communities and general society. Also sponsor TECHNOLOGICAL INNOVATION IN EDUCATION PROGRAM GRANTS to innovative educational television and communication technology in science education institu-

tions; PUBLIC UNDERSTANDING OF SCIENCE GRANTS.

VIDEO RESIDENCE GRANT: Science Public Service Television, Radio, $18,000-$35,000 (Prorated according to length of tenure) to scientific, educational, service, charitable organizations (or individuals through such organizations) not primarily for profit, for residencies allowing scientists, engineers to undertake up to 1 year's activities with organizations in need of their expertise, and resulting in TV-radio programs addressed to scientific needs of citizens.

JUDGING: Reviewed by scientists, engineers, professional, institutional leaders.

DEADLINES: Various

347

United States and Japan Exchange Fellowship Program
Japan United States Friendship Commission
Francis B. Tenny, Executive Director
1875 Connecticut Avenue N.W.
Suite 709
Washington, District of Columbia
20009 U.S.A. Tel: (202) 673-5295

April, October

National; **entry restricted to mid-career U.S. and Japanese artists;** semiannual; established 1975. Purpose: to aid education and culture at highest level; enhance reciprocal people-to-people understanding; support close friendship and mutuality of interests between U.S. and Japan. Sponsored by Japan United States Friendship Commission, NEA (U.S.), Agency for Cultural Affairs (Japan). Have fellowships in Dance, Design, Folk Arts, Music Composition, Theater, Visual Arts, Crafts. Also sponsor Journalism Fellowships, Book Translation Awards, American Performing Arts Tours in Japan, Japanese Cultural Performances in U.S. Second contact: Nippon Press Center Building, 2-1 Uchisaiwai-cho, 2 chrome, Chiyoda-ku, Tokyo; tel: 508-2380.

VIDEO-AUDIO RESIDENCE FELLOWSHIPS: Video, Audio Work Study in Japan. 5 fellowships of about $1600, plus round-trip transportation for 6 months minimum, to creative and practicing artists well established in field, to observe Japanese traditional and contemporary artistic developments. (Overseas travel fares for spouse, children to 18 also provided.) Require completed training; not recent resident or working in Japan at time of application. Funds also available for additional expenses. Written report required at conclusion. Not open to historians, scholars, art critics, students. Proficiency in Japanese not required.

VIDEO GRANTS: Japanese Culture Television, to organizations that help broaden understanding by American public of culture, society, history, institutions of Japanese people; of acceptable quality and interest for screening on national public broadcasting. Classroom-oriented materials should include plans for cooperative regionwide broadcasting over ETV stations, 4 states minimum.

JUDGING: Reviewed by private citizens, experts in respective fields. Selection committee chooses semifinalists.

ENTRY FEE: None.

DEADLINES: Entry, March, September. Grants, Fellowships, October, April.

348

Walter Bagehot Fellowship Program in Economics and Business Journalism
Columbia University
Chris Welles, Director
Graduate School of Journalism
New York, New York 10027 U.S.A.
Tel: (212) 287-2711

September-May

National; **open to U.S. professional journalists;** annual; established 1974. Named after Walter Bagehot, 19th-century British economist. Purpose: to provide mid-career study in economics and business for professional journalists. Sponsored by Columbia University Graduate School of Journalism. Supported by various corporations. Average statistics: 50 entrants, 10 awards.

BROADCASTING RESIDENCE FELLOWSHIP: Economic-Business Journalism Television, Radio, $14,000 stipend and free tuition, to full-time editorial employees with 4 years journalistic experience for 2 semester (8 course minimum) study in business economics, international affairs, law at Columbia University. Have guest speakers, twice weekly seminars, dinners. Require leave-of-absence (employers expected to make up salary loss differential). Columbia University Certificate to fellows. Applicants must submit 6 work samples, 3 references, professional career essay, paper on business or economic trend.

JUDGING: By Graduate School of Journalism faculty, based on demonstrated journalistic excellence.

ENTRY FEE: None.

DEADLINES: Entry, April. Notification, May. Award, September for academic year.

349

WNET Artists in Residence Program
Television Laboratory at WNET-13
Carol Brandenburg, Associate Director
356 West 58th Street
New York, New York 10019 U.S.A.
Tel: (212) 560-3193

Fall

State; **entry restricted to New York independents;** annual; established 1973. Purpose: to encourage projects that advance art of television, use of medium in new way. Sponsored by Television Laboratory at WNET-13. Supported by NYSCA, WNET-13. Average statistics: 175 entrants, 40 semifinalists, 15 finalists, 5-7 awards. Have videotape postproduction rental facilities. Publish *Vision News,* quarterly newsletter. Also sponsor INDEPENDENT DOCUMENTARY FUND.

VIDEO RESIDENCE PROGRAM: **Videotape Production,** $17,000-$20,-000 each for production, postproduction costs and stipend for 5-7 New York state residents for 7-month residence-work at TV Laboratory on video project of own design. 1 entry per entrant. Require written description of proposed project, budget estimate, resume (5 copies), 1 completed sample (film or videotape); if applying for completion funds, rough cut of work-in-progress. Format sample: 3/4-inch video cassette, 1/2-inch reel tape, or 16mm composite film print.

JUDGING: Preselection by panel of peers. Final by TV Lab Associate Director and 3-member panel. Based on originality, ability. Sponsor reserves exclusive broadcast rights (4 releases in 3 years); will insure for replacement value.

ENTRY FEE: None.

DEADLINES: Application, December. Notification, January. Residence, Fall.

350

Journalists in Europe Scholarships
Centre de Formation et de Perfectionnement des Journalistes (CFPJ)
Philippe Uiannay, Executive Manager
33 rue du Louvre
F-75002 Paris, FRANCE
Tel: 5088671

October-June

International; **entry restricted to professional journalists;** annual; established 1946. Purpose: to provide journalists with training, opportunity to study European community institutions and discover political, economic, social, cultural realities of EEC-member countries. Sponsored by CFPJ, nonprofit organization founded 1974 (Hubert Beuve-Mery, Founder). Supported by European Economic Community (EEC), UNESCO. Average statistics: 135 awarded, 40 countries. Held at Journalists in Europe International Training Center, Paris. Have study rooms, documentation service. Publish yearbook. Also sponsor preliminary language courses; summer retraining sessions (limited entry) in specialized journalism media.

BROADCASTING RESIDENCE SCHOLARSHIP: **European Journalism Television, Radio.** 40,000 francs for 8 months' living expenses (comparable to student lifestyle) to professional journalists to conduct inquiries on European current events, problems. Does not include transportation to, from Paris study base. Require letter in English, French, or German; university, work references; tapes or recordings; evidence of language proficiency; statement of study intent. All documents require signature of diplomatic or consular representative.

ELIGIBILITY: Professional journalists aged 25-35 with proficiency (speak and understand) French and English, 4 years experience with TV or radio station.

JUDGING: By professional committee.

ENTRY FEE: Varies.

DEADLINES: Application, February. Acceptance, June. Scholarship, October-June.

SCHOLARSHIPS, FELLOWSHIPS, STUDY-LOANS, RESEARCH GRANTS

Primarily for STUDY and RESEARCH. Includes TV-Radio Broadcasting, Video, Film, Audio, Audiovisual, Multimedia; and MINORITY, WOMEN, ENVIRONMENTAL, SCIENCE. (Also see GRANTS, RESIDENCE GRANTS.)

| 351 |

American Film Institute (AFI) Curriculum Program Tuition Deferment Loans

Robert F. Blumofe, Director AFI West
501 Doheny Road
Beverly Hills, California 90210 U.S.A.
Tel: (213) 278-8777

September-June

National; **entry restricted to U.S.**

permanent residents; annual; established 1967. Purpose: to identify, encourage, develop new talent. Sponsored by AFI (Jean Firstenburg, Director, John F. Kennedy Center for the Performing Arts, Washington D.C. 20566), founded 1967 as independent nonprofit organization to preserve heritage, advance art of film and TV in U.S. Supported by NEA, NEH, MPAA, Academy of Motion Picture Arts and Sciences. Held at AFI Center for Advanced Film Studies (Greystone Mansion, Beverly Hills, California). Have Charles K. Feldman Library, seminars, workshops, educational services. Publish books, *American Film Magazine.* Also sponsor INDEPENDENT FILMMAKER PROGRAM GRANTS, DIRECTING WORKSHOP FOR WOMEN, ACADEMY INTERNSHIP PROGRAM, ARTS ENDOWMENT FILM ARCHIVAL PROGRAM.

VIDEO STUDY LOAN: Videomaking Study Tuition Deferment, $3750 for 1-year curriculum program study in videomaking, including workshops, video analysis, production, writing, directing. Admission to study program requires videotapes (1/2-inch EIAJ, 1-inch IVC, 3/4-inch U-matic), scripts, other supporting material, resume of background in arts and humanities, previous video work, goals as videomaker. Tuition deferment requires financial need (repayment of $100 per month plus 5% interest per annum, begins 3 years after end of study). Categories: Directing, Producing, Videography, Screenwriting, Production Design. Have *Conservatory Program* to prepare videomakers for career in professional world; entry by recommendations of faculty among graduate fellows from curriculum program.

ELIGIBILITY: U.S. citizens or permanent residents, age 21 or older, with basic background in arts and humanities. Foreign students may enter study program but are not eligible for tuition deferment.

JUDGING: Study program by faculty; additional evaluations at middle and end of academic year based on quality of completed work, participation in curriculum, commitment to work assignments, professional attitude, creative potential. May change or modify curriculum, terminate enrollment. No leaves of absence.

ENTRY FEE: $20 application (nonrefundable).

DEADLINES: Entry, February. Admission reports, May. Academic year September-June.

352

Corporation for Public Broadcasting (CPB) Minorities' and Women's Telecommunications Feasibility Project Grants

Marlene Thorn, Director Training and Development Services
1111 Sixteenth Street N.W.
Washington, District of Columbia
20036 U.S.A. Tel: (202) 293-6160

February, August

National; **entry restricted to minority and women's nonprofit organizations;** semiannual. Purpose: to provide assistance to incorporated nonprofit minority or women's groups-organizations for diversifying control, expanding range of public telecommunications services available to American public. Sponsored by CPB, private, nonprofit corporation founded 1967 by Public Broadcasting Act. Supported by NEA, federal, private funds. Also sponsor Production and Residence Grants; Women's and Minority Training Grant Programs; Instructional TV Series Grants; Radio

Expansion Grants.

BROADCASTING   RESEARCH GRANT: Minority, Women Public Telecommunications, up to $5000 for feasibility studies in establishing public telecommunications service (defined as noncommercial educational-cultural radio, television program and related noncommercial instructional-informational material), establishing, operating public telecommunications entity (defined as public broadcast station, or noncommercial telecommunications entity, that is, a state, public or nonprofit entity for dissemination of audio-video educational-cultural programs by coaxial cable, optical fiber, broadcast translators, cassettes, discs, microwave, laser, other than primary broadcast station). Funding for phases subsequent to feasibility studies may be available through *CPB Coverage Expansion Grant Program* or National Telecommunications and Information Administration *Public Telecommunications Facilities Program.* Categories: Engineering, Legal, Financial Feasibility Studies.

ELIGIBILITY: Women's, minority (Blacks; Indians, including Native Americans, Eskimos, Aleuts; Hispanics; Asian-Pacific) nonprofit organizations, incorporated and recognized as nonprofit. Require articles of incorporation; race-sex statistical breakdown of board members, management; nonprofit certification; statement of purpose, objectives, schedule, completion dates; budget. Final report required 30 days after project completion. No recipients of National Telecommunications and Information Administration Public Telecommunications Facility Program Planning Grants.

JUDGING: Based on justification of need, scope, realistic budget, proposed use of funds, timetable, personnel qualifications. Grant recipients not committed to pursue CPB qualification or construct facility.

DEADLINES: Application, continuous. Notification, February, August.

| 353 |

Electrical Women's Round Table (EWRT) Julia Kiene Fellowship
Jean P. Keele, Chairman
Central Power & Light Company
P.O. Box 2190
Alice, Texas 78332 U.S.A. Tel: (512) 664-0961

Spring

International; **entry restricted to women;** annual; established 1956. Named for Julia Kiene, former National President of EWRT and member National Board of Directors. Purpose: to promote efficient use of electricity; encourage high-caliber college graduates to further study toward advanced degree in field of electrical energy. Sponsored by 800-member Electrical Women's Round Table, founded 1927 as independent national organization of women associated with electrical industry, allied fields.

BROADCASTING FELLOWSHIP: **Television, Radio.** $2000 (in 2 payments during 1 year to woman graduate student working toward advanced college degree in field related to electrical living. Require background, goals, 4 references, college transcript. No EWRT members.

JUDGING: By 5-member committee, based on academic aptitude, vocational promise, character, financial need, willingness to continue career in field related to electrical energy.

ENTRY FEE: None.

DEADLINES: Entry, March. Award, Spring.

| 354 |

Environmental Conservation Fellowships
National Wildlife Federation (NWF)
Thomas L. Kimball, Executive Vice President
1412 16th Street, N.W.
Washington, District of Columbia
20036 U.S.A. Tel: (202) 797-6800

April

International; **entry restricted to U.S., Canadian, Mexican graduate students;** annual; established 1957. Purpose: to encourage advanced study in wildlife, natural resource management, protection of environmental quality. Sponsored by NWF, founded 1938 to educate general public about resource, environmental problems; American Petroleum Institute (API). Also sponsor API Matching-Funds Grants for oil-related research; Conservation Research Grants.

RESEARCH FELLOWSHIP GRANT: **Environmental Conservation Journalism, Communications Research,** up to $4000 for 1 academic year to U.S., Canadian, Mexican graduate students in college, university graduate program or law school (accepted for fall semester to conduct course work). Half given in September, half in January upon receipt of satisfactory progress report. Submit 5 copies typed application; 5 copies transcripts, GRE scores; statement, references from major adviser, department head or chairman. Research may be conducted outside U.S. Upon completion provide copy of publication, thesis, report resulting from study or supported by program; acknowledgement of NWF support on 1-page abstract.

JUDGING: By NWF Board of Directors based on completeness, clarity of application; relevance of proposed project to NWF interests, programs; value of study to natural resource conservation; scholastic standing; satisfactory credentials.

ENTRY FEE: None.

DEADLINES: Application, December. Acceptance, April. Grant awarded, Fall for academic year.

355

Harold E. Fellows Memorial Scholarship
National Association of Broadcasters (NAB)
Dr. Bruce A. Linton, Chairman
Broadcast Education Association
217 Flint Hall, University of Kansas
Lawrence, Kansas 60045 U.S.A.
Tel: (913) 864-3991

Spring

National; **entry restricted to NAB radio and television station, network employees and children;** annual. Named after former president of NAB. Purpose: to promote development of broadcasting arts. Sponsored by NAB (1771 N Street, N.W., Washington, D.C. 20036); Broadcast Education Association (BEA). Held at NAB convention.

BROADCASTING SCHOLARSHIP: Television, Radio Broadcasting, 4 scholarships, $1250 each, for 1 year junior, senior, or graduate-level study as broadcasting degree major at BEA-member university or college.

ELIGIBILITY: NAB-member radio, television station or network employees and their children. Require statement of goals, references.

JUDGING: Based on ability, interest, academic performance, personal characteristics.

ENTRY FEE: None.

DEADLINES: Application, January. Notification, Spring.

356

IFPA Film and Video Communicators Scholarship
Information Film Producers of America (IFPA)
Wayne Weiss
750 East Colorado Blvd., Suite 6
Pasadena, California 91101 U.S.A.
Tel: (213) 795-7866

Fall

National; **Entry restricted to U.S. audiovisual students;** annual. Purpose: to educate students planning to make careers in audiovisual communications. Sponsored by IFPA (founded 1957), nation's largest (17 chapters) nonprofit association of documentary, educational, industrial, business filmmakers, dedicated to professional advancement, recognition of creators of film, video, audiovisual for communications as opposed to entertainment. Held at IFPA National Conference and Trade Show. Publish *The Communicator,* bimonthly newsletter; membership directory. Also sponsor CINDY COMPETITION for film and video, AUDIO VISUAL DEPARTMENT OF THE YEAR AWARDS COMPETITION, seminars.

VIDEO SCHOLARSHIP: Audiovisual Student, $1500 cash, and material-equipment-service GRANT for (1 year) **informational** video, film, or multimedia slide project (10 minutes maximum). Expense-paid trip to IFPA Conference. Require 30-45-minute project report and screening at Conference, accounting for production expenses. Other scholarships and grants at judges' discretion.

ELIGIBILITY: High school graduate or college student, 18-30 years, 3.0

grade point average minimum (based on 4.0 scale). Require project proposal, budget, script, schedule, purpose; grade transcripts, goal statement, biography, 4 recommendation letters.

JUDGING: By committee. May suspend or withdraw grants. Any profits from project go to IFPA Scholarship fund.

ENTRY FEE: $5.

DEADLINES: Entry, June. Awards, October.

357

Indiana University Audio-Visual Center Assistantships and Internships
Robert Heinich, Chairman
Department of Instructional Systems Technology
Mitchell Hall, 110, Indiana University
Bloomington, Indiana 47405 U.S.A.
Tel: (812) 337-1362

Fall-Spring

International; **entry restricted to graduate student applicants;** annual; established 1940. Purpose: to support graduate students who are potential leaders in AV field. Sponsored by Audio-Visual Center at Indiana University. Also sponsor NATIONAL AUDIO-VISUAL ASSOCIATION PAST PRESIDENTS MEMORIAL SCHOLARSHIPS for Indiana University AV graduate students.

VIDEO ASSISTANTSHIPS: Audio-Visual Graduate Assistant, $1500 minimum, and fee remission to graduate students with media design and production skills, for study at Indiana University Audio-Visual Center, specializing in Instructional Systems Technology. Require Bachelors or Masters Degree from recognized institution, experience in media field, 3.0 (B) grade point average, profes-

sional goal statement, leadership references.

VIDEO INTERNSHIPS: Audio-Visual Internship, $9000 maximum. Requirements same as for Assistantships.

DEADLINES: Not specified. Assistantship, Internship for academic year.

358

John and Mary R. Markle Foundation Mass Communications Grants
Dolores E. Miller, Assistant to President
50 Rockefeller Plaza
New York, New York 10020 U.S.A.
Tel: (212) 489-6655

March, June, November

National; **entry open to U.S. organizations;** tri-annual; established 1936. Purpose: to strengthen educational uses of mass media-communications technology, promote advancement, diffusion of knowledge and general good of mankind. Sponsored and supported by John and Mary Markle Foundation (Lloyd N. Morisett, President), founded 1927 by John Markle, coal millionaire. Average statistics: 748 entrants, 36 grants totaling $3,270,667.

TELEVISION-RADIO RESEARCH GRANT: Mass Communications Improvement Television, Radio, Film, for projects that expand research on mass communication role in society, analyze public policy issues and questions, improve professional performance, develop better media service to specialized groups (children, elderly minorities), explore media-politics relationship, enrich print-electronic journalism quality. Support publicaton of books-reports. Require project proposal, resources needed, personnel, timetable, budget, method descriptions; visit, interview with finalists.

JUDGING: By staff and directors. Foundation works as active partner on projects.

ENTRY FEE: None.

DEADLINES: Open. Response within 2 weeks. Grants awarded March, June, November.

| 359 |

Kaltenborn Foundation Grants for Scholarly Studies in Communications
Rolf Kaltenborn, Trustee
349 Seaview Avenue
Palm Beach, Florida 33480 U.S.A.
Tel: (305) 655-8024

Continous

National; entry open to all U.S.; continuous. Purpose: to promote scholarly studies in communications dealing with effectiveness of informing public through television, radio, press, magazines. Sponsored by Kaltenborn Foundation. Average statistics: 3-4 grants.

TELEVISION STUDY GRANT: Television Scholary Studies. 3-4 grants approximately $1500 each, for scholarly studies in communications. Require project proposal, background biographical material, 1-2 references.

RADIO STUDY GRANT: Radio Scholarly Studies. Requirements same as for Television.

ENTRY FEE: None.

DEADLINES: Open.

| 360 |

Nate Haseltine Fellowships in Science Writing
Council for the Advancement of Science Writing (CASW)
William J. Cromie, Executive Director
618 North Elmwood
Oak Park, Illinois 60302 U.S.A.
Tel: (312) 383-0820

Continuous

National; **entry restricted to U.S. journalists, journalism graduate students;** annual; established 1977, replaces AMERICAN MEDICAL ASSOCIATION SCIENCE JOURNALISM AWARDS (established 1964). Named for Nate Haseltine, late medical writer, for Washington Post Newspaper. Purpose: to teach science-medicine writing, reporting. Sponsored by CASW, organization of science journalists, scientists seeking to increase science public understanding by upgrading writing quality. Supported by American Medical Association. Also sponsor DR. MORRIS FISHBEIN FELLOWSHIPS IN MEDICAL JOURNALISM.

BROADDCASTING FELLOWSHIPS: Science Writing Television, Radio Journalism, up to $1500 per year to working journalists, journalism graduate students for career in mass media general-public science writing. Working journalists may use funds for part-time schooling-directed study, reference-science books, magazine subscriptions, science meeting travel, on-job training with science writer. Stipends awarded through school-employer.

ELIGIBILITY: Journalists should be employed by radio or television stations or networks. Students must have undergraduate degrees in science or journalism; proven ability, motivation to pursue science writing career. Priority to those with two years journalistic experience. No fellowships for public relations, public information work. Require resume, 3 employer-faculty recommendations, 3 writing samples, 500-word career-study goals. For students also require undergraduate journalism-science degree, transcripts, science writing-study resources available at school.

JUDGING: By selection committee.

ENTRY FEE: None.

DEADLINES: Open.

361

National Association of Broadcasters (NAB) Grants for Research in Broadcasting
Dr. W. Lawrence Patrick, Senior Vice President in Research
1771 N Street, N.W.
Washington, District of Columbia
20036 U.S.A. Tel: (202) 293-5104

February

International; **entry restricted to students and academic personnel;** annual; established 1966. Purpose: to stimulate broadcasting research, facilitate training qualified personnel in field, expand knowledge of broadcasting role and function. Sponsored and supported by NAB.

BROADCASTING RESEARCH GRANT: **Commercial Broadcasting Research,** maximum $1200 for out-of-pocket expenses incurred in research on American commercial broadcasting social, cultural, political, economic aspects. Require proposal, budget, faculty endorsement. No foreign broadcasting systems, instructional radio-television, advertising effectiveness studies. Research concerned with radio particularly encouraged.

JUDGING: By broadcasting industry, broadcast research professionals, academicians, based on problem conceptualization, research technique, clarity, thoroughness.

DEADLINES: Entry, January. Winners notified, February.

362

National Indian Media Conference Scholarships
Native American Public Broadcasting Consortium
Frank Blythe, Executive Director
1800 North 33rd Street
P.O. Box 83111
Lincoln, Nebraska 68501 U.S.A.
Tel: (402) 472-3522

March

National; **entry restricted to U.S., Canadian Native American college media students;** annual; established 1977. Purpose: access vehicle to exchange ideas on Indian Media issues to public broadcasting. Sponsored by Native American Public Broadcasting Consortium, American Indian Film Institute. Average statistics: 250 participants. Have workshops, distribution. Also sponsor National Indian Woman of the Year Award, National Indian Man of the Year Award. Second contact: Laurell E. Schuerman, Assistant Director.

BROADCASTING SCHOLARSHIP: **Indian Media Conference,** 20 scholarships to Native American students (includes 1/2 air travel per diem and registration). Open to upper college, graduate college students in prescribed media training programs.

JUDGING: By Native American Public Broadcasting Consortium staff.

ENTRY FEE: None.

DEADLINES: Scholarships awarded, March.

363

New York State Summer School of the Arts School of Film-Media Scholarships
New York State Education Department
Charles J. Trupia, Executive Director
Room 679 EBA
Albany, 12234 Tel: (518) 474-8773

July-August

State; **entry restricted to participants in New York State Youth Film-Media Show;** annual; established 1976. Purpose: to provide resident program for development of students with superior media-creation talent, capabilities. Sponsored by New York State Education Department, Division of Humanities and Arts, NEA. Summer School of Film-Media (Dr. Gerald O'Grady, Director) trains students in film, video, creative sound, photography, mixed media. Held at State University of New York at Buffalo for 6 weeks. Have 4-person dormitory rooms on 1200-acre Amherst Campus, 3 daily meals, health care, recreational facilities, library; film-video screenings, lecturers, instruction, field trips, workshop. Have schools of Choral, Dance, Orchestral, Theater, Visual Arts Studies. Also sponsor NEW YORK STATE YOUTH FILM MEDIA-SHOW.

VIDEO SCHOLARSHIP: Student. $75-$750 available to talented New York high school student participants in NEW YORK STATE YOUTH FILM-MEDIA REGIONAL SHOW, for room, board, tuition, supplies; based on need, ability, commitment, creative interest.

AUDIO-CREATIVE SOUND

SCHOLARSHIP: Student. Requirements same as for Video.

MIXED MEDIA SCHOLARSHIP: Student. Requirements same as for Video.

JUDGING: At Youth Film-Media Shows and workshops, 7 New York regional locations.

DEADLINES: Judging, February-March. School, July-August.

364

Scripps-Howard Foundation Scholarships and Grants
Edward Forte, Administrator
200 Park Avenue, Room 4310
New York, New York 10166 U.S.A.

Spring

National; **entry open to U.S.;** annual. Purpose: to encourage ambitious, talented young people to prepare for careers in journalism, allied arts. Sponsored by Scripps-Howard Foundation, founded 1962 as charitable nonprofit organization. Also sponsor Robert P. Scripps Graphic Arts Grants; awards for Public Service, Conservation, Editorial Writing; First Amendment Awards; Ernie Pyle Memorial Awards.

BROADCASTING SCHOLARSHIPS: Student Journalism Television, Radio (*Roy W. Howard-Margaret Rohe Howard Scholarships in Journalism and Allied Arts*) up to $2000 to students interested in editorial, business aspects of television or radio and willing to work to provide part of costs. Require application letter, transcripts of record, faculty recommendation.
Professional Journalism Television, Radio (*Ellen Browning Scripps Journalism Scholarships*) 10 yearly to persons now working in field who wish to increase their knowledge in

any other field through graduate work. Require accompaning letter stating purpose, goals.

BROADCASTING GRANTS: Journalism Special Projects Television, Radio. Projects including but not limited to seminars, minority student programs, internship programs.

ENTRY FEE: None.

DEADLINES: Application, April. Notifications, Spring.

365

Society of Motion Picture and Television Engineers (SMPTE) Scholarships and Grants
862 Scarsdale Avenue
Scarsdale, New York 10583 U.S.A.

Spring

International; **entry restricted to U.S., Canadian college students;** annual. Sponsored by Academy of Motion Picture Arts and Sciences; SMPTE, founded 1916 as Society of Motion Picture Engineers (SMPE), television added 1950, for theory, practice, advancement and standardization of motion picture, television, photographic engineering and allied arts-sciences. Have 8000 members in 62 countries; establish international technical standards; provide test film; have lectures, technical courses, exhibitions, semiannual technical conferences; publish magazine, books. Also sponsor Awards for Achievement in film, TV, photo engineering, documentary, color, sound, educational technology, instrumentation, high-speed photography, member papers (nomination by members only).

TELEVISION SCHOLARSHIP: Television Engineering or Science, up to $3250 for tuition, fees, living expenses, or as grant-in-aid for graduate research.

ELIGIBILITY: Must be full-time second-year undergraduate or graduate student in engineering, sciences related to motion pictures, televsion at recognized U.S., Canadian college or university, with 3.5 cumulative GPA minimum, background or interest in technical areas of motion pictures, television, photography or technical production. Require statement of need or study proposal, college transcripts, confirmation of registration or admission acceptance, agreement from school to administer scholarship or grant, if awarded.

ENTRY FEE: None.

DEADLINES: Application, January. Notification, March.

366

Western States Film Institute (WSFI) Scholarship Program
Bonita S. Trumbule, Executive Producer
1629 York Street
Denver, Colorado 80206 U.S.A.
Tel: (303) 320-0457

Continuous

International; entry open to all; continuous; established 1972. Formerly called COMMUNITY FILM to 1977. Purpose: to provide community media education and services. Sponsored by WSFI. Recognized by AFI. Also sponsor Apprenticeships, Training Programs.

VIDEO SCHOLARSHIPS: Video Study. Partial scholarships for study at WSFI to those in need, with talent, potential, education.

ENTRY FEE: None.

DEADLINES: Not specified.

| 367 |

Raymond Crepault Scholarship
Canadian Association of
Broadcasters (CAB)
P.O. Box 627, Station B
Ottawa, Ontario K1P 5S2 CANADA

Spring

National; **entry restricted to French-speaking Canadians;** annual; established 1975. Sponsored by CAB, Broadcast Executives Society, CTV Television Network. Also sponsor RUTH HANCOCK SCHOLARSHIP; membership awards to television, radio stations, as showcase of achievements.

BROADCASTING SCHOLAR-SHIP: Television, Radio, $2500 to French-speaking Canadian for full-time TV-radio university training. Require university graduation or current communication-journalism study and (or) broadcasting technology institute graduation and (or) current broadcast employment.

JUDGING: By journalism, academic, public service committee, based on motivation, ability, financial need, recommendations.

DEADLINES: Entry,   February. Awards, Spring.

| 368 |

Ruth Hancock Scholarships
Canadian Association of
Broadcasters (CAB)
P.O. Box 627, Station B
Ottawa, Ontario K1P 5S2 CANADA

Spring

National; **entry restricted to Canadian communications students;** annual; established 1975. Sponsored by CAB, Broadcast Executives Society, CTV Television Network. Also spon-

sor   RAYMOND   CREPAULT SCHOLARSHIP; membership awards to television, radio stations, as showcase of achievements.

BROADCASTING SCHOLAR-SHIP: Television, Radio, two $1000 each to Canadian students enrolled in Canadian communications. Require 500-word essay about course, goals, reasons; recommendation letters from course director, CAB station manager.

JUDGING: By journalism, academic, public service committee, based on character, leadership, communications career interest-activities, enthusiasm.

DEADLINES: Entry,   January. Awards, Spring.

SCIENTIFIC, TECHNICAL
TV-Radio Broadcasting (video, film, audio), Video and Film, including AVIATION-SPACE, CHEMISTRY, NUCLEAR ENERGY, (also see AGRICULTURE-CONSERVATION, BROADCASTING, BUSINESS-INDUSTRIAL, DOCUMENTARY, EDUCATIONAL, HEALTH-MEDICAL, INDEPENDENT, JOURNALISM, TELEVISION FILMS.)

| 369 |

American Science Film Association (ASFA) Science Film Festival
University City Science Center
3624 Market Street
Philadelphia, Pennsylvania 19104
U.S.A. Tel: (215) 387-2255

November

National; **entry open to U.S.;** biennial (even years); established 1974. Sponsored by ASFA, founded 1960 as professional organization devoted to advancement of science-technology through film, television, other related communications media. Also submit U.S. films-video to annual INTERNATIONAL SCIENTIFIC FILM ASSOCIATION FILM FESTIVAL (ISFA, Suzanne Duval, Director, 38 Avenue des Ternes, 75017 Paris, France) as official U.S. member. Held during ASFA Sci-Com Congress at various U.S. locations. Have conferences, symposia.

VIDEOTAPE CONTEST: **Science** (3/4-inch) released in previous 2 years. Categories: Science Research, Science Education, Public Service, Industry.

AWARDS: Merit Diplomas.

ENTRY FEE: $10 per film (free to ASFA members).

DEADLINES: Event, November.

370

Aviation-Space Writers Association Journalism Awards
William F. Kaiser, Executive Secretary
Cliffwood Road
Chester, New Jersey 07930 U.S.A.
Tel: (201) 879-5667

Spring

International; entry open to all; annual. Sponsored by Aviation-Space Writers Association (AWA).

VIDEOTAPE CONTEST: **Aviation, Space Documentary Television Broadcast** (3/4-inch cassette) 3 copies script in English. Categories: Documentary (Network-Syndicate, Locally Produced).

AUDIOTAPE CONTEST: **Avia-**

tion, Space Documentary Radio Broadcast (7 1/2 ips reel-to-reel) 3 copies script in English. Categories same as for Videotape.

ELIGIBILITY: Published, broadcast, televised, released for public consumption during previous calendar year.

AWARDS: $100 Honorarium plus Scroll for Aviation and Space, each category, 1 award per person per year. Robert S. Ball Memorial Award, $500 and Trophy, for Space writing, reporting, any media. Earl D. Osborn Award, $500 and Trophy, for General Aviation writing, reporting, any media. James J. Strebig Memorial Award, $500 and Trophy, Aviation writing, reporting, any media.

JUDGING: May withhold, omit awards, or provide recognition certificates.

ENTRY FEE: None.

DEADLINES: Entry, January. Awards given, Spring.

371

Forum Award
Atomic Industrial Forum (AIF)
Mary Ellen Warren, Coordinator
7101 Wisconsin Avenue
Washington, District of Columbia
20014 U.S.A. Tel: (301) 654-9260

Fall

International; **entry restricted to professional electronic or print media;** annual; established 1967. Purpose: to encourage factual news coverage, public understanding of peaceful nuclear application. Sponsored by AIF, international, nonprofit 600-member association concerned with peaceful application of nuclear energy. Recognized by Committee on Public Affairs and Information. Average statistics: 50 entries. Held at AIF

Annual Conference, Washington, D.C. for 1 day.

VIDEOTAPE CONTEST: Nuclear Energy Television (3/4-inch tape) in English, 4 transcripts.

FILM CONTEST: Nuclear Energy Television (gauge not specified) in English, 4 transcripts.

AUDIOTAPE CONTEST: Nuclear Energy Radio (width not specified), in English, 4 transcripts.

ELIGIBILITY: Professional nuclear related projects for general public, appearing August previous year to September of current year.

AWARDS: $1000 and Framed Certificates each, Best Print, Best Electronic Media. Money divided equally in case of tie.

JUDGING: By independent judges representing print, electronic media, trade press, industry, academic community; based on accuracy, balance, perspective, timeliness, creativity, ingenuity of approach, contribution to public understanding of peaceful nuclear energy. Entries returned upon written request.

ENTRY FEE: None.

DEADLINES: Entry, September. Judging, October. Event, November.

| 372 |

James T. Grady Award for Interpreting Chemistry for the Public
American Chemical Society
Dr. Justin W. Collat, Head Grants & Awards
1155 Sixteenth Street, N.W.
Washington, District of Columbia
20036 U.S.A. Tel: (202) 872-4481

March

International; entry open to all; annual; established 1955. Purpose: to recognize, encourage, stimulate outstanding reporting directly to American public; materially increase public's knowledge and understanding of chemistry, chemical engineering, related fields. Sponsored by 120,000-member American Chemical Society.

VIDEO AWARD: Chemistry Television. For noteworthy presentation by nominee through medium of public communication (television). Require biographical sketch of nominee (with birthdate); specific identification of work on which nomination is based; evaluation, appraisal of nominee's accomplishments. Seconding letters not necessary unless contain additional factual information about nominee (maximum of 2). Furnish 6 copies complete nominating document, letter size and unbound.

AUDIO AWARD: Chemistry Radio. For noteworthy presentation by nominee through medium of public communication (radio, public lecture). Nomination same as for Video.

AWARDS: $2000 James T. Grady Award and Gold Medal, Bronze Replica. $300 travel allowance.

JUDGING: 5-member award committee selects recipients.

ENTRY FEE: None.

DEADLINES: Nomination, March.

| 373 |

International Scientific and Technical Film Festival
University Center of Scientific Film (CUFS)
Anne De Pauw, Director
Universite Libre de Bruxelles
Avenue F. D. Roosevelt 50
B-1050 Brussels, BELGIUM
Tel: 02-649-00-30, ext. 3110

March

International; entry open to all; triennial; established 1961. Purpose: to promote diffusion, production of scientific, technical films, videotapes; demonstrate cinema, television as teaching, research aids. Sponsored by CUFS (Prof. L. de Brouckere, President). Average statistics: 210 entries, 22 countries, 93 finalists, 39 winners, 2500 attendance. Held at Free University of Brussels for 1 week.

VIDEOTAPE CONTEST: University Scientific-Technical Teaching Aid (normalized European standard CCIR Pal cassette, U-matic or VHS) 20 minutes maximum, produced in previous 4 years, to be used as teaching aid at university level during lectures, seminars. Require French or English explanation. No programmed learning or whole lecture.

AWARDS: Prizes for Best Film, Research, University Didactic. Special Prize, Best Secondary Teaching. Honorable Mentions, Special Awards.

JUDGING: Preselection by committee. Final by 2-7 university and scientific film specialists per category. Sponsor requests copies of winners for university, scientific, research institution showings.

ENTRY FEE: None. Entrant pays postage.

DEADLINES: Entry, December. Materials, January. Event, March.

| 374 |

Kalinga Prize for the Popularization of Science
UNESCO
7 Place de Fontenoy
75700 Paris, FRANCE
Tel: 331-577-1610

Spring

International; **entry restricted** (nomination through official science or science writers organizations in each country); annual; established 1951 by B. Patnaik (of Cuttack, Orissa, India), named for ancient Kalinga empire of India. Monetary award (for travel to India) to **Science Television, Radio Program Director, Writer, Editor, Speaker** for distinguished career in interpreting science, technology, research to public; limit 1 per entrant. Sponsored by UNESCO. Supported by Kalinga Trust Foundation of India. Also have Architecture Prize. Event, Spring.

| 375 |

Golden Antenna International Telecommunication and Electronics Film Festival
International Telecommunications Union (ITU) ORGEXPO
W. Wolter, Executive Director
18 Quai Ernest-Ansermet
Case Postale 65
CH-1211 Geneva 4, SWITZERLAND
Tel: 21-95-33

September

International; **entry restricted to Telecom entrants and ITU-member governments;** quadriennial (next 1983); established 1971. Purpose: to show growing integration of national networks in world telecommunications; inform of latest developments. Sponsored by 154-member country ITU (Place des Nations, CH-1211 Geneva 20, Switzerland; tel: 022-91-51-11), founded 1865 to plan, regulate, standardize, coordinate world communications. Average statistics: 43 films, 15 countries. Held during Telecom World Telecommunication Exhibition at Palace of Expositions in Geneva. Have World Book Fair on Telecommunications and Electronics, World Radio Conference, technical symposium, forums, exhibits. Publish official catalog, exhibition journal. Also sponsor YOUTH IN THE ELECTRONIC AGE COMPETITION for youth photography, art; ITV CENTENARY PRIZE to individuals in international telecommunications.

VIDEOTAPE CONTEST: Telecommunications, Electronics (cassette) 4 maximum per government, 3 per commercial enterprise; with English, French or Spanish commentary, synopsis. Categories: Telecommunications Public Information (by ITU-member countries), Commercially Produced Telecommunications-Electronics Documentaries, Promotional-Advertising (by participating companies), Training Films (by governments, companies).

ELIGIBILITY: Open to member governments of ITU, commercial enterprises participating as Telecom exhibitors. Commercial entries not over 5 years old.

AWARDS: Golden Antenna, Best of Festival. Prizes each category. Special Awards for Artistic Value, Technical Quality, Best by Public Vote. Honorable Mentions. Participation Certificates.

JUDGING: Prescreened by organizing committee. Final by international film-technical experts. Based on audiovisual impact, spirit of festival, contents. May change categories, reject entries likely to offend national feelings. Not responsible for loss or damage.

ENTRY FEE: Up to 15 minutes, 200 Swiss Francs for governments, 300 for individuals. To 30 minutes, 400, 600 SFr. To 60 minutes, 600, 900 SFr. Entrant pays postage.

DEADLINES: Entry, May. Materials, June. Prescreening, June-July. Event, September. Materials returned, December.

| 376 |

Belgrade International Festival of Scientific and Technical Films
Jugoslovensko Drustvo "Nikola Tesla."
P.O. Box 359
Kneza Milosa 10
11000 Belgrade, YUGOSLAVIA
Tel: 330-641, 331-938

January

International; entry open to all; biennial (even years); established 1958. Purpose: to exchange experiences in production, use of latest scientific-technical films. Sponsored by Yugoslav Society for Promotion of Scientific Knowledge "Nikola Tesla" Association of Engineers and Technicians of Yugoslavia (IT), Yugoslav Radio and Television (JRT). Average Statistics: 107 films, 20 countries, 73 shown, 20,500 attendance. Held at Yugoslav Engineers and Technicians Club (Kneza 9, Belgrade, Yugoslavia) and as traveling exhibition in Yugoslavia. Have meetings, conferences.

VIDEOTAPE CONTEST: Scientific, Technical (electronic tapes, 625 lines per frame) produced in last 2 years. Require dialog lists. Categories: Science Research, Popular Science, Science Fiction, Informative, Television Science.

AWARDS: Grand Prize Nikola Tesla Gold Statuette. Tesla Gold, Silver, Bronze Medals-Plaques for First, Second, Third, each category. Other Official Awards. Special Prizes, Honorary Certificates. Participation Certificates.

JUDGING: By 5 judges.

ENTRY FEE: None.

DEADLINES: Entry, October. Materials, December. Event, January. Materials returned, June.

SPORTS, TRAVEL, RECREATION

TV-Radio Broadcasting and Video, including CONSERVATION, OUTDOOR, PARKS, SAILING, SPECIAL OLYMPICS, WILDLIFE. (Also see BROADCASTING, DOCUMENTARY, INDEPENDENT, TELEVISION FILMS.)

377

Special Olympics Awards
Joseph Kennedy Jr. Foundation
Eunice Kennedy Shriver, President
1701 K Street, N.W., Suite 203
Washington, District of Columbia
20006 U.S.A. Tel: (202) 331-1731

Spring

International; entry open to all; annual; established 1973. Purpose: to honor those giving local, national, international support to Special Olympics (founded 1968 as world's first and largest international physical fitness, sports training, athletic competition program for mentally retarded children and adults, with 750,000 athletes, 250,000 volunteers in 22 countries). Sponsored by Joseph P. Kennedy Jr. Foundation. Have athlete, volunteer, organization categories.

TELEVISION-RADIO AWARD: **Special Olympics Broadcasting.** Categories: Sportswriter, Sportscaster, Photographer, Media Coverage.

AWARDS: Special Olympics Awards for distinguished service to mentally handicapped through Special Olympics sports programs.

ENTRY FEE: None.

DEADLINES: Entry, March. Awards given, Spring.

378

Wes Francis Audiovisual Excellence (WAVE) Contest
National Recreation and Park Association (NRPA)
Martha Nudel Winsor,
Communications Director
1601 North Kent Street, Suite 1100
Arlington, Virginia 22209 U.S.A.
Tel: (703) 525-0606

October

National; **entry open to U.S.;** annual; established 1977. Named after Mrs. George T. (Wes) Francis, Jr., of Philadelphia, NRPA trustee. Purpose: to recognize park and recreation audiovisuals. Theme: Park and recreation programs and concepts. Sponsored by NRPA. Average statistics: 40 entries, 50 entrants, 5 finalists, 10 awards, 7000 attendance. Held at University of Missouri-Columbia Media Center for Recreation for 3 days.

VIDEOTAPE CONTEST: **Parks, Recreation, Conservation, Leisure** (3/4-inch cassette) 25 minutes maximum. Categories: General, Public Service Announcements (maximum 3 per entrant), In-House, Commercial Production.

AWARDS: First, Second Place Plaques each category. Honorable Mentions each category. Special Awards, Best Student, In-House entries.

JUDGING: By 5-member panel, based on content, usefulness to park and recreation discipline, artistic achievement. All entries viewed in entirety. Not responsible for loss or damage.

SALES TERMS: Must be released to University of Missouri-Columbia Media Center for rental on nonprofit basis to park and recreation professionals. Require permission for duplication of audiovisual presentations.

ENTRY FEE: None. Sponsor pays return postage.

DEADLINES: Entry, May. Judging, August. Event, October. Materials returned, November.

379

World Wildlife Film Festival

International Wildlife Foundation
Eric S. Hubbell, Public Relations
Director
5151 East Broadway, Suite 1680
Tucson, Arizona 85711 U.S.A.
Tel: (602) 745-9109

July

International; entry open to all; annual; established 1980. Purpose: to promote better understanding of world wildlife problems; expose general populace to wildlife films and videotapes. Theme: varies. Supported by International Wildlife Museum Foundation. Average statistics: 85-100 entries, 15 countries, 12 semifinalists, 4 winners, 400-800 attendance. Held at MGM Grand Hotel, Reno, Nevada, for 4 days. Tickets: $5-$400. Second contact: Liz Osborne.

VIDEOTAPE CONTEST: Wildlife, Outdoor (3/4-inch) no feature entertainment or TV spot commercial entries. Categories: Professional; Amateur; Big, Small Game Hunting; Wildlife Documentary; Shooting Sports; Wildlife Management; Outdoor-Travel, General Outdoor Recreation; Archery; Fishing; Fisheries Management.

AWARDS: Golden, Silver, Bronze Tusker Awards and cash ($500-$5000) to top 3 each main category. Viewer's Choice Trophy. Special Recognition Plaques for subcategories. Certificates of Excellence. Door Prizes.

JUDGING: Regional prescreening. Final by 3 from film, broadcast, photography, wildlife fields, based on technical excellence, creativity, originality, outstanding qualities. Festival keeps copies of winners. Not responsible for loss or damage.

ENTRY FEE: Varies, $50 average (considered donation to World Wildlife Foundation).

DEADLINES: Entry, June. Event, July.

380

Explore Canada Travel Film Awards

Travel Industry Association of
Canada (TIAC)
Suite 1016, 130 Albert Street
Ottawa, Ontario K1P 5G4 CANADA
Tel: (613) 238-3883

Spring

International; entry open to all; annual; established 1962. Purpose: to award films and videotapes encouraging Canadian tourism. Sponsored by TIAC. Held at TIAC National Conference for 3 days. Also sponsor AWARDS FOR CANADIAN PUBLICATIONS, CANADIAN TOURIST AND TRAVEL WRITING IN U.S. NEWSPAPERS, MAGAZINES, promotion, conservation.

VIDEOTAPE CONTEST: Canadian Travel, Recreation (3/4-inch) encouraging travel to and within Canada (including travel promotion, travelogues, leisure time activities, and tapes for TV), released for general showing between March and December current year.

AWARDS: Maple Leaf Award, Best Film. Canuck Award, Runner-Up.

ENTRY FEE: None.

DEADLINES: Entry, December. Materials, January. Awards, February.

381

La Rochelle International Sailing Film Festival
Hotel de Ville
17000 La Rochelle, FRANCE
Tel: (46) 41 90 44

October-November

International; entry open to all; biennial; established 1977. Purpose: to promote knowledge of sailing and sea-environment through visual media. Sponsored by La Rochelle Yacht Club and other organizations. Have slide shows, discussions, conferences, workshops. Also sponsor photo exhibition. Second contact: Rose Marie Richard, 71 Avenue de Rompsay, 17000 La Rochelle, France; tel: (46) 41 45 52.

VIDEOTAPE FESTIVAL: Sailing (width not specified) productions devoted to sailing and sea-environment.

AWARDS: Noncompetitive.

JUDGING: Preselection by committee. Final by jury of sailing, film, media personalities. Not responsible for loss or damage.

ENTRY FEE: None. Entrant pays postage.

DEADLINES: Entry, May. Tapes, September. Event, October-November. Materials returned, November.

382

Yugoslavian International Festival of Sports Television Programs
RTV Ljubljana
Beno Hvala, Secretary
Tavcarjeva 17
61000 Ljubljana, YUGOSLAVIA
Tel: 061-311-922

May

International; **entry restricted** (nomination by official televison broadcasting organizations in each country); biennial; established 1971. Gold, Silver Shot Awards to **Sports Television Videotape** (VCR 625 PAL, Sony U-matic 3/4-inch low band HB 625 PAL). Purpose: to improve knowledge of sports; promote international exchange of programs and experience. Alternates with LAUSANNE INTERNATIONAL CONTEST OF TELEVISED SPORTS. Sponsored by JRT, EBU. Recognized by International Olympic Committee, Executive Council of SFR Yugoslavia. Held in Portoroz, Slovenia, Yugoslavia for 5 days. Second contact: JRT, Milan Milosavljevic, 11000, Belgrad, Borisa Kidrica 70, Yugoslavia. Event, May.

STUDENT, YOUTH, AMATEUR
Includes Video, Audio, Multimedia. Amateur is usually defined as made entirely for fun and pleasure, with no commercial purpose or profit in mind, by persons not engaged in video-making as their main source of income at the time of production; and which has not been sold, commissioned, sponsored, or subsidized. However, these definitions may vary. (Also see AMERICANISM-PATRIOTIC, DOCUMENTARY-SHORT, TELEVISION FILMS.)

383

California Student Media Festival
California Media & Library Educators Association (CMLEA)
Phoebe Webb, Division of

Educational Media
Los Angeles County Superintendent
of Schools
9300 East Imperial Highway
Downey, California 90242 U.S.A.
Tel: (213) 922-6107

June

State; **entry restricted to California students;** annual; established 1966. Formerly called CALIFORNIA STUDENT 8MM FILM FESTIVAL. Purpose: to encourage California educators to offer filmmaking, videomaking, recognize student films, videotapes. Theme varies yearly. Sponsored and supported by CMLEA, California Audio Visual Educational Distributors Association. Average statistics: (film and video): 175-200 entries, 100 finalists, 12 winners, over 200 attendance. Held at various educational facilities. Tickets: free. Publish free handbook *Film-Making & Videotape Production for the Student.*

VIDEOTAPE CONTEST: Student (1/2-inch reel, Beta or VHS; 3/4-inch U-matic cassette) 10 minutes maximum. Categories: General, Festival Theme. Age Division per category: K-3, 4-6, 7-9, 10-12, Community College 13-14. Divisions: Individual, Group, Class.

ELIGIBILITY: Student produced and photogaphed, certified by school administrator.

AWARDS: First, Second, Third Place Award Plaques, each age division and category. Sweepstakes Award, Best in Festival. First, Second, Third Place, Best on Theme. One prize per entrant per grade level.

JUDGING: All entries viewed in entirety by 50 educator, media industry judges, based on content, organization, originality, creativity, technical quality, effectiveness. Films over 10 minutes lose points. Festival may disqualify, change, cancel awards; make copy of any entry. Winners copied for publicity and promotion. Not responsible for loss or damage.

ENTRY FEE: None.

DEADLINES: Entry, May. Festival, June.

| 384 |

JVC Student Video Festival
Burson-Marsteller Public Relations
Paula Petti
866 Third Avenue
New York, New York 10022 U.S.A.
Tel: (212) 752-8610

Winter-Spring

National; **entry restricted to U.S. art school students;** annual; established 1980. Purpose: to recognize, encourage efforts of aspiring video artists, news-entertainment producers, corporate communicators. Sponsored by U.S. JVC Corporation (Victor Company of Japan). Average statistics: 9 awards. Held in New York City. Also sponsor JVC TOKYO VIDEO FESTIVAL, JVC BUSINESS AND INDUSTRY VIDEO FESTIVAL. Second contact: Stuart Rose.

VIDEOTAPE CONTEST: Student (1/2-inch EIAJ, VHS, Beta or 3/4-inch U-matic) 30 seconds to 20 minutes, produced with video camera; no professional assistance. No JVC employees or relatives. Categories: Documentary, Creative, News Short.

AWARDS: First, Second, Third Place Certificates plus trip to New York City, each category. Video equipment to winning students' schools.

JUDGING: By 5 professionals in video, film, news. Not responsible for loss or damage.

ENTRY FEE: None.

DEADLINES: Entries, February.

385

Maine Student Film and Video Festival
Maine Alliance of Media Arts (MAMA)
Huey (James Coleman), Director
Box 4320, Station A
Portland, Maine 04103 U.S.A.
Tel: (207) 773-1130

May

State; **entry restricted to Maine students 19 and younger;** annual; established 1977 (film), 1980 (video). Purpose: to promote filmmaking and video arts among young people in Maine. Sponsored by MAMA, nonprofit, tax-exempt membership corporation supporting media education, production, distribution, exhibition in Maine. Supported by Maine State Commission on the Arts and Humanities; WCSH-TV, Portland, Maine. Average statistics (includes video): 80 entries, 200 entrants, 20 finalists, 7 awards, 200 attendance. Also sponsor MAMA MEDIA ARTS FAIR, MAMA SUMMER FILM AND VIDEO INSTITUTE. Second contact: Ned Lightner, TV3, 189 Water Street, Augusta, Maine 04330.

VIDEOTAPE CONTEST: Maine Student (widths not specified), 30 minutes maximum. Categories: Preteen (to 11 years), Junior (12-15), Senior (16-19).

AUDIOTAPE CONTEST: Maine Student (format not specified). Categories same as for Videotape.

AWARDS: First Place $25; Second Place $15. Special Merit Awards at judges' discretion.

JUDGING: By 3 professional film-makers, educators, based on originality, content, style, technique. Copies made for promotion. Not responsible for loss or damage.

ENTRY FEE: None. Festival pays return postage.

DEADLINES: Entry and Event, May.

386

National Student Media Festival
Association for Educational Communications & Technology (AECT)
Dr. William D. Schmidt, Chairperson
Instructional Media Center
Central Washington University
Ellensburg, Washington 98926
U.S.A. Tel: (509) 963-1842

Spring

National; **entry restricted to U.S. students;** annual; established 1976. Purpose: to recognize creative activity by students in media production. Sponsored and supported by AECT. Average statistics: 200-300 entries, 45 awards, 450 attendance. Held at AECT convention for 5 days. Tickets: free.

VIDEOTAPE CONTEST: Student (1/2-inch reel, Beta or VHS; 3/4-inch cassette) 10 minutes maximum. Divisions: Individual, Group, Class, Club. Categories: K-3, 4-6, 7-9, 10-12, College or University.

ELIGIBILITY: Certified student-produced and photographed; original work not previously entered in AECT competition.

AWARDS: Best of Festival. Framed Certificates, each category.

JUDGING: By 4-5 judges. Entries over 10 minutes penalized. May make copies for future motivation, promotion, PBS television broadcasting.

ENTRY FEE: None.

DEADLINES: Entry, March. Event, April. Materials returned, June.

| 387 |

New England High School Film and Video Festival

Mount Wachusett Community College
Professor Vincent S. Ialenti, Director
444 Green Street
Gardner, Massachusetts 01440
U.S.A. Tel: (617) 632-6600

May

Regional; **entry restricted to New England high school students;** annual; established 1977. Purpose: to showcase works of New England high school filmmakers and video artists. Sponsored by Mount Wachusett Community College. Supported by 3M Company, Sony Video Products. Average statistics: 50 entries, 24 finalists, 7 winners, 250 attendance. Held at Mount Wachusett Community College, Fine Arts Center, Gardner, Massachusetts. Also sponsor TWO-YEAR COLLEGE FILM AND VIDEO FESTIVAL.

VIDEOTAPE CONTEST: Student (3/4-inch, 1/2-inch reel-to-reel, Beta 1/2-inch, VHS 1/2-inch). By enrolled, certified New England high school students.

AWARDS: $500 in cash prizes to students. $1000 in video equipment, tape to colleges.

JUDGING: By panel, viewed in entirety. Final by 3 judges, each awarding one-third of cash prizes. Not responsible for loss or damage.

ENTRY FEE: $3 per film. Festival pays return postage.

DEADLINES: Entry, judging, event, May.

| 388 |

New York State Youth Film-Media Shows

New York State Education Department
James V. Gilliland, Administrative Director
Bureau of Visual Arts and Humanities Education
Room 681 EBA
Albany, New York 12234 U.S.A.
Tel: (518) 393-9230

January-March

State; **entry restricted to New York young film and media makers;** annual; established 1969. Purpose: to provide training and viewing of creative film, video media. Sponsored by New York State Education Department, Bureau of Art Education and Humanities Education Unit, Division of Humanities and Arts Education. Supported by NYSCA, New York State Art Teachers Association. Held in 7 New York regions. Have demonstration workshops. Also sponsor NEW YORK STATE SUMMER SCHOOL OF THE ARTS SCHOOL OF FILM MEDIA SCHOLARSHIPS for talented students.

VIDEOTAPE CONTEST: Youth Color (1/2-inch, 3/4-inch, 2-inch) 15 minutes maximum.

AUDIOTAPE CONTEST: Youth Creative Sound 15 minutes maximum, original music compositions, manipulated electronic sound, voice overs, radio.

MIXED MEDIA CONTEST: Youth , 15 minutes maximum, combinations of film, video, audio, photography.

ELIGIBILITY: Independent projects, made with or without school or teacher involvement, by New York State elementary or secondary school-age youth. No college, higher learning institution students, ex-students.

AWARDS: Scholarships to New York State Summer School of the Arts.

JUDGING: By film-media teachers, artists.

ENTRY FEE: None.

DEADLINES: Entry, 3 weeks prior to show date. Regional Shows, January-March. All-State Show, April.

389
North Carolina Film Festival
North Carolina Museum of Art
Lorraine Laslett, Jen Wilson,
Coordinators
Department of Cultural Resources
Raleigh, North Carolina 27611
U.S.A. Tel: (919) 733-7568

April

State; **entry restricted to North Carolina;** biennial (even years); established 1972. Alternates with NORTH CAROLINA FILM SYMPOSIUM. Purpose: to provide forum for independent film and video artists in state. Sponsored by North Carolina Museum of Art. Supported by North Carolina Arts Council, North Carolina Art Society. Held in Raleigh, North Carolina, for 2 days. Also sponsor exhibitions, lectures, concerts, arts programs, conferences, professional seminars.

VIDEOTAPE CONTEST: **Student, Commercial-Sponsored** (3/4-inch) unlimited entries. Artist must be North Carolina resident when entry completed.

AWARDS: Grand Prize, $1000. $1000 prize monies awarded at juror's discretion. Student Prize, $150.

JUDGING: By out-of-state profes-

sional juror; viewed in Entirety. Request right to duplicate winner at lab cost for exhibition, education.

ENTRY FEE: $5 each.

DEADLINES: Entry, March. Judging, March-April. Event, April.

390
Two Year College Film and Video Festival
Mount Wachusett Community College
Professor Vincent S. Ialenti, Director
444 Green Street
Gardner, Massachusetts 01440
U.S.A. Tel: (617) 632-6600

May

National; **entry restricted to U.S. Community or Junior college students;** annual; established 1972. Purpose: to showcase works of young filmmakers and video artists. Sponsored by Mount Wachusett Community College. Supported by 3M Company, Sony Video Products. Average statistics: 40 entries, 20 finalists, 6 winners, 250 attendance. Held at Mount Wachusett Community College Fine Arts Center, Gardner, Massachusetts. Also sponsor NEW ENGLAND HIGH SCHOOL FILM AND VIDEO FESTIVAL.

VIDEOTAPE CONTEST: **Student** (3/4-inch, 1/2-inch reel-to-reel, Beta 1/2-inch VHS 1/2-inch) by community or junior college student as of January previous year.

AWARDS: Cash prizes to students ($500). Video equipment and tape to colleges ($1000 value).

JUDGING: By screening panel. Final by 3 judges, each awarding one-third of cash prizes. All entries viewed in entirety. Not responsible for loss or damage.

ENTRY FEE: $3 each. Sponsor pays return postage.

DEADLINES: Entry and event, May.

391

Young Peoples Film and Video Festival
Northwest Film Study Center
Bill Foster, Associate Director
Portland Art Museum
1219 Southwest Park
Portland, Oregon 97205 U.S.A.
Tel: (503) 221-1156

February-March

Regional; **entry restricted to Oregon students**; annual; established 1972. Purpose: to survey new work by Northwest students. Sponsored by Northwest Film Study Center, Oregon Educational and Public Broadcasting Service, Oregon Educational Media Association, Washington Library Media Association. Recognized by National Student Film Festival. Average statistics: 175 entries, 15-20 winners. Held at Portland Art Museum. Also sponsor year-round film and video exhibitions, NORTHWEST FILM AND VIDEO FESTIVAL, PORTLAND FILM FESTIVAL.

VIDEOTAPE CONTEST: **Student** (3/4-inch, 1/2-inch EIAJ standard) sound, silent. Categories: Grades K-3, 4-6, 7-9, 10-12, College.

AWARDS: Top winners broadcast over PBS stations. Some winners entered in *AECT National Student Media Festival.*

JUDGING: By 3 judges, each category. Sponsor may make copies of winners for archival, educational broadcast, publicity purposes. Not responsible for loss or damage.

ENTRY FEE: None. Entrant pays return postage.

DEADLINES: Entry and Event, February.

392

Liege International Festival of Picture and Sound
Francois Oury, Chairman
62-106 Voie de l'Ardenne
4920 Embourg, BELGIUM Tel: (041) 65-93-19

November

International; **entry restricted to amateurs;** biennial; established 1977. Formerly called LIEGE AUDIO VISUAL FESTIVAL to 1979. Purpose: to promote nonprofessional works; establish contacts among amateurs. Sponsored by University of Liege, Belgium. Supported by State of Belgium, Province and City of Liege. Recognized by FIAP, PSA, UNICA. Average statistics: 250 entries, 2000 entrants, 10 countries, 112 finalists, 35 awards. Held at Palais des Congres (Esplanade de l'Europe, 4020 Liege) for 5 days. Have hotel accommodations, projection equipment. Also sponsor workshops, exhibition, slide shows, computer categories. Second contact: Yvonne Briart, 5 Heid des Chenes, 4052 Dolembreux, Belgium; tel: (041) 68-73-63.

VIDEOTAPE CONTEST: **Amateur** (VHS system) 15 minutes maximum. Nonprofessional only, any language.

AWARDS: Not specified.

JUDGING: By 3-5 judges. Entries viewed in entirety once during preselection, twice by main jury if selected. Not responsible for loss or damage.

ENTRY FEE: 200 Belgian francs per

work. Receipt acknowledged. Festival pays return postage.

DEADLINES: Entry, September. Materials, acceptance, judging, October. Event, November.

393

West of England International Film Festival

Ballard Center Cine Group
A. J. Dawson, Administrator
28 Belle Vue Road
Saltash, Cornwall PL12 5DG,
ENGLAND

October

International; **entry restricted to amateurs, students;** biennial; established 1970. Sponsored by Ballard Center Cine Group (25 the Crescent, Plymouth, England). Supported by Westward Television, BBC, Plymouth City Council. Recognized by IAC. Average statistics: 115 entries, 11 countries.

VIDEOTAPE CONTEST: Amateur, Student (width not specified) any speed, produced without professional assistance. Categories: Fiction, Documentary, Young People (18 and under), Animation, Family, Open.

AWARDS: $4000 in trophies, cash, equipment. Ceramic Oscars to Top Ten.

JUDGING: By 5 judges.

ENTRY FEE: 1.50 pounds. Entrant pays return postage.

DEADLINES: Entry, August. Judging, September. Event, October.

394

Marburg International Amateur Film Festival

Dr. Herman Schreiner
Georg-Voight-Strasse 37
D-3550 Marburg Lahn, WEST
GERMANY(FRG)

October

International; **entry restricted to amateurs;** annual; established 1970. Sponsored by Filmteam Marburg. Supported by UNICA, BDFA, Hessian Cultural Affairs Minister. Held in Marburg on Lahn.

VIDEOTAPE CONTEST: Amateur (Video-Recording-Tapes) 20 minutes maximum; produced within last 3 years, not sold or in financial negotiation, 2 maximum per entrant. Require summary in English, French or German, stills, photos. Categories: Documentary, Travelog, Theatrical-Fictional, Animated-Experimental-Abstract.

AWARDS: Gold, Silver, Bronze Medals, each category. Prizes for special film achievements. Special prizes by Foreign Minister of the German Republic, Lord Mayor of Marburg. Competition Certificates.

JUDGING: International panel of film amateurs, journalists, club members. May change categories. One copy of Gold-Medal films kept for archives. Not responsible for loss or damage.

ENTRY FEE: $5 per film.

DEADLINES: Entry, September. Festival, October.

TELEVISION FILMS
Films for Television, including

AMATEUR, ANIMATED, DOCUMENTARY, EDUCATIONAL, EXPERIMENTAL, FEATURE, SHORT, STUDENT. (Also see Television Films included in most other categories.)

| 395 |

CINE Golden Eagle Film Awards
Council on International Nontheatrical Events (CINE)
Shreeniwas R. Tamhane, Executive Director
1201 Sixteenth Street, N.W.
Washington, District of Columbia
20036 U.S.A. Tel: (202) 785-1136

November-December

National; **entry open to U.S.;** annual (semiannual judging); established 1957. Purpose: to represent American film artists abroad; contribute to better international understanding; award excellence. Sponsored by CINE (Pennie Collins, Secretary; Indra de Silva, Film Librarian), voluntary, nonprofit educational-cultural organization, founded 1957 at initiative of National Education Association Department of Audio-visual Instruction, to coordinate selection, paperwork, shipment of U.S. nontheatrical films to foreign film festivals. Average statistics: 800 entries, 12,000 total entries, 1600 international awards to date. Held at CINE Showcase, Washington D.C. Have exhibitions. Publish illustrated yearbook of winners.

TELEVISION FILM CONTEST: Television Documentary, Nontheatrical, Theatrical Short Subject (35mm, 16mm, Super 8mm, 8mm) any length; optical, silent; any subject. Categories: Agriculture, Amateur-Student, Animation, Architecture, Arts-Crafts, Biography, Children's Films, Documentary, Education, Entertainment-Short Subject, Environment, Experimental-Avant-Garde, History, Industry-Commerce, Maritime, Medicine-Dental, Public Health-Drugs, Religion, Safety, Science, Social Documentary, Sports, Technology, Tourism, Training, Travel. Request 1 or more prints of winners for foreign entry.

ELIGIBILITY: Principle creation by U.S. citizen, photographed anywhere in world; basic ownership by U.S. citizen, partnership, corporation, or organization. No foreign festival entry of film by foreign nationals.

AWARDS: Golden Eagle (professional); Eagle (amateur-student). Certificates and listing in Library of Congress, each selected. Film submitted to foreign festivals with entrant's approval. Foreign Awards given by foreign diplomats at CINE Showcase in following years.

JUDGING: Preliminary by about 35 regional juries comprised of over 300 film subject matter specialists. Semifinal judging. Final in Washington D.C. by CINE Board of Directors and Regional Jury Chairmen, based on imagination, creativity, cinematographic excellence, authenticity, honesty, sensitivity, objectivity, brevity, uniqueness, revelation of new insights, visual-sound imagery. Sponsor insures while in U.S.; not responsible for loss or damage by foreign festivals.

ENTRY FEE: Amateur-Student, $15. Professional, 15 minutes maximum, $50; 15-30, $75; over 30, $100. Amateur-Student, $15; Professional, $35 per foreign festival entered (for handling); foreign entry fees additional.

DEADLINES: Entry, February, August. Judges reports, May, October. Awards, November.

396

Melbourne Film Festival
Victorian Federation of Film Societies
Geoffrey Gardner, Director
53 Cardigan Street
P.O. Box 357
Carlton South, Victoria 3053,
AUSTRALIA Tel: (03) 347-4828

June

International; entry open to all; annual; established 1952. Purpose: to present broad spectrum of modern international cinema, with emphasis on young directors, new developments, films from Asia. Sponsored and supported by Australian Film Commission, Victorian Film Corporation, Peter Stuyvesant Cultural Foundation. Recognized by FIAPF. Held at Palais, National and State Film Theaters, Melbourne, Australia, for 16 days. Average statistics: 116 shorts, 59 features, 30 countries. Tickets: $70 Aust. admits to all sessions. Second contact: R. Rothols.

TELEVISION FILM CONTEST: **Television, Feature, Short** (35mm, 16mm) optical, dialog or subtitles in English; produced after January, 6 years prior; unscreened in Melbourne (Australian films excepted). Request poster, stills, press sheets. Categories: Features, noncompetitive; Shorts, Competitive (Fiction, 30 minutes maximum; Nonfiction, 60 minutes maximum).

AWARDS: To short only. Grand Prize, Gold Boomerang Trophy, $4000. Second Prize, Silver Boomerang, $2500. Third Silver, $1500. Peter Stuyvesant Cultural Foundation Awards, $1000 each for Best Film on Art, Best Animated. Erwin Rado Prize, Best Australian Film, $1000. Special Jury Award, Television Prize, Diplomas of Merit. Festival assists in placing films for local distribution and print sales.

JUDGING: Preliminary by selection board. Awards by 5 international judges. All entries insured.

ENTRY FEE: None. Festival pays return postage.

DEADLINES: Entry, March. Materials, April. Judging, May. Event, June.

397

Effigy Film Awards
Canadian Film Editors Guild (CFE)
Lynette McPeake, Business Manager
P.O. Box 46, Station A
Toronto, Ontario M5W 1A2 CANADA
Tel: (416) 485-3222

November

National; **entry restricted to CFE members;** annual; established 1968. Effigy Awards for **Canadian Television Feature, Documentary, Student Film Editing.** Purpose: to recognize outstanding achievements of CFE members. Theme: Advance the Art and Craft of Film Editing. Sponsored by various film labs, postproduction companies. Recognized by Academy of Canadian Cinema, Canadian Film Sound Society, Canadian Society of Cinematographers. Average statistics: 50 entries, 40 entrants, 7 winners, 500 attendance. Held in various Canadian cities. Publish annual newsletter. Event, November.

398

Leipzig International Documentary and Short Film Festival for Cinema and Television
Ronald Trisch, Director
Christburger Strasse 38
1055 Berlin, EAST GERMANY (GDR)
Tel: 4-39-19-02

November

International; entry open to all; annual; established 1958. Purpose: to promote presentation of television, cinema films; personal contacts; exchange of opinions among film, television filmmakers, critics, historians. Motto: "Films of the world for the peace of the world." Sponsored by Committee of the International Leipzig Documentary and Short Film Festival for Cinema and Television. Have information programs, retrospectives, press conferences, meetings, tradeshows.

TELEVISION FILM CONTEST: Television, Documentary, Animation (70mm, 35mm, 16mm) not shown publicly before one year prior, shown in original version with simultaneous translations in German, Russian, English, French. Require synopses; narration list in German, Russian, English or French; stills; advertising materials. Categories: Documentary, Animation, Television Reports and Documentation, Documentaries with Staged Reconstructions, Television Journalistic Magazines, Animation.

ELIGIBILITY: Convincing, creative, journalistic cinema and TV films telling story of struggle for peace, development of man in existing socialistic society; illustrate efforts to achieve freedom from imperialist and colonial oppression, for national sovereignty, democracy, security, social progress, dignity of man. No technology, natural science, advertising or films directed against human dignity, or propagating racial hatred, discrimination.

AWARDS: 2 Golden Doves, 5000 Marks each. 4 Silver Doves, 3000 Marks each. Special Animation Prize, 3000 Marks. International Organization Prize, 2500 Marks. Special Prize of International Jury, 4000 Marks. 2 Special Prizes, 2500 Marks each. Organizing Committee Prize, 2500 Marks to young filmmaker, first-time participant. Honorary Diplomas.

JUDGING: Selection by commission; final by international jury of film and TV makers. Judges may not have contributed to films in competition. Sponsor may negotiate for winners for festival archives; show entries at noncommercial events, and clips free on TV for festival promotion. Festival insures for replacement value during event.

ENTRY FEE: None. Festival pays postage.

DEADLINES: Entry, October. Event, November.

399

Mannheim International Film Week
Fee Vaillant, Hanns Maier, Directors
Stadt Mannheim
Rathaus E-5
D-6800 Mannheim 1, WEST
GERMANY (FRG) Tel: 293-2745,
293-3799

October

International; entry open to all; annual; established 1952. Purpose: to provide competition for films showing new developments. Supported by Mannheim Cultural Committee. Held at 5-theater Planken-Film-Center in Mannheim (with simultaneous translations). Also sponsor MANNHEIM INTERNATIONAL YOUTH FILM CONTEST, retrospectives, seminars. Second contact: Marc Weiss, c/o Association of Independent Filmmakers, Inc., 140 Waverly Place, New York, New York 10014.

TELEVISION FILM CONTEST: Television, Fiction Feature, Documentary (35mm, 16mm) first fiction features over 60 minutes, social-

political documentaries over 45 minutes; no separate magnetic sound; released after November 1 of previous year; unshown and unreleased for cinema-TV in West Germany or West Berlin. Non-German language films subtitled or accompanied by dialog list in German, English, or French.

AWARDS: Mannheim Grand Prize and 10,000 DM, Best Fiction Film. 6,-000 DM Prize, Best Documentary. Sternberg Prize, 3,500 DM, Most Original. 5 Mannheim Film Ducats, 2,000 DM each. Special Prize, Best TV Film. Participation Certificates.

JUDGING: By 7-member selection committee; final by 7 international judges. Sponsor retains winners for archives and noncommercial exhibition.

ENTRY FEE: None. Entrant pays postage.

DEADLINES: Entry, August. Event, October.

400

Hong Kong International Film Festival
Urban Council of Hong Kong
City Hall
Edinburgh Place
HONG KONG Tel: 5-261528

April

International; **entry restricted** (selection by official organizations in each country); annual; established 1977. Merit Certificates to **Television, Feature and Documentary Films** (35mm, 16mm). Purpose: to develop and encourage the art, enjoyment, appreciation of cinema in Hong Kong. Sponsored by Urban Council of Hong Kong. Recognized by IFFPA, FIAPF. Average statistics: 120 entries, 30 countries, 60,000 attendance, 166 screenings. Held in Hong Kong City

Hall. Have seminars, discussions, exhibitions. Event, April.

WOMEN, MINORITY
TV-Radio Broadcasting, Video and Film, including BLACK, HISPANIC, NATIVE AMERICAN.

401

Black Film and Video Maker Cooperative Distribution
Black Filmmaker Foundation
Denise Oliver, Executive Director
79 Madison Avenue, Suite 906
New York, New York 10016 U.S.A.
Tel: (212) 686-4145

Continuous

National; **entry open to U.S.;** continuous; established 1978 as nonprofit, tax-exempt service organization for black independent film, video makers. Purpose: to increase visibility, expand rental and sales markets of black independent film, video makers. Supported by grants. Publish annual catalog. Have summer film exhibition, project sponsorship, information library, programming assistance (to community groups, museums, educational institutions, public television). Second contact: P.O. Box 315, Franklin Lakes, New Jersey 07417; tel: (201) 891-8240.

VIDEOTAPE-FILM DISTRIBUTION: By or about Blacks (gauges-widths not specified).

SALES TERMS: Vary by film, tape.

DEADLINES: Open.

402

By, For, About Native Americans Video Distribution
Native American Public Broadcasting Consortium
Frank Blythe, Executive Director
1800 North 33rd Street
P.O. Box 83111
Lincoln, Nebraska 68501 U.S.A.
Tel: (402) 472-3522

Continuous

National; **entry open to U.S., Canada;** continuous; established 1975. Purpose: to provide, encourage high-quality programs by, for, about Native Americans through distribution. Sponsored by Native American Public Broadcasting Consortium, CPB. Supported by CPB, ESAA, NEH. Held at Nebraska Educational Telecommunications Center, Lincoln, Nebraska. Have TV production training. Publish catalog. Second contact: Laurell E. Schuerman, Assistant Director.

VIDEOTAPE DISTRIBUTION: By, For, About Native Americans (widths not specified).

JUDGING: By screening committee of Native American TV professionals, public television managers.

ENTRY FEE: None.

DEADLINES: Open.

403

San Antonio Cine Festival
Oblate College of the Southwest
Ken Amerson, Director
285 Oblate Drive
San Antonio, Texas 78216 U.S.A.
Tel: (512) 736-1685

August

International; entry open to all; annual; established 1976. Formerly called CHICANO FILM FESTIVAL. Purpose: to recognize, promote excellence in film and video production within U.S. Hispanic community. Sponsored by Oblate College of the Southwest. Supported by NEA, individual business organizations. Average statistics: 75 entries, 4000 attendance. Held in San Antonio, Texas, for 2-3 days. Have workshops. Also sponsor EMERGING ARTIST GRANTS PROGRAM. Second contact: Adan Medrano.

VIDEOTAPE FESTIVAL: Hispanic (3/4-inch cassette, 1/2-inch reel-to-reel) any language; produced by Hispanics or on Hispanic theme; unlimited entries. Require synopsis (100 words maximum), credits, photos.

AWARDS: None.

JUDGING: May show excerpts of program for promotion. Sponsor insures during Festival only.

ENTRY FEE: None.

DEADLINES: Entry, July. Event, August.

404

Vanguard Award
Women in Communications, Inc. (WICI)
Ruth Massingill, Communications Director
P.O. Box 9561
Austin, Texas 78766 U.S.A.
Tel: (512) 345-8922

October

International; entry open to all; annual; established 1980. Purpose: to reward films and institutions for positive, nonstereotypical portrayals of women in advertisements; heighten awareness of factors that enhance women's image and status. Theme varies yearly. Sponsored by WICI.

Held in various U.S. cities at WICI national conference. Have print, billboard, special categories. Also sponsor CLARION COMPETITION.

VIDEOTAPE CONTEST: Women Television Broadcast (3/4-inch cassette). Require script. Must be paid advertisement publicized within previous year. No public service announcements.

AUDIOTAPE CONTEST: Women Radio Broadcast (1/4-inch cassette). Requirements same as for Videotape.

AWARDS: Vanguard Trophy. Commendation Certificates to finalists.

JUDGING: Preselection of 5-7 finalists by panel of professional communicators. Selection by 8 WICI regional vice presidents. All entries except audiovisual become WICI property.

ENTRY FEE: None.

DEADLINES: Entry, March. Winners announced, September. Awards given, October.

| 405 |

Women at Work Broadcast Awards
National Commission on Working Women
Sally Steenland
1211 Connecticut Avenue N.W.
Suite 310
Washington, District of Columbia
20036 U.S.A. Tel: (202) 887-6820

Fall

National; **entry restricted to U.S. TV and radio stations;** annual; established 1979. Purpose: to recognize broadcasters for exceptional reporting and programming on concerns of working women; promote new coverage and programs about, encourage

greater recognition of working women. Sponsored by National Commission on Working Women. Supported by AFL-CIO, AFSCME, CBS, IBM. Average statistics: 200 entries, 25-30 awards. Held in Washington, D.C.

VIDEOTAPE CONTEST: Working Women Television Broadcast (3/4-inch cassette) aired within one year before August. "Women at Work" includes participation of women in work force, as well as social, educational, economic needs related to their participation (child care, career counseling, occupational health-safety, wages-benefits). Categories: Spot News (5 minutes maximum); New Series (30 minutes maximum); Public Affair or Documentary (1 hour maximum); Portrait (1 hour maximum); Entertainment; Special Categories.

FILM CONTEST: Working Women Television Broadcast (16mm). Requirements, definition, categories same as for Videotape.

AUDIOTAPE CONTEST: Working Women Radio Broadcast (typewritten copy, cassette or tape). Requirements, definition, categories same as for Videotape.

AWARDS: First, Second, Third Place, each category. Honorable Mentions.

JUDGING: By representatives from business, labor, academia, the media, working women. Not responsible for loss or damage.

ENTRY FEE: $10 handling fee if return of material requested; otherwise materials become property of NCWW.

DEADLINES: Entry, September. Event, Fall.

406

**Vancouver Women In Focus
Society Exhibitions of New Films
and Video**
Michelle Nickel, Director
6-45 Kingsway
Vancouver, British Columbia V5T
3H7 CANADA Tel: (604) 872-2250
Continuous

International; **entry restricted to
women**; continuous; established 1974.
Also called VANCOUVER WOM-
EN'S VIDEO & FILM FESTIVAL.
Purpose: to produce, support, exhibit
art and media from women's perspec-
tive. Held in Vancouver, British Co-
lumbia. Publish distribution catalog.
Also sponsor WOMEN IN FOCUS
GALLERY.

**VIDEOTAPE EXHIBITION: By
women** (width not specified).

AWARDS: Recognition of colleagues.

ENTRY FEE: None. Entrant pays
postage.

DEADLINES: Open.

OTHER
*TV-Radio Broadcasting (video, film,
audio), Video and Film, including
ANIMAL, FANTASY, JUSTICE,
LEGAL-JUDICIAL, MARITIME.*

407

**Captain Donald T. Wright
Maritime Journalism Awards**
Southern Illinois University at
Edwardsville
John A. Regnell, Chairman
Department of Mass
Communications, Box 73
Edwardsville, Illinois 62026 U.S.A.
Tel: (618) 692-2230
Winter

International; entry open to all; annual; established 1970. Named after
Captain Donald T. Wright, riverboat
pilot, publisher of *Waterways Journal.*
Purpose: to recognize outstanding
achievement in maritime journalism
contributing to better understanding
of U.S. inland and intracoastal waterways. Sponsored by Southern Illinois
University at Edwardsville (SIUE)
Foundation, SIUE Department of
Mass Communications. Supported by
Mrs. Donald T. Wright. Average statistics: 20 entries, 2 awards. Held at
various River Association meetings.

**VIDEOTAPE CONTEST: U.S.
Maritime Television Broadcast,**
about inland or intracoastal waterways, previously produced.

**FILM CONTEST: U.S. Maritime
Television Broadcast,** about inland or
intracoastal waterways, previously
produced.

**AUDIOTAPE CONTEST: U.S.
Maritime Radio Broadcast,** about inland or intracoastal waterways, previously produced.

AWARDS: 2 or more Bronze
Plaques (showing river transportation) for maritime journalism contributing to better understanding of
contributions of U.S. inland or intracoastal waterways industry to welfare of our society.

JUDGING: By SIUE Department of
Mass Communication faculty. Not responsible for loss or damage.

ENTRY FEE: None.

DEADLINES: Entry, September.
Awards, February-March.

408

Gavel Awards
American Bar Association, Division
of Communications
Dean Tyler Jenks, Special Events
Director
77 South Wacker Drive
Chicago, Illinois 60606 U.S.A.
Tel: (312) 621-9249

Fall

National; **entry restricted to U.S.
news and entertainment media;** annual; established 1958. Purpose: to recognize U.S. news, entertainment media that educate, increase public understanding of American legal and judicial system; promote correction, improvement of laws, courts, law enforcement, legal goals. Sponsored and supported by 270,000-member American Bar Association (ABA). Average statistics: 378 entries, 235 entrants, 25 Gavel Awards, 42 certificates. Held at ABA annual meeting in various U.S. cities. Tickets: $15-$20. Second contact: Richard S. Collins, Director of Communications.

VIDEOTAPE CONTEST: Legal and Judicial Television Broadcast (3/4-inch cassette, 2-inch quadruplex standard). Require 4 copies of program synopsis, subject summary, biography. Sections: Syndicated; Local and Independent Productions (nonsyndicated) Top 10 Markets, 11-50, over 50; Local and Independent Productions; Local Noncommercial; Cable. Categories: Documentary, Educational, Dramatic, Editorial.

AUDIOTAPE CONTEST: Legal and Judicial Radio Broadcast. Require 4 copies program synopsis, subject summary (including listener reactions and views), biography. Sections: Network, Syndicated, Local and Independent Productions (nonsyndicated), Top 10 metro areas, 11-50, 51 and over, Local Noncommercial. Categories: Documentary, Educational, Dramatic, News, Interviews, Editorials.

ELIGIBILITY: Broadcast January to December of previous year. Entries should relate to work of the bench, bar, law enforcement, law itself, current, historical, or futuristic. Actual courtroom broadcast must be produced in compliance with courtroom requirements and authorized by judge. ABA staff members, awards committee members not eligible. 5 entries maximum.

AWARDS: Silver Gavel Awards for outstanding contribution to public understanding of American law and justice, top executives, each winning organization. Gavel Awards Certificate of Merit to noteworthy examples of distinguished public service.

JUDGING: By lawyers, judges, teachers, based on informational value, educational merit, creativity, thoroughness, reportorial and technical skills, impact. All entries viewed in entirety. May withhold awards.

ENTRY FEE: None.

DEADLINES: Entry, February. Awards, August. Entries returned (upon request), Summer.

409

International Conference on the Fantastic in the Arts
Thomas Burnett Swann Fund
Dr. Robert A. Collins, Coordinator
College of Humanities
Florida Atlantic University
Boca Raton, Florida 33431 U.S.A.

March

International; **entry restricted** (invitation by Conference); annual; established 1979. **Exhibitions of Fantasy Videotapes and Films.** Purpose: to recognize, emphasize, explore tradition of the fantastic. Sponsored by Thomas Burnett Swann Fund. Average statistics: 7 countries, 500 attendance. Held at Florida Atlantic University for 4 days. Have workshops, shows, exhibits, presentations, lectures. Event, March.

410

New York State Bar Association (NYSBA) Media Awards Contest
1 Elk Street
Albany, New York 12207 U.S.A.
Tel: (518) 445-1251, 445-1242

Fall

National; **entry open to U.S.;** annual. Purpose: to encourage reporting that educates citizens about roles of law, courts, law enforcement agencies in society, discloses practices in legal system needing correction, promotes legislative efforts to improve law. Sponsored by NYSBA.

VIDEOTAPE CONTEST: Justice, **Legal Television Broadcast** (3/4-inch cassette) 6 copies script or synopsis; no commercials. Categories: New York State, National (any medium).

AUDIOTAPE CONTEST: Justice, **Legal Radio Broadcast** (cassette) 6 copies script. Categories: New York State, National (any medium).

ELIGIBILITY: Appearing October 1 previous year to September 30 current year.

AWARDS: $250 and Plaques, Best Reporting on Administration of Justice, each category. Merit Certificates.

JUDGING: Based on informational value, educational merit, creativity, courage, thoroughness, reportorial and technical skills.

ENTRY FEE: None.

DEADLINES: Entry, October. Awards, Fall.

411

PATSY (Performing Animal Top Star of the Year) Awards
American Humane Association (AHA)
Carmelita Pope, Hollywood Director
8480 Beverly Blvd., Room 20
Los Angeles, California 90048 U.S.A.
Tel: (213) 653-3394

June

International; **entry restricted** (nomination by sponsor); annual; established 1951. PATSY Awards to **Videotape and Film Television, Theatrical, and Advertising Animal Performances.** Purpose: to recognize noteworthy performances by humanely trained animals, skill and ability in animal handling, compliance with AHA standards; promote better animal stories. Sponsored by AHA. Average statistics: 50 entries, 4-5 winners, 350 attendance. Event, June.

ALPHABETICAL
EVENT/SPONSOR/AWARD INDEX

Alphabetical index to each EVENT, SPONSOR, and AWARD (followed by identifying CODE NUMBER of the event).

A

J

SUBJECT/CATEGORY INDEX

Index to AREAS OF SPECIAL INTEREST (followed by identifying CODE NUMBER of each event).

HAVE WE MISSED A CONTEST/EVENT?

Please let us know so that we may
correct our future editions. Thank you.

FESTIVAL PUBLICATIONS
P.O. Box 10180
Glendale, California 91209 U.S.A